SOCIAL IDENTITIES IN THE
CLASSIC MAYA NORTHERN LOWLANDS

The Linda Schele Series in Maya and Pre-Columbian Studies

SOCIAL IDENTITIES IN THE CLASSIC MAYA NORTHERN LOWLANDS

Gender, Age, Memory, and Place

TRACI ARDREN

UNIVERSITY OF TEXAS PRESS
Austin

This series was made possible through the generosity of William C. Nowlin, Jr., and Bettye H. Nowlin, the National Endowment for the Humanities, and various individual donors.

Copyright © 2015 by the University of Texas Press
All rights reserved

First edition, 2015
First paperback printing, 2016

Requests for permission to reproduce material from this work should be sent to:
  Permissions
  University of Texas Press
  P.O. Box 7819
  Austin, TX 78713-7819
  http://utpress.utexas.edu/index.php/rp-form

♾ The paper used in this book meets the minimum requirements of ANSI/NISO Z39.48-1992 (R1997) (Permanence of Paper).

LIBRARY OF CONGRESS CATALOGING-IN-PUBLICATION DATA

Ardren, Traci.
  Social identities in the classic Maya northern lowlands : gender, age, memory, and place / by Traci Ardren. — First edition.
      pages cm. — (The Linda Schele series in Maya and pre-Columbian studies)
  Includes bibliographical references and index.
  ISBN 978-0-292-76811-6 (cl. : alk. paper)
  1. Mayas—Yucatán Peninsula—Social conditions. 2. Maya—Yucatán Peninsula—Antiquities. 3. Group identity—Yucatán Peninsula—History. 4. Social structure—Yucatán Peninsula—History. 5. Social archaeology—Yucatán Peninsula. 6. Yucatán Peninsula—Antiquities. I. Title.
  F1435.3.S68A73 2015
  305.897′4207265—dc23
                                                  2014025626

ISBN 978-1-4773-1132-5, paperback
doi:10.7560/768116

CONTENTS

ACKNOWLEDGMENTS	vii
Chapter 1 SOCIAL IMAGINARIES AND THE CONSTRUCTION OF CLASSIC MAYA IDENTITIES	1
Chapter 2 CIRCULATIONS AND THE URBAN IMAGINARY OF CHUNCHUCMIL	21
Chapter 3 MEMORY, REINVENTION, AND THE SOCIAL IMAGINARY OF LATER YAXUNA	51
Chapter 4 BURIAL RITUALS AND THE SOCIAL IMAGINARY OF CHILDHOOD	83
Chapter 5 GENDERED IMAGINARIES AND ARCHITECTURAL SPACE	117
Chapter 6 WHY SOCIAL IDENTITIES?	153
REFERENCES CITED	177
INDEX	207

ACKNOWLEDGMENTS

Most of the data included in this book was recovered as part of collaborative research projects. I have been fortunate to work with many wonderful colleagues on field projects within the northern Maya lowlands, and to conduct long-term investigations at a number of truly significant archaeological sites. As a member and later codirector of the Selz Foundation Yaxuna Archaeological Project, I had the opportunity to collaborate with excellent codirectors, talented graduate students, and many members of the village of Yaxunah. In particular I wish to thank Charles Suhler, Phil Hofstetter, Jeanne Randall, Lilia Fernández Souza, José Fernando Robles Castellanos, Rafael Cobos, and of course David Freidel, who all taught me how truly collaborative research is more than the sum of its parts. I thank Grace Bascope and Elias Alcocer for our continued collaborations in the village of Yaxunah with the Cultural Center. I was invited to join the Pakbeh Regional Archaeology Project by my codirector, the late Bruce Dahlin, and I will always be grateful for this turn of fortune. Again I was privileged to collaborate with an outstanding group of scholars, many of whom I continue to consider my closest colleagues and most trusted critics. Special thanks are extended to Scott R. Hutson, Aline Magnoni, Travis W. Stanton, David Hixson, Tara Bond Freeman, Eugenia Mansell, Socorro Jiménez, and Jaime Forde for all the fruitful conversations and collaborative spirit. On my current project, the Proyecto Arqueológico Xuenkal, I wish to thank my codirector T. Kam Manahan, my colleagues Vera Tiesler, Andrea Cucina, Christopher M. Götz, Christopher T. Morehart, and Mandy Munro-Stasiuk, but especially our graduate students Alejandra Alonso Olvera, Justin Lowry, Daniel Vallejo, Trent Stockton, and Eric Stockdell for the superb atmosphere of cooperative research we share. My gratitude is also extended to the many dedicated undergraduate students who contributed to the field projects mentioned above, especially Julie K. Wesp and Joe Stevenson.

The field research that enabled this volume has been supported by the Consejo de Arqueología of the Instituto Nacional de Antropología e Historia in México, and by the Centro Regional de Yucatán, in Mérida. I wish to express my gratitude to the members of the Consejo and especially to Arglo. Alfredo Barrera and Arglo. Luis Millet, both former directors of the Centro Regional de Yucatán, for their untiring support of this research. Members of the *ejidos* of Yaxunah, Chunchucmil, Kochol, San Mateo, Halacho, Coahuila, and Espita graciously granted me and my colleagues permission to conduct field investigations on their land, and I hope they have found the results interesting. Alejandro Patron Laviada first brought me to the site of Xuenkal, and introduced me to her guardian, Miguel Rosado Kuk. Generous support for the fieldwork presented here was provided by the National Geographic Society, the National Science Foundation, the Foundation for the Advancement of Mesoamerican Studies, Sigma Xi, the Miami Consortium for Urban Studies, the College of Arts and Sciences, Research Council and Office of the Provost of the University of Miami, the Selz Foundation, and private donors.

Many individuals at the University of Miami have contributed to the ideas presented here, and to the final form of this book. My colleagues in the Department of Anthropology, in addition to offering constructive comments, have provided a welcome and supportive environment conducive to scholarly activity. J. Bryan Page, former chair of the Department of Anthropology, has been a true advocate for my intellectual career, and for that I will always be thankful. Particular thanks are due to Louis Herns Marcelin, as well as Edward LiPuma, Will Pestle, Linda Taylor, Pamela Geller, and Caleb Everett, who all offered ideas that they will see incorporated in the final text. Thank you, Steve Butterman, for being a writing partner and for our lunchtime discussions of the writing process. My deepest appreciation goes to my colleague Dexter Callender of the Department of Religious Studies, for his intellectual ambition, dedication, and support as a writing partner during the final year in which this book was completed. Dean Leonidas Bachas of the College of Arts and Sciences at the University of Miami granted me a semester of research leave in which to finish the preparation of this manuscript, and I will be forever grateful for his mentorship and vision. Jessica Figueroa was a superb research assistant and chased down many bibliographic references.

I wish to acknowledge my wonderful colleagues in the Society for the Study of Childhood in the Past, who have provided many hours of inspiration over cups of tea and child-centered artifacts. A scholar is lucky to find such a cohort, and I wish to thank in particular Mike Lally, Jane Eva Baxter, Sally Crawford, Eileen Murphy, Dawn Hadley, and Carenza

Lewis for their research and collaboration. Many of my colleagues who direct research in the northern Maya lowlands have shared unpublished data or provided invaluable feedback, and I am proud to work in a region where there is such a high degree of mutual support. Special thanks for references or data incorporated in this book are due to George J. Bey III, Rubén Maldonado Cardenas, Anthony P. Andrews, Tomas Gallareta Negron, William M. Ringle, Rafael Burgos Villanueva, Socorro Jiménez, Eduardo Pérez de Heredia, Miguel Covarrubias Reina, Matthew Restall, Amara Solari, John Chuchiak, Stanley Serafin, Susan Milbrath, Marilyn Masson, Christopher Götz, E. Wyllis Andrews V, Vera Tiesler, Andrea Cucina, Gabrielle Vail, Virginia Miller, Karl Taube, Michael E. Smith, Christopher T. Morehart, Charles Golden, Paul E. Hoffman, Mary Pohl, Jeff Kowalski, Payson Sheets, Kathleen R. Martin, Quetzil Castañeda, Patricia McAnany, and Julia Hendon. I am deeply appreciative of the support shown by editor Theresa May at the University of Texas Press, the efforts of copyeditor John Brenner, and the thoughtful comments on the manuscript offered by Scott R. Hutson and an anonymous reviewer. Jack Scott produced excellent illustrations that far surpass the field sketches he was provided, and I thank him for his patience and expertise.

I am grateful to all the writers in my family, past, present, and future. Yes, Cyrus, I'm talking to you! My family is patient and understanding, and I thank Mike, Morgan, Cyrus, my mother Marty, and my *suegra* Kathy for all their support and their participation in the fieldwork presented in this volume. My research is richer for their contributions, and I am very thankful for their presence in Yucatán while I was excavating. I put this book aside in 2007 when my father, Bob Ardren, was diagnosed with cancer, and recently he let it be known he was watching over me as I returned to finish this work. So in his honor, this book is dedicated lovingly to all gonzo journalists who meet deadlines and protect the innocent. Thank you for hitchhiking to Caracol to check on me, for the Guatemala border crossing without your passport, for afternoons eating our way through the Mérida market, and for teaching me how to show no fear.

SOCIAL IDENTITIES IN THE
CLASSIC MAYA NORTHERN LOWLANDS

SOCIAL IMAGINARIES AND THE CONSTRUCTION OF CLASSIC MAYA IDENTITIES

Chapter 1

INTRODUCTION

This is a book about social identities, and specifically about trying to recover and understand the social identities at play in Classic Maya culture of southern México during the period from approximately 600–1100 CE. Social identities are interesting for reasons that have to do with the history of archaeological research, as I discuss more fully below. They are also familiar aspects of our lives today. I use the term "social identities" to make explicit the perspective that identities are not inherent (i.e., deriving from so-called biological characteristics such as race, gender, ethnicity, etc.) but rather are based in human interactions that make sense of such factors, as well as many others, by forming categories of social relations. Identities may have indeterminate borders, but they mark difference and help make sense of its importance (Alcoff 2006). To be a member of a social identity group does not entail an ascription of unrelenting sameness, but it does imply a constitutive relation of the individual to the Other, as well as between self and community (Alcoff 2006:85).

A great professor of mine once said that students of ancient cultures see either the differences between those cultures and their own, or they see the similarities, a glass half empty or half full explanation that gets to the heart of why I do archaeological research. My own feelings of being an outsider led me to explore how women in cultures radically different than my own fit, or did not fit, into their socially sanctioned roles. When we look at social identities in the past, we rarely see ideas about social relationships that are identical to those held in the modern West, but this kind of focus allows us to approach aspects of human social experience with which all of us have direct knowledge. Identities are the ideas we hold and relationships we form to explain difference and navigate social structures. Humans are social beings and we are a product of our relationships—this is true of both our own lives today and the lives of ancient people.

Every culture has a unique set of shared ideas and practices that are deployed, and at times resisted, to define social relationships. We create communities around gender, age, ethnicity, residence, race, shared history, etc. — these social identities are the result of a dialogue about membership and how individuals come to understand or make sense of their similarity and difference (Alcoff 2006, Moore 1994, Sørensen 2000). I want to make clear that identities are never inherent or given, but are constructed, reproduced, and resisted through relations with other people, with objects, and with various aspects of the landscape. As the mother of two boys, I cannot deny that there is some biological basis for certain male behavior, but as an anthropologist I know with equal certainty that the biological component, the brain differences or musculature, are interpreted and shaped with such a range of options across cultures that they become only a small part of the resulting social identity group we describe as masculinity. In fact it is the apparently unending ways in which cultures of the past and present have understood and manipulated the biological realities of human life that makes the study of social identities so fascinating and this field so important to anthropological archaeology.

The investigation of social identities is crucial to modern social archaeology, which is concerned with understanding the ways in which human social relationships have been expressed through the objects and architecture we make, and how we understand or utilize the past in the present (Hall 2001, Preucel and Meskell 2004:3, Renfrew 1984). As noted, identities are an expedient way that almost anyone can connect with the lives and experiences of ancient people, thereby partially dissolving the arbitrary line we have erected between past and present. But perhaps more importantly, identity construction is a fundamental human process of great interest to anthropology and many other social sciences because it reflects one of the basic ways in which cultures reproduce themselves, as well as how they change. The ideas any culture holds about how young people are made into adults involve a set of interlocking identities we choose to call gender, age, and even nation, which have to be reproduced through a shared understanding of mutual participation (Taylor 2004). Identities, as a form of social community building, are one of the primary mechanisms by which cultures reproduce themselves through instruction and performance of values, goals, behaviors, etc. Such actions and beliefs leave a material residue available to archaeologists, and these data are reflections of common understandings, worked out through dialogue and interaction (Taylor 2002:106). As Sørensen (2000) has explained, archaeology is very well suited to look at how social identities such as gender or childhood are constructed and lived, as these practices involve material things and physical arrangements or practices. But we should never lose sight of the fact that what we recover are materializations of shared ideas, or, more accurately, the materialization of individual negotiation or dialogue around shared ideas.

Recent social theory has explored the concept of the social imaginary, which is broader and deeper than either ideas or practices alone. Charles Taylor describes the social imaginary as "the ways in which people imagine their social existence, how they fit together with others, how things go on between them and their fellows, the expectations that are normally met, and the deeper normative notions and images that underlie these expectations" (Taylor 2002:106). What Benedict Anderson also makes clear is that the social imaginary is imagined because most members of a shared identity will not know other members, yet all will share an awareness of some sort of communion with others (Anderson 1991:6). Viewing the social identities of ancient societies as forms of the social imaginary allows us to see material culture and its circulations as part of a discourse about identity and membership, and this book will explore the use of objects and spaces to prop up and shape various identities. This can promote a study of contingent change rather than universal cultural evolution as well as an ancient past filled with interested agents who make strategic choices (Isbell 2000). William Isbell has suggested that for the study of past societies, the social imaginary moves the focus from innate or given identities to identities as a process of dialogue, something constructed through practice and interaction (Isbell 2000:252). I will explore the application of the social imaginary in more detail throughout the book as a framework in which to understand how gender, age, memory, and community were deployed or rejected within ancient Maya society of the northern lowlands.

The title of this book is *Social Identities in the Classic Maya Northern Lowlands: Gender, Age, Memory, and Place*, and throughout the next five chapters we will explore how social identities share certain characteristics, especially the use of material objects to help create and reinforce the meaning of key behaviors and relations. Social relationships, whether they are organized around ideas of gender, community, or history, leave a material residue. My interest in social identities began with a fascination with gender and a desire to know how historically specific ideas were entangled with aspects of the human body. How had the female body I was born into and our culture's ideas about natural abilities made it impossible for me to enroll in wood shop or auto mechanics during high school? From this rather trivial personal experience I began to see the myriad ways in which my culture naturalized a gendered division of labor and made it seem self-evident. In the modern West, gender is a social identity around which we have created tremendous dialogue and a sense of difference that is perhaps the most durable. Despite increasingly less gender-specific work habits, religious practices, modes of dress, or architectural spaces, our ways of understanding the differences between male and female bodies remain deeply relevant in the modern West and elsewhere. Understanding the human fascination with gender is a puzzle to solve, and we are still in the initial stages of looking at the many ways gender was conceptualized within the ancient world. The study of gender and its intricate intersections with other social conditions requires that we open the door to understanding other equally complex social identities, and hence this book explores four intersecting forms of social identity.

This book has three primary objectives. First, I embrace the goals of modern social or relational archaeology to address and debate issues of power in social relationships and the construction of knowledge about the past. Archaeology has much to contribute to wider discussions about the exercise of power, the construction of memory, and the manipulation of social identities, and I hope this volume will contribute in some way to those discussions. I explore populations that have been historically marginalized in mainstream representations of Classic Maya society as a remedy to certain patterns of how knowledge is constructed. Second, the patterned material culture discussed here will provide a series of case studies for how social identities are created, shared, and manipulated. Other case studies of social identity in the ancient world have appeared, and the present work attempts to provide an additional example from a large and complex state-level society of how identity can be understood within the theoretical framework of the social imaginary (Bernardini 2005, Cuddy 2007, Gardner 2007, Hendon 2010, Hutson 2010, Janusek 2004, Orser 2001, Varien and Potter 2008). Each time we deconstruct identities that have been naturalized or made to seem self-evident, we learn more about how human social actors exert power and control over one another and about how they resist such control. We are also better able to see heterarchical relations and variation when identity groups are viewed as historically contingent constructions. Third, this volume will present new primary data from my excavations in the northern Maya lowlands, specifically at the sites of Yaxuna, Chunchucmil, and Xuenkal, in Yucatán, México, over the last fifteen years (Figure 1.1).

Despite being very well known within the social imaginary of modern tourism, the archaeological record of the northern lowlands has been

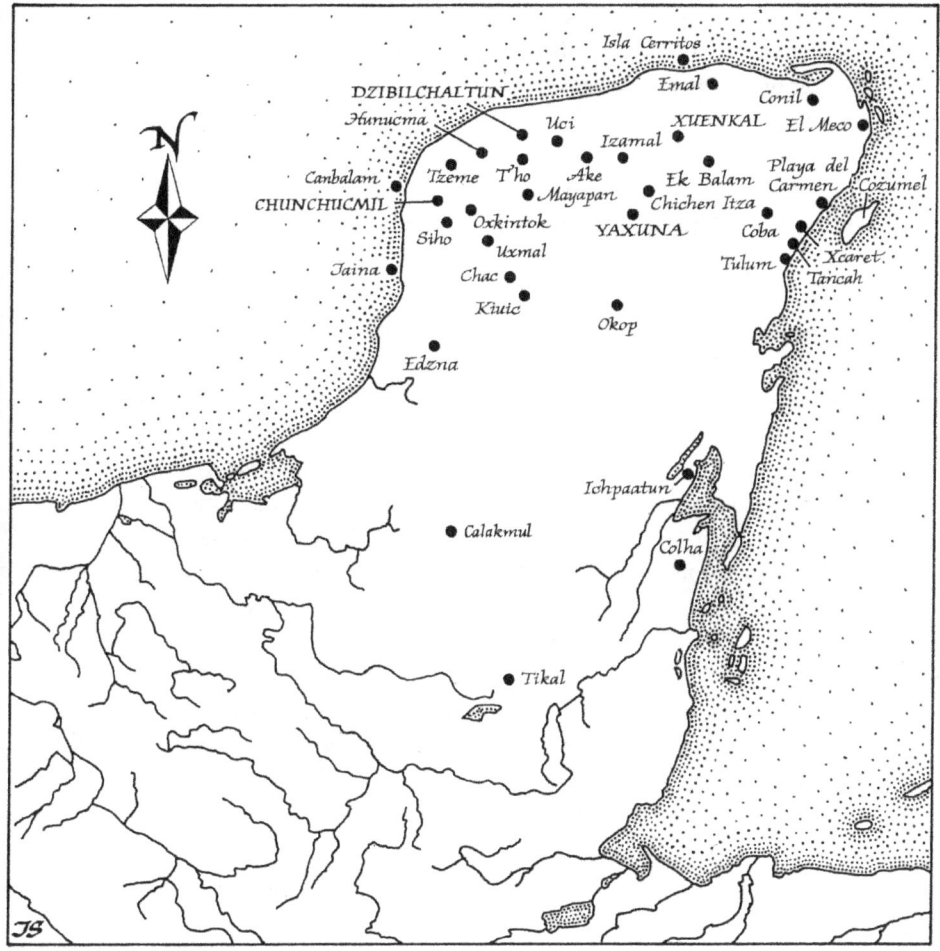

FIGURE 1.1. *Map of the Maya area with archaeological sites mentioned in the text. Illustration by Jack Scott.*

overshadowed in academic discourse about the Maya, perhaps due to the tradition within Maya studies of focusing on lengthy inscriptions and rich royal tombs. I hope that the publication of data from this culturally rich and diverse area will act as a corrective to the perception that Yucatán was in any way peripheral to Classic Maya society.

I feel it is worthwhile to explain briefly my interest in social identities in order to situate myself in relation to the data recovered by my research. A central contribution of the post-processualist movement in archaeology was to argue for an acknowledgment that our recovery of data from the archaeological record is driven in part by our personal interests and thus is never fully objective (Hodder and Hutson 2003; Johnson 1999; Shanks 1992, 2001). As the child of self-proclaimed hippies growing up in a small midwestern town, I was poignantly aware of the long hair and embroidered caftans worn by my parents and their friends as deliberate markers of an identity at odds with, but situated within, the qualified tolerance of conservative farming communities. My parents were civil rights activists and feminists and struggled against many of the hegemonic values and identities they felt were imposed by a small community. When we moved to Florida, identities were deliberately shifted and my parents layered a new regional identity on top of the others with self-conscious practices such as decorating palm trees for Christmas and wearing flowery Hawaiian shirts. As a teenager, when I became aware that I was both queer (not strictly heterosexual) and pagan (not of a monotheistic faith), the world of strategic decision making in regards to social identity and performance opened up. I had the choice to reveal or conceal, and "passing," as well as the condemnation by peers for "passing," became part of my social negotiations (Alexander 2006, Hoffman 2009). When introduced in college to the ancient cultures of the Maya world, a culture so complex and multifaceted yet with very clearly conveyed identities along axes of age, gender, and status, I found a counterpoint to my own complex negotiations of identity within the modern West. Ancient Maya lives were structured along a continuum of choices about social identities, and those choices were always entangled with the material world. In exploring ancient Maya culture, I have both learned how social imaginaries can provide a conservative and supportive framework for cultural perpetuation as well as how those same structures can change or be manipulated by the interests of a powerful minority.

ARCHAEOLOGY OF IDENTITY

The archaeology of identity has become a vast and diverse field of research, with many divergent theoretical perspectives. As scholars began to think about material culture as actively engaged in the construction and negotiation of identities, an awareness of the rich data available in the archaological record has inspired a generation of scholars to explore the social identities of past societies. But this line of questioning has evolved tremendously over the last twenty-five years, and like so much social archaeology, it is a product of a fertile cross-pollination of social theory and the long history of material culture studies.

Prehistorians have noted the association of material culture with social groups since the beginnings of the discipline of archaeology. Early twentieth-century attempts to link material culture with social evolution had as their premise that identity was visible in artifactual remains, although the interpretation of identity was often simplistic and determinative. In Mesoamerica, the presence of certain ceramic types or artifact groups represented or indicated the presence of an ethnic group. The Sotuta ceramic complex, a set of unique forms and ceramic pastes defined at Chichen Itza, is still used as an indication of "the Itza," a mythical group of non-Maya people, presumed to have been present at sites where this pottery is found (cf. Pool Cab 2013). There was little deconstruction of why certain materials were used or preferred by groups of ancient people, or to what degree those same people had exercised choice in the selection of such a material or design. This was because, as many scholars have noted, the individual was of less interest to processualist archaeology, which emphasized cultural systems on a broad scale. The processualists of the 1950s to 1970s made important and significant contributions to the field of archaeology by regularizing explicit hypothesis testing, multidisciplinary collaborative research projects, and the application of archaeological knowledge to wider social scientific questions. However, they did so at the expense of attention to the role of the individual within society, an understandable if unfortunate consequence of a focus on societies as a collection of smoothly functioning systems rather than a collectivity of individual actors. Little interest in the individual's experience of membership in social groups led to little recognition of individual ambition or resistance in the archaeological record, which in turn led to a rather unproblematic and direct association between material culture and status or roles. As early engendered studies of Maya households showed, the processual focus on systems failed to capture that economic relations were inextricable from gendered practices and most domestic production of food, crafts, and other goods took place within highly gender-specific spatial and social relations (Hendon 1992, 1997; Joyce 1993; Pohl and Feldman 1982). Uncritical interpretations of gender or age as purely limiting factors of identity are still present in the field of Mesoamerican archaeology today. Luckily these are balanced by an increasing number of publications oriented toward the individual as a social actor who made strategic decisions about how to enact social options.

In the last twenty-five years, social theory has moved far from the view of cultures as bounded and homogeneous, with an order that is natural and unconscious on the part of its members. Although certainly imperfect, especially regarding the concerns of feminists, the work of social theorists such as Pierre Bourdieu, Michel Foucault, Anthony Giddens, and colleagues set in motion an intellectual movement that argued human society does not exist apart from the members who create it. Rather, individuals' actions and struggles in relation to the expectations of their peers should be the focus of research that aims to understand human society. This relational approach emphasizes daily practices and interpersonal relationships as the foundation for an individual's understanding of the world. From a relational perspective, identity is contingent and strategic, rather than implicit or static.

The study of embodied practices has developed into a rich field within anthropology, and a focus on the body as the site of cultural inscription has deepened our understanding of cultural reproduction. However, an embodied approach alone often does not aim to get at the ways in which members of a society participate in communities or identities that are larger than a single individual's own experience, such as the processes by which we share citations about mutual social identities and become part of a collectivity. Embodiment is a crucial aspect of a relational approach but does not always facilitate a focus on the broader shared social imaginary to which this present work is directed.

An emphasis on the central role of individuals within society had enormous influence on the development of the study of identities within all the social sciences, including anthropological archaeology. The long-standing interest in class and status within archaeology was expanded to encompass a series of single-issue studies of social identities such as gender or nationality, as for example my book on ancient Maya women (Ardren 2002a), Sian Jones's (1997) in-depth examination of ethnicity, or Jane Eva Baxter's (2005) exploration of childhood. Recently archaeologists have followed the progression of social theory toward complicating the boundaries of identity categories and their intersections (Geller 2009, Meskell 2001). Where at first there were perhaps too many studies of social categories important to modern Westerners, such as "women" or "ethnic groups," now there is a more sensitive attention to the intersection of social identities and their mutual negotiation (Hutson 2010, Voss 2008).

SOCIAL IMAGINARIES

The social imaginary framework opens up the archaeology of identity to find evidence of competing discourses and contingent change while still allowing for the existence of a broader interpretive community that determines options and sets boundaries (Lee and LiPuma 2002:192). In his brilliant contribution to what is now known as the theory of social imaginaries, *Imagined Communities: Reflections on the Origin and Spread of Nationalism* (1991), Benedict Anderson explores the rise of nationalism after World War II in the West and in Southeast Asia. Anderson sought to explain three key components of nationalism: the disjunction between how the relative modernity of nations is viewed by its members versus by later historians, the universality of nationalism as a social concept and how it came to be naturalized like gender or age so that everyone must have a national identity, and the political power of nationalism despite philosophical impoverishment (Anderson 1991:5). The second and third goals are the most relevant for exploring the social imaginary and bear directly on how identities are created, maintained, and transformed as well as their intersections with relations of power and inequality.

Building on earlier conceptualizations of "the imaginary" in the work of Cornelius Castoriadis (1987) and Jacques Lacan (1977), Anderson shared with Castoriadis an emphasis on the creative aspects of the imaginary, but his focus on national identities broadened the concept to allow for the existence of multiple and simultaneous social imaginaries (Strauss 2006:329). Anderson defined a nation as an "imagined political community" and used the term "imagined" to convey that most members of a nation will not know the other members, yet they will share an image of connection and mutual purpose (Anderson 1991:6). This was not just true of nationalisms; Anderson argued that all shared social communities were imagined and this made them no less real or influential. The nation as a social identity had boundaries, power, and meaning. It was a self-evident horizontal fraternity that obscured real inequalities, limitations, and difference. From 1820 to 1920, the rise of nationalisms in Europe served to consolidate political power and expand capitalism in the hands of newly emergent elites (Anderson 1991:64, 110). Vernacular print media was the primary tool by which this new identity was enacted in Anderson's analysis, through such processes as the development of lexicons, the dissemination of dictionaries, and especially through the practice of reading popular newspapers. The convergence of capitalism and print media on a diverse set of languages to anoint a dominant language as the property of a specific group created a shared imaginary community. Each day as an emergent middle class read the newspaper in the dominant language to which they were a party, they were aware of millions of other people like themselves doing the same thing, which created a daily ritual of participation that reassured and reinforced the imagined community of nationalism. At the same time these people experienced membership in the social imaginary of their gender, an acknowledgment of the simultaneous existence of parallel imaginaries or identities (Anderson 1991:5).

Reading the newspaper alone was not enough to sustain a sense of shared identity, and Anderson suggests that understanding membership in an imagined community was confirmed by other means as well, such as habits, expectations, and performances which are seen to be linked. These linkages are often not explicitly visible but exist with real force in people's minds, through their practices, and in relations between members. A central aspect of his theory is the capacity of language to create and reinforce shared ideas that become naturalized through language use (Anderson 1991:141). For archaeologists, however, it may be Anderson's identification of shared rituals, especially private daily acts repeated habitually, that is of most importance. All cultures past and present have rituals of inclusion, like reading the newspaper, that circulate ideas about identity and shared membership. The fetching of water from a well or river, the preparation of food, or the proper care of infants are all daily acts that constitute rituals of inclusion present in most societies, including ancient Maya society. In large complex societies, some of these rituals are performed without knowledge of who else is also performing them, although with the certainty that they are doing so. In the Maya area, at many large urban sites household groups have burial platforms located on the eastern side of the compound that were used as ancestral shrines (Ashmore 1991, Becker 1991, Leventhal 1983, McAnany 1995). The shrines were integrated into household groups, and daily activities were carried out on their platforms. At Chunchucmil or Tikal, large urban cities of more than thirty thousand inhabitants, individuals did not know the details of every other citizen's religious life, although they shared in a system of practices that had certain elements in common. The presence of ancestral shrines in household groups of the ancient Maya is a clear materialization of a shared social imaginary, one which we will explore further in chapter 2.

Charles Taylor has elaborated upon the concept of the social imaginary, emphasizing that social practices are essential to the ability to "imagine" one's social surroundings and membership (Taylor 2002:106). Taylor is explicit that this is not a matter of theory but of practice: "theory is usually the possession of a small minority, whereas what is interesting in the social imagination is that it is shared by a large group of people, if not the whole society" (Taylor 2002:106). Images, stories, daily rituals: these are the places where the social imaginary is encountered and reproduced, in contexts both mundane and extraordinary. These practices may start off as theories held by a minority, such as the elite, but they come to infiltrate society as a whole, in a process similar to what Anderson identified for the creation and nurturance of nationalisms. Taylor is worth quoting at length:

> Our social imaginary at any given time is complex. It incorporates a sense of the normal expectations that we have of one another, the kind of common understanding which enables us to carry out the collective practices that make up our social life. This incorporates some sense of how we all fit together in carrying out the common practice. This understanding is both factual and "normative"; that is, we have a sense of how things usually go, but this is interwoven with an idea of how they ought to go, of what missteps would invalidate the practice. (Taylor 2002:106)

Taylor elaborates a theory of how we enact the social imaginary by participation in "macrodecisions" or actions that all members of the imaginary understand and practice. We know intuitively the boundaries of such macrodecisions and the consequences of stepping beyond those boundaries, and we share the knowledge that other members of our social imaginary possess this same knowledge base. He gives the example of choosing governments in a modern Western democracy, where each citizen understands their individual action is repeated simultaneously by others with the same choices, rules, and consequences. Members recognize an ideal behavior or practice guided by a shared moral order or principle as well as the reality of the imperfect practice. Perhaps most importantly for archaeology, where we are left with an imperfect record of only those actions that carried a durable material aspect, for Taylor the relation between practices and background understanding is central and reciprocal. "If the understanding makes the practice possible, it is also true that the practice largely carries the understanding" (Taylor 2002:107). The understanding, or what philosophers such as Martin Heidegger have called the "background," is in a reciprocal relationship with the behaviors or practices of which it is composed (Dreyfus 1991, Strauss 2006). People who share a social imaginary possess a common repertory of possible actions as well as the knowledge of how to choose among them and the consequences of an alternative choice. Members of ancient Maya society shared a background understanding of what was considered palatable food, tailored to their geography yet centered around the symbolically charged (and nutritious) holy trinity of corn, beans, and squash. They also understood the social repercussions for choosing to consume food considered inedible, and based on widespread studies of archaeofaunal remains we know they only very rarely made the choice to eat monkeys or raptors, while dogs and seabirds were considered edible (Götz 2008, 2011; Götz and Stanton 2013). Food choices are a powerful means by which cultures reproduce themselves and the reciprocal relationship between Taylor's practice and understanding.

Taylor gives the example of a political demonstration. When we choose to organize such an event, we know it is within our repertoire of possible means by which to express an opinion; we know how to make signs and choose a location that does not break the laws of assembly yet draws attention; in other words, we understand the ritual. Taylor could have easily used funerals as his example, and for my purpose I will substitute an ancient Maya funeral. Guided by background knowledge of options that make sense within a moral order, ancient Maya people made choices about how to commemorate the dead that were often very similar. The bulk of the population chose to bury the dead in close association with the residential spaces of the living—under floors or in small free-standing shrines (Becker 1999, McAnany 1995). They very often placed ceramic vessels with the dead and chose from a selection of gender-appropriate artifacts that will be discussed further in chapter 5. But the choice to inter a relative in the house group and to place a ceramic vessel with the body, especially when repeated by thousands of individuals in a private manner not visible to the entire population, only makes sense within a wider understanding or schema. This practice perpetuates the understanding, gives it an experiential and material basis, and circulates the knowledge among a fictionalized set of interpersonal relationships within the imaginary. From this perspective, the identity that members of a Maya city shared was not innate or given, but rather the result of a process of dialogue and construction, and the material evidence of those identities is not a static reflection but rather a record of discourse.

Taylor's ideas about the dialogue between background and behavior clearly owe much to the practice theory of Pierre Bourdieu (1977) and his contemporaries who struggled to understand the subject within objective social structures. Both Taylor and Bourdieu share an emphasis on actions or behaviors that create meaning and perpetuate membership, and both reject the existence of overarching rules that dictate the activities of social actors. The sensory experience of repeated actions (habitus) is important to both theorists as a way to understanding, and coordination with the actions and bodies of others plays a profound role in the enactment and perpetuation of the social imaginary; indeed Taylor says "practice largely carries the understanding" (Taylor 2002:107).

What Taylor adds to practice theory is a greater emphasis on the mental schemas or shared cognitive models, what might also be described as the understanding of shared membership (Strauss 2006:330). Although Taylor makes clear that theories are of less interest because they are only held by a minority, his inclusion of theories, or what he describes as the ideas held by a small and dominant group that may (or may not) come to infiltrate society as a whole, illustrates an emphasis on ideas that is not seen as strongly in Bourdieu. Where Bourdieu's practice theory allows for change or transformation in ways of being primarily through an individual's sensory experiences, the social imaginary as articulated by Taylor and Anderson incorporates competing discourses and contingent change from the outset, because each individual is empowered to understand and participate in their social imaginaries. These competing discourses might be the understanding of modernity held by Québécois versus Canadian citizens (Taylor's context) or the understanding of masculinity held by juvenile boys versus elder men (as discussed in chapter 5), but they exist within a broader interpretive community that can be influenced by ideas that shape practice, then imaginaries. In speaking about the rise of modern Western moral order, Taylor explains that what he wants to do is "sketch the changeover process in which the modern theory of moral order gradually infiltrates and transforms our social imaginary. In this process, what is originally just an idealization grows into a complex imaginary through being taken up and associated with social practices, in part traditional ones, which are transformed by the contact" (Taylor 2002:110).

In our efforts to understand the nature of power in the social relationships of past societies, the social imaginary provides a means by which to explore how group membership, which is never natural and effortless but rather always a dialogic process, could be influenced by certain dominant groups or ideas, the processes by which membership is achieved, and how the understanding of membership changes over time. Taylor fits within a relational practice theory approach to understanding the subject, but the social imaginary expands our discussion of the means by which ancient individuals thought about and experienced their fit with others to include participation in multiple and simultaneous imaginaries. Some may find Taylor's emphasis on shared ideas too abstract or intangible, even too homogenous, but since archaeology has a ready body of materialized ideas and practices in the architecture and artifacts we recover, a person-centered study is possible and promises to uncover real coherence as well as variance. The social imaginary approach is fully able to explore the practices that underscore and generate shared social understanding, as I show in the following case study chapters.

The role of circulations, or the overlapping experiences that emerge from an exchange of ideas, goods, stories, or rituals that lead to a specific and shared everyday understanding, has been elaborated by Benjamin Lee and Edward LiPuma (2002). The acknowledgment of circulations as key constitutive factors in a social imaginary contributes to a relational approach to understanding social identities and the processes by which cultural membership is achieved. Circulations are performed, whether through exchange of trade items or a rite of passage, and thus they both construct and constitute the imaginary and are constructed by it. A focus on circulations shifts us away from seeing the unit of analysis, whether that be a city or a social institution like a market, as bounded and stable and forces an analysis of how shared imaginaries like citizenship are fluid and evolving (LiPuma and Koelbe 2005:154). Lee and LiPuma address how the dynamics of circulation drive globalization and the resultant challenges to local notions of language, culture, etc. (Lee and LiPuma 2002:191), but their model of circulations as a mechanism of social imaginaries is applicable to the material record. Noting that circulations, especially of goods, have been of interest to anthropologists since Levi Strauss (with important modern contributions from Annette Weiner and others), nonetheless anthropologists did not see circulations and exchange as creating meaning but merely as transmitting meaning ascribed by other constituencies (Lee and LiPuma 2002:192). Their model of circulations is performative and sees circulations as cultural phenomena with their own forms of abstraction, evaluation, and restraint: "Cultures of circulation are created and animated by the cultural forms that circulate through them . . . and always presuppose the existence of their respective interpretive communities" (Lee and LiPuma 2002:192). Thus what Lee and LiPuma have added to the conceptualization of the social imaginary is another mechanism by which materializations can be used to read how the social imaginary is maintained and constituted. "Cultures" do not just exist; they are created and maintained by items and ideas moving between people along a gradient of consumption or participation. Some individuals in ancient Maya cities created domestic serving vessels that were exquisite and consistent, while other potters created lopsided and poorly fired vessels. Because of background similarities such as the identical paste, manufacturing method, and decoration, we understand them to be points along an identifiable spectrum of possible artistic choices. A ceramic style still has boundaries, for example in Fine Orange Ware of the Terminal Classic period only orange paste and volcanic ash temper were used to build the pot, and the decoration was always carved or applique. However, the results are not a single point but rather a spread. In this way the concept of circulations accommodates the choice and change we see within the material record by suggesting that artistic choice ("culture") was both suggested and perpetuated by the ideas and practices exchanged between members as they created a common style of ceramic serving vessel.

The identification of circulations gives us one more tool to understand what Taylor called the background understanding that makes practices possible and which is created by these same repeated practices. If both the background, or what Lee and LiPuma call the "interpretive community," and the practices, or what Lee and LiPuma call the "forms," are relational and created through a series of repeated circulations, then these circulations should leave a material residue available in the archaeological record. In more practical terms, the exchange of objects within an ancient Maya city, such as the distribution of imported obsidian, should be read as not merely a reflection of social interactions but as constitutive of a social identity or shared imaginary that provided a way for the people of that city to make sense of their choices and lives. While archaeologists are known for focusing on the circulation of an easily sourced trade item such as obsidian, we can also perform the same analysis on funerary rituals or ceramic styles that were circulated between people. Through such circulations, these materialized ideas confirmed the expectation of membership in a shared imaginary as well as perpetuated the interpretive community of that imaginary.

A wide variety of behaviors qualify as circulations that constitute and perpetuate social imaginaries. It may appear that everything is a circulation or that the concept is so broad as to lose interpretive usefulness. Circulations are inherently social and interactive; they are performative, meaning they are witnessed and ritualized. Through ritualization, consent of the participants is implied even if it is not completely in place. There is no reason to question the consent of participants since through their presence they are perpetuating the transmission of the imaginary along a gradient of involvement. Consequently, behaviors that are undertaken alone, outside the margins of society as defined in the moment or unintelligible, are likely not circulations and exist outside a shared social imaginary.

Circulations are obviously very important in understanding the way in which people lived together within an urban setting, imagining and acting as collective agents. The shared urban imaginary of the trading center of Chunchucmil will be explored in chapter 2.

VISUAL PARTNERS/BITS AND PIECES

The perspective on social identities and their construction, maintenance, and transformation presented here also owes a debt to recent scholarship on material culture that questions the Cartesian separation between people and things. If one embraces the idea that human interpersonal relationships occur within a framework of shared imaginations about the world and that dialogue or debate about that social imaginary is how we determine our place or membership within a shared social identity as well as how we maintain and change that imaginary, then we must agree that the materializations of those discourses—the choice to wear family jewelry or not, the choice to dress along gendered lines or not—are likewise powerfully implicated in the dialogue about membership. Material culture plays a special role in social reproduction—objects link generations, families, and individuals and are fundamental partners in the mediation of tradition or other cultural institutions (Sørensen 2000). Objects can be used as visual memories or props for commemoration or renegotiation of relationships and are often deployed in a strategic manner. Viewed in this light, it is difficult to deny that objects have some form of agency and are central to the experience of social interaction. Bruno Latour (1993, 1999, 2005) questions the division between people and objects, highlighting their interdependence, and claims that objects, as characterized by Scott Hutson, are not "second-class agents" (Hutson 2010:22). In 1988, writing under the fictional name Jim Johnson, Latour posed an important question:

> But anyway, who are you, you the sociologists, to decide forever the real and final shape of humans . . . are you aware of your discriminatory biases? You discriminate between the human and the inhuman. I do not hold this bias but see only actors—some human, some nonhuman, some skilled, some unskilled—that exchange their properties. (Johnson 1988:303)

As Latour highlights, human actors cannot be our only focus of analysis when understanding the meaning and experience of identities, an idea with obvious resonance for scholars of material culture. But the predominant model within modern archaeology is to see objects as simply the products of human activity, not as reciprocal agents locked in a relational network (Lally and Ardren 2008). Yet premodern non-Western cultures often did not ascribe the same lack of agency to objects, or, to phrase it more accurately, objects were empowered or even agitated agents in other cultures. As Julian Thomas and others have noted, archaeology has probably overemphasized the modern Western notion of the bounded individual in our interpretations of the past (Thomas 2002). Because we tend to think of ourselves as self-contained and having free agency, a center point from which meanings and actions emerge, we have projected the same bounded, stable notion of the individual into the past. This interpretive fallacy obscures the relational aspects of material culture in ancient societies as well as the role such objects play in our own culture. There are abundant examples of the inherent power and agency ancient Maya people understood certain materials to possess, independent of their use in highly charged arenas. Jade, whether worn by a queen in an elaborate beaded skirt or imitated by a commoner in a simple pebble painted blue-green, had an inherent agency to connect the wearer with the fertile power of the Maize Deity and a related set of regenerative forces. Pottery vessels were ritually killed with drilled holes before being placed in a burial and houses were animated with offerings before they could be occupied. As humans performed these actions, they circulated a knowledge and set of practices that confirmed their expectation of living within a universe of animate actor-objects. At every level of ancient Maya society, objects were agents and co-constituted the social identities of members of that society. I am not arguing that objects had the same capabilities as humans, but rather that we must acknowledge a deeper interdependence between objects and human identities and refrain from interpreting objects as a reflection of status or identity when in fact objects were created with far greater intention than to reflect. The complex life histories of especially portable objects make an argument for any single meaning impossible to sustain.

The object biography approach adds a further dimension to our understanding of the interactions between humans and objects because it posits that as people and objects gather time, they are constantly transformed, and such transformations of person and object are tied up with one another (Appadurai 1986, Gosden and Marshall 1999, Meskell 2004). The notion of the biography of objects originates in a 1986 article by Igor Kopytoff, who argued that things could not be fully understood at just one point in their existence. It was better, he argued, to look at cultural processes such as cycles of production, exchange, and consumption as a whole (Kopytoff 1986). This is because objects, like people, have the ability to accumulate history and meaning, so that the present significance of a Maya incense burner on display in a European museum derives from not only its current aesthetic impact but also its original maker and his or her intent, the people who used it in the ancient past, manipulations of the global antiquities market, and its radical removal from the Maya area to reside in a foreign museum. Each of these social interactions can be illuminated by seeing them as interconnected moments along a continuum. Likewise, in the same way that no individual has a single biography, there will never be a single narrative or biography that captures the entire spectrum of an individual object.

The object biography approach is particularly relevant in the study of ancient Mesoamerican art since we know objects held life force and were animate in the eyes of the ancient Maya (Harrison-Buck 2012, Lucero 2010, Stuart 1998). Given the Maya perspective on material culture, we can begin to talk about mutual biographies, where material objects are not fully external to the lives of humans but rather people and objects shaped and transformed each other permanently. From hieroglyphic inscriptions and material evidence, we know ancient Maya people performed ceremonies to animate, sustain, and even terminate certain material objects such as stelae, buildings, and ceramic vessels. The artist who created these pieces or the priest who performed the initial dedication gave birth, in a sense, to these objects and thus was permanently transformed by the interaction. Melanesians see objects as detached parts of the people who made them, and in this culture artists are ultimately composed of all the objects they have made and their associated transactions or circulations throughout the culture (Gosden and Marshall 1999:173). This idea illuminates the relational way in which an object is never wholly distinct from the person who "made" it, nor is the person able to fully disengage from the materialized idea we tend to call an object. For this reason, I consider objects agitated, because this term calls to mind the opposite of the static and inanimate view of objects utilized within much of modern archaeology. The perspective employed here enables us to understand the archaeological record as the visible materialization of ideas and interactions shared or contested by a vast array of agents.

CONCLUSION

This chapter has introduced the relational framework to be employed in this volume as a means of beginning the dialogue about how social identities were materialized in Classic Maya culture. Situated within the aims of modern social archaeology to explore relations of power and representation at all levels of society including the individual, I have suggested that the concept of the social imaginary captures the contingent ways in which identities form and change as well as how we can view material culture and its circulations as part of a discourse about identity and membership. The following chapters present case studies of some of the major social imaginaries at play in Classic Maya society. As Taylor makes clear, each of us participate in multiple or parallel social imaginaries, as we simultaneously experience ourselves as members of a gender, an age cohort, a community, and various other social groups. While gender- and age-based identities are relatively familiar to most archaeologists, in the following chapters I argue that the ways in which memory is deployed within settlements and the experience of living in an urban setting are also both constitutive of identities we share with others. I hope to show how these parallel social identities intersect or exist simultaneously in order to move away from a notion of identity as fixed or determined by inherent biological characteristics. Certainly when someone moves to a city, like ancient Chunchucmil or Yaxuna, they experience a process of identity transformation, moving from outsider to marginal to member. The patterned remains in the material record can reveal how this process occurs, how culture is created and maintained, through circulations of strategic behaviors linked to key objects.

Chapter 2 will debate the urban imaginary and the social experience of living in an ancient Maya city through the data from my excavations at Chunchucmil, where more than thirty thousand people lived in an environmentally demanding location in order to benefit from trade in salt and other coastal resources. Travel to and from the coast created a literal circulation that came to define an important characteristic of life in ancient Chunchucmil. I also identify important architectural features that shaped how citizens interacted and thus how they perpetuated a sense of belonging to such a place. Chapter 3 interrogates how memories are used to perform, perpetuate, and transform social identities late in Classic Maya culture. With data from Postclassic architectural shrines and their associated offerings at Yaxuna, I look at the powerful connection between memory and identity and how local elites remembered or reimagined their collective past disappointments in order to breathe life into their social identity as leaders and survive in a new social order. In chapter 4, I explore the social identity of childhood, and through the data from juvenile burials at Yaxuna, Xuenkal, and Dzibilchaltun, as well as the sacrifice of children at

Chichen Itza, I discover how the social imaginary of childhood in Classic Maya cities of the north included practices and beliefs centered in the sacred or numinous power of infancy. Certain infant burials placed into architectural settings across the northern lowlands communicate a perception of the inherent value of the child as a substance to connect the living with the dead. Chapter 5 takes up the subject of gender and the manner in which specific architectural spaces were used to help instill a sense of gender and gender-specific activities as natural and significant. By exploring domestic compounds from Yaxuna and Chunchucmil as well as the civic architecture of Dzibilchaltun, I argue that unequal access to power was mediated by conversations about gender difference. In the final chapter I review other recent work on social identities within the Maya area and their relevance to modern Maya writers. I argue for the emergence of a unified approach to identity studies and show how this would deepen both our analyses of material remains and our comprehension of ancient cultures. The social imaginary is a powerful tool with which to approach how identities are constructed and maintained. As a concept, it allows for contingent change rather than natural evolution, and for understanding material objects as active partners in the negotiation of larger social interactions. It is my hope that the rich data I have had the privilege of gathering from these impressive ancient cities will be illuminated in a new and insightful way through the lens offered here.

CIRCULATIONS AND THE URBAN IMAGINARY OF CHUNCHUCMIL

Chapter 2

INTRODUCTION

What was daily life like in the ancient cities of Classic Maya society? Did ancient people face the challenges of urban life many of us know today—was their neighborhood noisy, did they meet strangers when they went out, did they feel they belonged? Did they share a sense of membership or identity with the other people who lived in their city? What experiences shaped a sense of connection with their city? This chapter explores the social experience of urbanism in ancient Chunchucmil, a large urban trading center in northwestern Yucatán. To tackle this challenge I assemble information from a variety of sources including architecture, artifacts, and geography that all contribute to reconstructing the urban imaginary of this unusual community.

I summarize artifactual and architectural data in order to demonstrate the truly immense size of this ancient city and its social landscape, with a focus on the residential house-lot known as the Lool group. The environmental challenges of living not far inland from the coast on the dry northwestern plains provided a key motivation for a social imaginary centered on exchange. I attempt to reconstruct some of the interaction between the people of Chunchucmil and the coast, and the ways urban leaders controlled vital coastal resources, especially salt, as a means to comprehend the background understandings and practices shared by members of this very unusual place. Finally, I offer some conclusions on experiences that would have helped shape how citizens of the ancient city saw themselves as part of the social entity known today as ancient Chunchucmil.

THE LANDSCAPE OF THE CITY

Previous research by members of the Pakbeh Regional Economy Program (PREP), which I codirected from 1997–2002, has demonstrated that Chunchucmil was a demographically large urban center that functioned as a central place for the surrounding region (Ardren 2002b; Dahlin et al. 2005; Dahlin and Ardren 2002; Hutson 2010; Hutson, Magnoni, and Stanton 2004; Hutson et al. 2008; Magnoni 2007; Magnoni, Hutson, and Dahlin 2013). Most definitions of urbanism require both a demographic threshold and the demonstration of a variety of functions; Chunchucmil meets both of these characteristics. Early definitions of urbanism in the contemporary world (Weber 1958, Wirth 1938) or in the prehistoric past (Childe 1950) also emphasized the social adjustments that are at the heart of the development of urbanism. There has always been recognition that it is not only physical features, like large settlement size, high population density, and monumental architecture that define the urban nature of a city. Urban settings are the stages for elaborate social networks that draw residents, supporting rural populations, and visitors into shared relationships and often shared identities.

The analyses and interpretations of ancient Chunchucmil presented by members of the Pakbeh Regional Economy Program are based on a detailed map of almost 12 square kilometers including 8.5 square kilometers of dense urban settlement, maps of regional settlement, satellite imagery, environmental reconstructions including soil and water sampling, and extensive excavations in both household and monumental groups at Chunchucmil (see Hutson 2010 for a comprehensive bibliography). The site of Chunchucmil was occupied throughout the entirety of the Classic period, or almost two millennia from approximately 500 BCE to 1100 CE. There is limited ceramic evidence to suggest the city was initially occupied during the end of the Middle Preclassic period (700–350 BCE) and grew steadily throughout the Late Preclassic period (350 BCE–200 CE) to reach a peak of population during the Early Classic period (200–600 CE). Most of the materials to be discussed in this chapter—the architecture and artifacts left in household groups—date to the Early Classic period and the first part of the Late Classic (600–900 CE), especially the three hundred years from 400–700 CE. People continued to reside and build architecture at Chunchucmil during the Late and Terminal Classic (900–1150 CE) periods, with a dramatic shift in the settlement pattern (Magnoni, Hutson, and Stanton 2008). Fewer people seem to have lived in a less dense arrangement on large platforms within the center of the site. Like so many other ancient cities in the northern Maya lowlands, evidence for Postclassic occupation appears at only a few key locations scattered across the site (see chapter 3).

My colleague Aline Magnoni has done a brilliant job estimating the ancient population of Chunchucmil, a notoriously difficult exercise that often yields unreliable results given the incomplete nature of the archaeological record. But by a series of corrections and the application of GIS technology, Magnoni proves Chunchucmil was one of the most densely occupied cities of the ancient Maya world (Magnoni 2007). Based on mapped data from over six thousand structures within an area of twenty-five square kilometers, and utilizing only contemporaneously occupied structures and a well-accepted figure of five occupants per residential structure, Magnoni suggests the population reached from thirty-one thousand to forty-three thousand people during the period from 400-600 CE when the city was at its height (Magnoni 2007:163). The overall population of the famous Maya city of Tikal was larger, but it was spread over an area twice the size of greater Chunchucmil (Magnoni 2007:165). Like most cities, the central urban core of Chunchucmil, an area of approximately 8.5 kilometers square, was the most densely occupied, with many residential groups clustered around large monumental architecture and elite residential compounds. This zone is surrounded by a residential periphery in which the settlement is almost exclusively domestic and finally by a hinterland or rural supporting population, for a total area of 64 kilometers square for greater Chunchucmil (Hutson et al. 2008, Magnoni et al. 2014)

The high figures estimated for the Chunchucmil urban population are even more striking when the poor agricultural potential of the landscape around the site is considered. Chunchucmil is located in semi-arid terrain twenty-seven kilometers inland from the Gulf of Mexico, not far north of the modern border between the states of Yucatán and Campeche, México. This particular environmental zone is among the driest in all of the Maya area, with annual rainfall varying from 700 to 1,000 millimeters (Beach 1998:762). High rates of evapotranspiration further reduce this figure to 600-800 millimeters to create an annual precipitation deficit (Beach 1998:762). The typical tropical rainy season from May through October provides some relief from these conditions, but due to microenvironmental conditions, rainfall is highly variable from year to year and consequently corn agriculture is unreliable (although there is plenty of evidence that agriculture was practiced in ancient times, as discussed below) (Dahlin et al. 2005). Nearly a third of the surface around Chunchucmil is exposed limestone bedrock, and even when soil is present, it is shallow and not particularly productive unless enhanced by human modification (Hutson 2010:41, Beach 1998).

To the west of Chunchucmil are the shifting sand dunes and salt flats of the coast with adjacent mangrove swamps that can be traversed in canoes.

In between the mangrove swamps and the semi-desertic zone around Chunchucmil lies a seasonally inundated zone of scrub forest and savanna grassland punctuated by freshwater springs. This zone is waterlogged for much of the year and has evidence for small-scale human habitation in prehistory (Hixson 2011). Even today it is utilized primarily for its natural resources such as palm fibers and wildlife. To the east of the site, there is a very modest improvement in soils, and the density of ancient and modern settlement increases. Twenty-seven kilometers to the east of Chunchucmil, and visible from the highest pyramids of the site, is the only significant topographical feature of the Yucatán peninsula, a low limestone ridge that rises one hundred meters above otherwise flat topography known as the Puuc hills. On the summit of this ridge is the ancient site of Oxkintok, a compact settlement whose elaborate standing palaces and hieroglyphic inscriptions give it a very different character from the dense and sprawling city on the edge of the swamp (Rivera Dorado 1989, Varela Torrecilla 1998). From a regional perspective, the urban core of Chunchucmil is situated at the westernmost edge of inhabitable land within the absolute worst area for agriculture, but as close to the coast and wetlands as possible without significant risk of regular flooding.

David Vlcek and other members of the Archaeological Atlas Survey were the first to propose that this unusual location and settlement pattern could be explained by a focus on coastal resources, especially the salt trade (Vlcek et al. 1978). The salt flats of Celestun, located immediately to the west of Chunchucmil on the coast, are the second-largest saltworks in all of Mesoamerica (Dahlin et al. 1998) and would have provided a major economic return for those in control of this resource, probably enough to compensate for the marginal agricultural productivity in the region. This hypothesis has been tested and explored in many earlier publications by members of the Pakbeh Regional Economy Program and the economic basis of the city as a center for trade is now firmly established (Dahlin et al. 2005; Mansell et al. 2006).

THE PICH QUADRANGLE

The basic component of the monumental architectural plan at Chunchucmil was the quadrangle—a relatively large, quadrangular patio with low range structures on three sides and a monumental pyramid on the fourth side (9 to 14 meters high), often with a low freestanding platform in the center of the patio. Fifteen of these quadrangles exist within greater Chunchucmil, eleven of which are in the site center, while four are located at varying distances of 800 meters to 2 kilometers from the site center (Dahlin and Ardren 2002, Magnoni et al. 2014). Most of these quadrangles, even those located at a distance from the site center, are connected by ancient road systems that radiate out from an open area at the heart of the city to terminate at the patio of a quadrangle group. Given the absence of other freestanding pyramids or palace compounds usually found at Classic-period sites across the Maya area, the quadrangle groups represent the primary civic and ceremonial architecture of the city. Access to the interior patio areas would have been easily controlled, perhaps more so than the large open plazas characteristic of other Maya cities of comparable size. Access is so restricted that it is possible the quadrangles would have been defensible. Most of the quadrangle groups were occupied during the Early Classic period and may be the architectural manifestation of multiple powerful social units operating at the site simultaneously.

In most cases, the pyramids of these quadrangles are located on the eastern side of the group and face west. It is common at many Maya sites that the ceremonial structure is located on the eastern side of an architectural group, as east was understood as the first direction (Ashmore 1991, Becker 1991, Leventhal 1983, McAnany 1995). The only exceptions are three pyramids located either on the western or southern side of quadrangles and facing the site center. Thus, in a few instances, facing the site center was a more salient consideration for the pyramidal structure than a location on the eastern side of the quadrangle group (Hutson et al. 2008).

Excavations have shown that the range structures located around three sides of the quadrangle patios are a combination of open platforms and roomed structures. At the Pich quadrangle, two range structures on the central patio were excavated (Figure 2.1). One was a long platform with an open summit (N1E1-23), reached by stairs on both sides. The other (N1E1-22) was a large room reached by a small staircase that opened onto the central patio of the quadrangle. Like other similar Classic Maya monumental constructions, the function of such rooms is always difficult to determine precisely due to the lack of associated artifacts and activity area residues. The dimensions are consistent with the area needed to gather small groups of people or store goods, and the lack of artifactual evidence for craft or food production argues against domestic use. In both cases these structures were well built with the architectural hallmarks of substantial investment such as well-cut stones, thick plaster surfaces, and cinnabar painted surfaces. The plaster floor of the large open room on the west of the quadrangle was elevated and resurfaced several times during the Early Classic period.

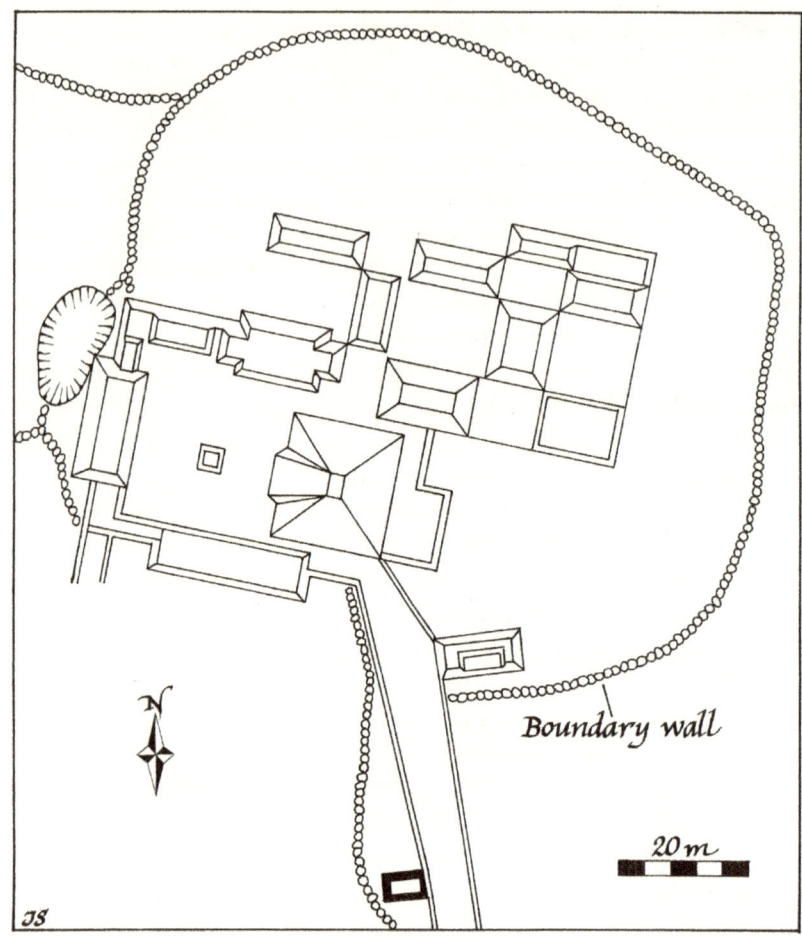

FIGURE 2.1. *Pich quadrangle group, Chunchucmil. Illustration by Jack Scott based on Pakbeh Regional Economy Program (PREP) field drawings.*

Immediately adjacent to the quadrangle groups are clusters of mid-elite domestic structures. To the north of the Pich quadrangle, we excavated an elaborate four-room structure (N1E1-29) with an interior bench, multiple doorways, and associated domestic refuse. This set of rooms had a perishable roof and opened onto a restricted patio area immediately to the north of the main Pich quadrangle patio. Ceramic debris, household tools such as broken obsidian blades, and worn grinding stones indicate this was a living area (Blackmore and Ardren 2002). Residential areas associated with the quadrangles are a variation on the more typical palace compound found at other Maya sites. This architectural difference, of elite residences attached to quadrangles rather than palaces, indicates a conceptual difference as well, one that emphasizes the particular social identity of people who lived at Chunchucmil and controlled the architectural landscape. At many Classic Maya cities it is easy to identify a succession of royal palaces or compounds associated with the funerary pyramids of important dynastic founders and rulers. At Chunchucmil we find a large number of quadrangle compounds that were occupied simultaneously, an indication that multiple elite social groups, each of whom held significant economic, political, and social power at the site, were present concurrently. The large number of quadrangles at Chunchucmil as well as the lack of any typical Classic-period palace architecture indicates the organization of the city around multiple power holders was an enduring tradition at least throughout the four hundred years of the Early Classic period. One of the quadrangles is somewhat more elaborate than the others and includes an attached ball court (the only one known from Chunchucmil), multiple courtyards, and the highest pyramidal structure. Known as the Chakah group, the additional resources evident in the elaboration of this quadrangle suggest it may have been the loci of a social group considered first among equals (Dahlin and Ardren 2002:269). The differences between the Chakah group and the other large quadrangles are not as dramatic as the differences between a royal compound and secondary elite domestic groups at other Maya sites, and we believe this indicates a modest stratification among economic equals rather than the more common dynastic stratification evident in the monumental architecture of many ancient Maya cities.

Quadrangles are known at other sites in western Yucatán, although not in the numbers documented at Chunchucmil, and other recent studies have explored the connections between quadrangles and expressions of political power. Nicolas Dunning (1992) identified two common site plans for the western Puuc area, one of which is the quadrangle complex connected by *sacbe* to a palace, the other the quadrangle group so common at Chunchucmil: a large pyramid structure fronted by a series of range structures and courts. William Ringle and George Bey have suggested that quadrangle areas, especially their interior patios or courtyards, were the primary meeting areas for northern Maya royalty, the settings for performative activities that demonstrated elite status (Ringle and Bey 2001:281). They support this interpretation by citing the relative lack of domestic refuse at quadrangles, their association with clearly civic features such as raised roads and pyramidal structures, and their highly formalized and restricted entryways.

These interpretations are supported by architectural and artifactual data from Chunchucmil where excavations at the Pich quadrangle show the interior patio area of the main quadrangle was the focus of the flanking structures. At this quadrangle, the large pyramid is located on the eastern side of the patio. Across from it on the western side, a set of stairs leads to a single open room. To the north, extensive horizontal excavation showed another set of stairs leading up to a long open platform that ran the length of the patio area. The stairs on both of these structures face into the patio area where there is a small central "shrine," which Ringle and Bey suggest may have been a throne platform (Ringle and Bey 2001:278). The presence of stairs accentuates the possibilities for this central patio area to have been a performative space for Maya elite, either as a place to receive tribute payments, as suggested by Bey and Ringle based upon ethnohistoric literature, or as a place from which to conduct trading negotiations and bestow or consume exotic gifts, as we think may have been the case at Chunchucmil. Both actions would have been key components in rituals of status reinforcement and reciprocal social reproduction that were important throughout the Classic Maya world in royal courts. The dramatized and ritualized exchange of trade goods, or even commodities, at a city dedicated to trade and exchange in order to survive would have constituted one of the core rituals of inclusion by which people became citizens of Chunchucmil. The prevalence of quadrangles throughout the city, especially as indicated by their occurrence nearly two kilometers outside the urban center, is a materialized expression of a discourse about identity. Quadrangles were core components in the reproduction of a social identity based on trade and exchange. They were part of both the "understanding"—the background values that frame behavior—and the practice—the activities that perpetuate the understanding, as Taylor would suggest. Moving from one quadrangle to another or being prohibited from entering a quadrangle was a performative circulation that created a shared understanding of the city and what it meant to live there.

At Chunchucmil as well as other sites in the western Puuc region, quadrangles and more modest domestic patio groups share the same organizational or spatial principles—an interior patio enclosed by architecture—and we are certain that the expression of this principle at the elite level in often elaborate monumental architecture signaled an essential conceptual unity between the ruling population and the ruled (Magnoni, Hutson, and Dahlin 2013; Magnoni et al. 2014). This is not to say there were not severe status differences in the population, but to highlight that these differences were deliberately muted in the choices evident in elite architecture.

The dispersed settlement of urban Maya sites is generally understood to be the result of a gradual incorporation of rural zones into an urban setting due to the need to retain agricultural fields for intensive suprahousehold cultivation (Chase and Chase 1998, Chase et al. 2001, Cobos 2001, Drennan 1988, Dunning 1992, Killion et al. 1989). Retention of space for household production activities, such as gardens or stone working, is clearly visible at Chunchucmil, even though the structural density is extremely high in comparison to other Maya sites (Hutson et al. 2007). Throughout the city, domestic groups including elite quadrangles as well as modest house-lots were delimited and enclosed by stone boundary walls—*albarradas*—an unusual feature found at only a few other Maya sites and usually later in time, such as Classic-period Coba (Folan et al. 1983), Postclassic Mayapan (Bullard 1952, 1954), and small Postclassic sites along the east coast of the Yucatán peninsula like Tulum (Benavides Castillo 1981, Freidel and Sabloff 1984, Silva Rhoads and Hernandez 1991, Sierra Sosa 1994, Vargas et al. 1985). Most of Chunchucmil's architectural groups shared these stone boundary walls, perhaps because of the high structure density. Both density and barriers like boundary walls are best understood as materializations of social values and interactions. The presence of stone walls at Chunchucmil, but not at contemporary neighboring sites, is another indication of the particular social identity under construction at this unique place. At a certain distance from the site center, when the structure density diminishes, open spaces were left between bounded residential groups. But within the urban core, streets created by parallel stone walls that intersected raised roads directed traffic in the crowded urban landscape. These features are literally the boundaries created by the community of Chunchucmil as it managed competing discourses about access, opportunity, and space. The walls were a strategic decision, and not an inevitable one, given that such walls do not appear at other large urban centers of the time. They constitute a key component to understanding the urban identity attached to this particular city.

Stone walls surround hundreds and hundreds of house-lots at Chunchucmil. These modest groups are usually a set of small structures around an open patio, and four such groups within the urban core have been intensively investigated through mapping, horizontal excavation, and geochemical testing. The nature of the 'Aak, Muuch, and Kaab domestic groups has been extensively discussed in a series of publications, and here

I will explore a fourth house-lot, the Lool group (Hutson, Magnoni, and Stanton 2004; Hutson et al. 2006; Hutson et al. 2008; Hutson 2010). It has much in common with the other three in terms of overall scale, design, and function, and thus contributes to our understanding of the way urban life was materialized at Chunchucmil.

THE LOOL GROUP

The Lool group is located in an area of the ancient urban core approximately thirty meters to the northeast of the Pich quadrangle. It shares a stone boundary wall with the Pich structure. The two groups were occupied simultaneously, and their physical proximity suggests a shared social proximity as well. This house-lot group consists of three structures situated around the northern, eastern, and southern sides of a small central patio (Figure 2.2). A very low rubble pile can be found on the fourth side of the patio. The northern structure (N2E2-74) is a very low platform with the remains of a small circular enclosure on its western edge. The eastern structure (N2E2-75) is a platform approximately three meters tall with damage due to looting. The southern structure (N2E2-76) is an elaborate four-room building designed in a manner consistent with other residential architecture at Chunchucmil. The Lool group was damaged by the construction in the 1950s of an unpaved gravel road that bisected the group immediately to the east of Structure 75, and it is likely that looting of this structure for its worked stone happened at this time.

Just like the arrangement found at the 'Aak, Muuch, and Kaab groups, the Lool group has a nonresidential structure on the eastern side that was the focus of ritual activities (Hutson, Magnoni, and Stanton 2004:81). Structure 75 is a small platform approximately four by six meters at the base with a single staircase on the western or patio side that leads halfway up the structure. There are no other points of access to the summit of the shrine. The walls of Structure 75 were made of evenly cut worked stone set in thick plaster, and the most notable aspect of the building is its distinctive talud-tablero design: outward sloping walls topped with slab stones, originally covered in modeled stucco (Ardren and Blackmore 2002, Ardren 2003a, Ardren and Lowry 2011a). This architectural style was defined at the Early Classic central Mexican site of Teotihuacan, but local variations are found throughout Mesoamerica from the Late Preclassic through the Postclassic period (Giddens 1995, Gendrop 1984, Heyden and Gendrop 1980, Marquina 1964, Stanton 2005, Varela T. and Braswell 2003).

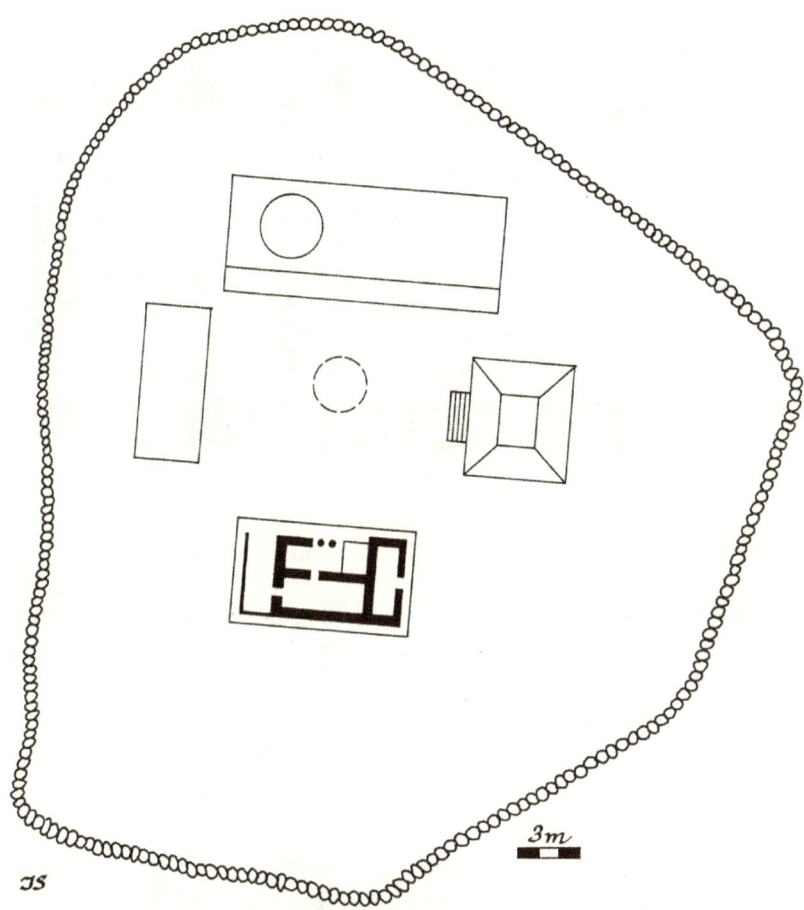

FIGURE 2.2. *Residential group, Chunchucmil. Illustration by Jack Scott based on Pakbeh Regional Economy Program field drawings.*

Ceramics recovered around the base of Structure 75 and from interior construction fill indicate that it was constructed during the Early Classic period, which is consistent with this style of architecture, as well as the main period of occupation at the nearby Pich quadrangle (Hutson in prep). A radiocarbon date of 530 CE from the adjacent residential structure (N2E2-76) in the Lool group (Beta-177740 of bone collagen via AMS, 2 sigma calibration AD 420 to 610 [Cal BP 1530 to 1340]) suggests the latter part of the Early Classic period. Ceramics from Structure 75 fall within a regional complex, and both local and imported wares were recovered. Excavation into the area behind the stairs on the western (patio) side of Structure 75 revealed a very small substructure and cache completely en-

FIGURE 2.3. *Tripod cylinder vessel from Structure 75, Lool residential group, Chunchucmil. Photograph by Phillip Hofstetter, used with permission.*

cased by the construction of the stairs and talud-tablero walls of Structure 75. The small dimensions of the substructure suggest it may have been created for the deliberate protection of an offering, much as the architectural boxes found at the 'Aak group of Chunchucmil (Hutson 2010).

A cylindrical vase fifteen centimeters tall with a small inverted bowl for a lid was placed by the ancient inhabitants of Lool as a cache offering just in front of the substructure (Figure 2.3). The soil surrounding the vase had been stained with hematite, and the vase contained similar soil as well as a large quantity of small bone fragments that have been identified as cremated human remains (V. Tiesler personal communication). Restoration of the vase revealed polychrome hieroglyphic painting on the exterior. While small glyphic elements are recognizably Maya, others are not identifiable and the text is both very early and very poorly preserved. Epigraphic analysis indicates that it is Early Classic in date, a very unusual finding and currently not decipherable (A. Lacadena personal communication, D. Stuart personal communication). The tripod slab-footed design of the cylindrical vase is a diagnostic form associated often with the Early Classic site of Teotihuacan.

As noted recently by Travis Stanton, no solid evidence has been recovered to support the model that people from the central Mexican city of Teotihuacan lived permanently in the Classic Maya northern lowlands during the sixth century (Stanton 2005, cf. Smyth and Rogart 2004). Following Carmen Varela and Geoffrey Braswell, Stanton favors a model of appropriation by Yucatec Maya of traits circulating throughout Mesoamerica during the Early Classic period (Varela T. and Braswell 2003). Many of these traits are best known from Teotihuacan but are also present at a wide variety of other ancient sites throughout Mesoamerica. The evidence from Structure 75 of the Lool group fits easily within the Oxkintok Regional phase as defined by Varela, which consists of local Maya traditions augmented by a regional variation of the talud-tablero architectural style and cylindrical tripod ceramics. Such traits were defined at Oxkintok, only twenty-seven kilometers from Chunchucmil, but are known from Early Classic deposits at other sites within the region such as Yaxuna, Dzibilchaltun, T'ho, and Chac II among others.

Joseph Ball (1983) was the first to write about "homologies," or local copies of foreign wares within Classic Maya culture. Ball defined this concept in order to distinguish true imports from local copies in a sample of ceramic vessels that all utilize the same style. In Ball's study of Early Classic Maya ceramics, local copies far outnumbered foreign imports, which not only reveals useful economic information about the limits of trade but also illuminates the central importance of stylistic change and imitation, especially at elite levels of material culture. Likewise, the prevalence of the local Yucatecan version of talud-tablero architecture, in which, as Varela noted, the tablero is not present on all sides of a structure, is much more common in the northern lowlands than the Teotihuacanoid version that has an inset upper talud and steeply sloping lower talud (Varela T. and Braswell 2003). Thus the balance of evidence from the northern lowlands argues for a local tradition using these design elements, just as there is a southern lowland tradition, a Gulf coast tradition, and a central Mexican tradition.

But what motivates people to adopt a new architectural style when hundreds of years of architectural history and knowledge are already available? The unusual nature of Chunchucmil, now well documented as a center of Classic-period commerce and trade with close economic ties to the Gulf coast and farther afield, presents a particular historical context for identity formation and maintenance. At landlocked Maya cities of the interior, elites interacted with small groups of their peers through ceremonialized royal visits in which trade was conducted. The social context of the trade site of Chunchucmil was fundamentally different and likely brought many segments of the city together with visitors from outside the Maya region (Dahlin et al. 1998, Dahlin and Ardren 2002, Magnoni et al. 2014). Likewise the Chunchucmileños likely traveled along the Gulf coast to obtain trade goods in exchange for salt and other commodities.

The dependence of Chunchucmil upon imports for food, its location near a strategic saltworks, and the presence of possible market areas and craft workshops have all been documented in earlier studies (Dahlin et al. 2005, etc.). This economically driven settlement was likely more pluralistic and diverse than many Classic Maya cities, and identity groups were likely composed along more fluid lines than was generally true for Classic cities where a small minority of local elites ruled a large majority of local commoners. I suggest that within this diverse and shifting social environment identity markers took on great importance as midlevel household groups within the epicenter of the city, whose occupants were largely dependent upon trade and other nonagricultural activities, struggled to position themselves within a varied population of similar merchants.

A CULTURE OF EXCHANGE

There is no scholarly agreement on a universal definition of cities, ancient or modern (Knox and Taylor 1995, Smith 2003). Even today, after a century of scholarship, the criteria for defining a city are regionally and culturally specific. Population size, population density, aerial extent, and presence of specialization are the major criteria used by most researchers for the definition of ancient cities (Childe 1950, Sanders and Webster 1988, Magnoni et al. 2014). Yet to other scholars the role of cities as central places that fulfill political, economic, religious, and sociocultural functions to the hinterland are more important than their absolute population (Blanton 1981, Golden and Scherer 2013, Marcus 1983, Yoffee 1995). But the thorny issues of city size and boundaries return us to the social. There are very few ways in which to delimit the so-called true boundary of a city beyond its linkage to the social identity of its inhabitants. And because boundaries are linked closely to identities, they are always shifting given the variety of criteria used by inhabitants and outsiders to communicate a sense of place (Golden and Scherer 2013, Smith 2003, Yaeger 2003). Monica Smith has argued that a city always represents a new and evolving social order, since it is constituted by the fluid social networks of people drawn together despite their differences (Smith 2003:1). These same social aspects are the key to the longevity and success of any city, since the vast majority of an urban population has chosen to reside together despite the disadvantages of city life. New shared rituals of inclusion, like the daily practices of fetching water or food, come to constitute and construct a shared identity of a place. But in addition to these shared habits, and in part because of their repetition, cities take on a significance or authority as places that are able to generate collective beliefs. In part this authority is the result of what Harold James Dyos and David Reeder (1973:362) described poetically as "a more persuasive legend of opportunity," held by cities, which helps lure immigrants and the economically disadvantaged into urban citizenship. The authority of the city is formed also through the "implicit contracts" that hold disparate members of a city together in mutual dependencies crisscrossing differences of economic power, occupation, age, etc. (Smith 2003:7). Charles Golden and Andrew Scherer have described this process as "trust building," given that as Classic Maya polities such as Yaxchilan and Piedras Negras grew, the daily interactions between a king and his subjects diminished (Golden and Scherer 2013:399). In this model community identity was built through shared social experiences, and when the dispersal of populations into nearby hinterlands reached a peak in the Late Classic, such bonds of trust were weakened and social fragmentation resulted. Even basic subsistence takes on charged social content in cities, especially ancient cities located in marginal environments where competition for resources had to be mediated socially (Lucero 2006). The background understanding, as Charles Taylor would say, shared by all citizens, is that a contract exists whereby each citizen of a city knows roughly how much water, land, and other resources they need and, more importantly, how to negotiate such demands with their fellow citizens. These social interactions produce the material patterns available to us as archaeologists interested in ancient urbanism. While earlier scholars suggested urbanism arose as a result of abstract cultural forces such as agricultural intensification or population growth, my perspective, like that of Smith and others, is that urbanism is the materialization of social transformations in how power, resources, and space are allocated.

Chunchucmil is the only large, urban city in the far western part of the northern Maya lowlands (Garza T. and Kurjack 1980). Because of its size and the lack of any similarly complex site in the area, Chunchucmil must have provided urban functions for a wide hinterland population. The emergence of Chunchucmil as a densely inhabited urban city was the result of social negotiations and innovations on the part of emergent elites who maximized connections between a strategic location with respect to the exploitation of coastal and savannah resources, especially salt; the need for redistribution of goods to the interior; and the elites' ability to provision maritime and overland traders. These connections were held together by a shared understanding of the city as dedicated to exchange, and were performed through various discourses such as the value of exotic commodities, the performance of redistribution and market exchange, or arguments over foodstuffs. The social imaginary of Chunchucmil was centered in a culture of exchange that made these discussions possible. In Taylor's terms, both the background and the practice were at their core economic—there were few reasons for so many people to live in this place other than to practice exchange, and trading activities circulated this perception on a daily basis.

Chunchucmil's location midway between the coastal port site of Canbalam and the inland regal city of Oxkintok illuminates its role within the broader region (Dahlin et al. 1998). Chunchucmil is located as far west, or toward the Gulf coast, as possible, in a transition zone between arable upland soils and the annually inundated savannah. This strategic choice of location, as a gateway to the rich savannah and coastal resources, positioned Chunchucmil to dominate coastal-inland trade as well as most urban functions for the surrounding region. If the relative size of a site within its region reflects its functional size, meaning the number and variation of activities undertaken there, then Chunchucmil clearly dominated the surrounding zone as far inland as the Puuc hills and for at least twenty-five to thirty kilometers north and south of the city. Other nearby centers such as Siho, Tzeme, and Oxkintok, although much smaller, were also occupied during the Early Classic period. The occupation and urbanization of the extreme western part of the Yucatán peninsula during the Early Classic period can be explained in part by a flourishing system of economic and cultural exchange that occurred around the Gulf coast and throughout Mesoamerica at this time. The central Mexican urban capital of Teotihuacan is often identified as the driving force behind this interaction, but the evidence increasingly points to Teotihuacan as a primary center among many important regional players interconnected in a system of commerce and exchange that included western Yucatán, southern Veracruz, the Pacific coastal highlands, and the southern Maya lowlands.

One arena in which Chunchucmil shows noticeable similarities to its closest neighbors is in the artifactual classes of obsidian and ceramics. The ceramic sequence of Chunchucmil has many strong parallels with the Oxkintok Regional phase identified by Carmen Varela, and current estimates suggest one-third to one-half of the ceramics at Chunchucmil are identical to types present at Oxkintok in the Early Classic period (Varela T. 1998, Bond and Mansell 2001). Neutron activation analysis is currently underway to identify the source of some of the rare types at Chunchucmil, and a Veracruz or Gulf coast origin is suspected. The ceramic traditions of Campeche and sites south along the Gulf coast are a major influence in the sequence (Jiménez in prep). Oxkintok and Chunchucmil also share patterns of obsidian consumption, at least in terms of the source of the material. This is consistent with our observation that obsidian is the most visible traded good in the Chunchucmil record and is present in large quantities. Over 80 percent of the obsidian from the Early Classic period at Oxkintok and 90 percent of the obsidian from Chunchucmil is from the El Chayal source in Guatemala (Mazeau and Ford 2003, Braswell 2003). Both sites show small amounts of obsidian from other sources in the Guatemalan highlands and the Veracruz Gulf coast. Both cities also have very little evidence of chert utilization (Oxkintok has four artifacts, Chunchucmil has 140) despite a relative abundance of chert sources in the area around the Puuc hills. When waste flakes are eliminated and only tools are considered, Chunchucmil has a ratio of forty-one obsidian tools to every chert tool (Mazeau 2002). This striking preference for obsidian is characteristic of a Classic-period Maya center with access to traded obsidian but also speaks to a deep reliance or even dependence upon non-local resources at Chunchucmil. The fact that there are no shell tools from the Chunchucmil excavations, despite easy access to shell, underscores this observation and the conclusion that a culture of commercialism in which traded items were plentiful and preferred dominated the economy and perhaps the history of the city.

Research by David Hixson and other members of the Pakbeh Regional Economy Program documented the presence of a network of stone pathways amidst small camp sites in the wetlands between Chunchucmil and the Gulf of Mexico coast, where the ancient Maya port town of Canbalam was located (Hixson 2011). Investigation of Canbalam, where the natural coastline opens into an estuary and could have provided a port for seafaring vessels, testifies to its participation in long-distance exchange (Dahlin et al. 1998). Was this, then, a thriving trade route with caravans of seasonal laborers and merchants crossing the wetlands to work the salt flats and bring foreign goods into the city? Using Landsat satellite photographs and radar imagery, Hixson located camp sites within the western wetlands and surveyed their micro-environments (Hixson 2005, 2011). Using the remote data to identify similar micro-environments, Hixson was able to verify the presence of prehistoric habitation in a number of locations throughout the savannah. Small hamlets were found on many pockets of higher ground in the wetlands, and ancient field houses were found even in the most isolated locations within the swamp (Hixson 2005:4). Rock alignments of human manufacture but unknown function in the savannah were also documented by Pakbeh Program members.

These alignments are the physical manifestation of Chunchucmil's regional communication and trade network, outlining a dendritic system of local and regional interchange.

It is interesting to compare this scenario with oral histories of modern Chunchucmileños collected by Hixson. Wealthy ranchers who built and occupied the early twentieth-century hacienda in the village of Chunchucmil, adjacent to the ruins, created an infrastructure for regular communication and trade with the coast. A canal from the coast that likely predated the hacienda led inland to an elevated platform, in turn leading to a pushcart rail system that ended at the center of town. While a major communication artery, this historic trail was never more than a couple of meters wide. It was traveled regularly by both inland and coastal villagers. For local economies, the route to the coast brought salt, fish, and shellfish into the interior, while the coastal fishermen traded for inland garden products that did not grow in the sandy soils of the coast such as spices, fruits, corn, and beans (Hixson 2011). The passage also became part of the Catholic seasonal religious pilgrimage, with members of the coastal communities building strong religious ties with inland churches and vice-versa. Men from Chunchucmil would occasionally seek extra work at the salt flats of the coast during the dry season, a time when farmers were otherwise waiting for the cleared cornfields to dry. Intermarriage between people of the coast and the interior was not uncommon, as can be seen today during family gatherings and Catholic fiestas. Together, this paints a fascinating picture of the integrative potential of a single path on the social, religious, and economic systems across the region. The results of the PREP regional survey indicate that such paths likely existed in pre-Hispanic times, leading from city to town to country, then on to the coast, linking the people of Chunchucmil to the resources of the wetlands, the trade routes of the coast, and the saltworks.

The solar-evaporation saltworks of Yucatán have long been noted for both the quality of their salt and their strategic location. The semi-arid conditions of northern Yucatán combine with highly saline estuary waters to allow high-quality sodium chloride crystals to form on the shores of the estuaries. During the dry season, these crystals can be raked up and collected using simple technology that is demanding but a less labor-intensive process than boiling salt brine or leaching brine from salt-rich earth, the other two techniques known in pre-Hispanic Mesoamerica (Andrews 1983, McKillop 2002). It is not unreasonable to estimate that more salt could be harvested in a dry-season day at the Celestun salt flats than in an entire season of boiling salt brine on the southern Belizean coast or leaching brine from earth in the highlands (cf. Kepecs 2003). The two main salt beds of Yucatán are the Celestun salt flats and the even larger string of salt flats located on the north coast near the ancient site of Emal. Both areas have dense urban settlements in close proximity to the saltworks, an indication that large labor pools were available to harvest salt during the short window of time each year when it was available on the surface.

While the north coast salt beds are more extensive, they are also farther away from the rest of Mesoamerica. The Celestun salt flat is the first source of solar-evaporation salt to be encountered in sailing around the Gulf of Mexico, or up from the Chontalpa basin—two of the primary water routes during the Classic period. The Celestun salt flat is also better protected by a natural harbor and would have offered a safer provisioning location for merchants than the open waters of the north coast.

There is ample evidence that Yucatecan salt was widely traded in ancient Mesoamerica (Andrews 1983, McKillop 2002). When the Spanish arrived, Yucatecan salt was traded as far as Honduras and Veracruz, and during the Aztec period it was found in central Mexican markets like Coyaxtlahuaca and Huexotla (Andrews 1983, Kepecs 2003:129). The reasons for the extensive demand for Yucatecan salt are many: one is the quality, which is far higher than salt produced by other techniques. This naturally high purity means the salt tastes better and goes further in culinary dishes. While most of us today are unaware of the variations in table salt, solar-evaporation salt from the coast of Brittany continues to be sold worldwide for the same reasons that Yucatecan salt was preferred by Aztec royals—it has a superior texture and taste. A second stimulus to the demand for Yucatecan salt was the high dietary requirements for salt in a tropical environment and the many uses to which salt was put. Inland people living on primarily plant-based diets of corn and beans received very little naturally occurring salt in their diet and would have needed to supplement with salty salsas or meats. Add to this the need for salt to treat medical conditions (Franciscan friar Sahagún described thirteen different medical uses in Aztec culture) and to cure meats and leathers, fortify cotton armor, and be offered on ritual occasions, and it is clear that salt was a true economic necessity.

A final stimulus to the demand for Yucatecan salt was the pervasive culture of trade and commerce that existed in the northern lowlands during the Classic period, especially in coastal areas. Salt was traded in part because people responded to dietary and cultural demands by organizing into large production units to extract and transport salt crystals. Yet once organized, such a system required constantly seeking new markets to ensure against the collapse of its investment. The wide circulation of goods along the western coast of Yucatán, and from there to interior sites, demonstrates a significant culture of commerce and exchange, well before the rise of Chichen Itza in the Terminal Classic or the Postclassic coastal trading sites of the east coast. Two forms of data illustrate this point. Ceramic assemblages from Chunchucmil are consistent with a regional ceramic tradition that demonstrates a substantial degree of exchange between the northern Yucatecan ceramic wares and those from Campeche and the rest of the Gulf coast. I prefer not to call these imported wares, since they are common at other sites in the region, but instead call attention to the heterogeneity of western, especially coastal, peninsular assemblages when compared to the more homogenous assemblages at interior or even eastern Yucatecan sites. This heterogeneity indicates frequent, pervasive exchange on a regional level during the Classic period.

Further evidence for the culture of trade and exchange in this area of Chunchucmil during the Classic period is the iconography found on one class of elite ceramic vessels from the region. The Chochola carved ceramics were long thought to originate in the southern lowlands because of their elaborate iconography. A systematic study of the limited provenience information available as well as their paste and slip indicated they were made in the western Puuc region, near the modern village of Chochola (Ardren 1996). The most common iconographic image on the 107 examples of these beautiful bowls examined is God L, the trading god of the Classic period who often appears with his broad-brimmed hat to protect him from the sun and his trading bundle packed onto his back. Images of God L are most common along the western Maya area of the Gulf coast, and there are definite connections between God L and the Postclassic god Ek Chuah, known as the patron of merchants (Coe 1973, Taube 1992). The appearance of God L with trader paraphernalia on these highly portable elite objects often exchanged between elites of the western Yucatán indicates again that commerce and trade were pervasive and powerful mechanisms of elite legitimization in Classic-period Yucatán.

Thus trade in salt at Chunchucmil occurred within a regional cultural setting that emphasized exchange as a means for the legitimization of social hierarchy. In addition to salt, all manner of items could have been traded at the city—coastal products such as shell blanks, stingray spines, fresh and salted fish and shellfish, and savannah products such as waterfowl, caiman, monkey or jaguar, as well as their pelts or feathers. Jaguar pelts and flamingo feathers alone would have been rare and precious commodities coming out of the savanna adjacent to Chunchucmil. But it was the salt trade that moved the city beyond a household level of specialization into the status of a regional trade center which supplied a naturally occurring commodity to a large region. Even though salt processing and trade may have occurred at Chunchucmil in a household or quadrangle context, with the salt perhaps ground in the numerous *metates* or stored in the range structures around quadrangles, the scale of regional trade was such that production must have been organized at a supra-household level.

There are other examples of ancient Maya centers dedicated to specialized production and distribution of a natural resource. The best known is Colha, a small community in northern Belize located near natural outcroppings of high-quality chert. At Colha, excavation documented chert tool production in a wide array of forms and at levels far beyond domestic needs. Shafer and Hester argue for mass production at Colha in the agricultural off-season, and the wide distribution of Colha chert tools throughout Belize and elsewhere support this position (Shafer and Hester 1983). A significant part of the distribution pattern of Colha chert is that sites closer to Colha in northern Belize have domestic tool kits made exclusively of Colha chert, while at sites outside northern Belize, Colha chert tools appear only in elite contexts in forms such as eccentrics. The scale and political control of production in Classic Maya culture is a matter of ongoing debate, but there is strong evidence to demonstrate that some Maya cities acted more or less independently to maximize gain from monopolization of a given economic necessity. Chunchucmil monopolized the highly prized salt from the Celestun salinas, and from this grew tremendously in size and wealth during the Early Classic period. In fact, the opportunity to benefit from participation in the salt trade, and the associated culture of commerce, was one of the reasons urban Chunchucmil attracted such an immense supporting population. Perhaps in part because Classic Maya economic systems were not strictly regulated by the state, fluid social networks of people drawn together by trade in commodities evolved and formed the basis for settlements like Chunchucmil.

EXPERIENCING THE CITY

In urban contexts, human relations no longer operate primarily within kin-based social networks as they do in smaller settlements, but such relations become part of other types of social networks (Smith 2003). Individuals can increase their networks of contacts through participation in groups outside of their households, and this may often be the only way for them to actively participate in urban life (Wirth 1938). Cooperative efforts and voluntary associations based on common trades and crafts, neighborhood groups, and religious traditions allow a more pervasive involvement in civic activities, which can in turn create a restructuring of power relations within the city's diverse groups. This also creates a high level of economic and social interdependence between a variety of economic and social groups (Hutson and Magnoni 2011).

As discussed more fully in chapter 3, recent advances in the study of Contact-period Maya political organization by ethnohistorians Matthew Restall, Sergio Quezada, and Tsubasa Okoshi make clear that social relationships were at the heart of Maya conceptualizations of settled life (Okoshi 1995, Quezada 1993, Restall 1997). Restall has argued persuasively that the fundamental unit of Yucatec Maya society in the Late Postclassic and Contact periods was the *cah*, or town (Restall 1997). Quezada has elaborated on the Maya concept of the *batabil* or single central place administered as the central unit by a lord with dependents, although at certain times *batabils* joined together into the larger administrative unit of the *cuchcabal*. Both iterations rely upon extended kin networks that perpetuated systems of elite privilege well into the Colonial period with certain patronymic groups holding most of the offices of *batab*, or governor, in Maya settlements. Maya nobles continued to recognize one another and grant one another respect in ways they had utilized for perhaps centuries before Spanish contact. These interactions were upheld by the majority of the population, the Maya occupants of villages and towns who understood and believed in the privileges of certain families. Thus social arrangements that made possible land tenure, tribute, and social stratification were all aspects of colonial settled life that likely originated in indigenous concepts of urbanism and relied upon shared social contracts. I do not mean to argue that elite privilege was at the heart of the social networks that sustained Chunchucmil, but to demonstrate that social relations were such a fundamental motivation for settled life in the Maya area that they survived the societal cataclysm of the Contact period.

Architectural groups enclosed by boundary walls are a materialization of the basic social networks present in the ancient city of Chunchucmil. Differences in area enclosed by the boundary walls and the number of structures included within them indicate that the compositions of the households may have varied considerably. Despite these differences, we expect walled groups to be equivalent social units, since extensive excavations at four house-lot groups revealed that each group shared relatively similar patterns of consumption, production, transmission of wealth, and social reproduction (Ashmore and Wilk 1988; Hutson, Magnoni, and Stanton 2004; Wilk and Rathje 1982). Cooperation or even voluntary association above the household level, such as participation in neighborhood groups or the design of raised roads and boundary walls, was probably an important element in the urban life of Chunchucmil. However, the overall design of the city does not demonstrate a high degree of planning. The major raised roads that originate in the site center and terminate at quadrangles may have been planned, possibly starting in the Late Preclassic, but the rest of the site consists of a dense settlement of bounded residential groups with meandering streets, built without a central planning effort. The impression is of a city that grew irregularly over time, as people migrated to live there and take advantage of the opportunities urban life presented. Despite the impressive growth and the lack of a centralized planning effort, Chunchucmil managed to remain easily accessible and navigable. Streets connected with *sacbeob* that provided an efficient way to reach different parts of the dense urban settlement. Some of these streets extended for kilometers across the landscape, integrating even the rural areas with the site center. Coordination and management by adjacent household groups and neighborhoods must have been exercised in order to maintain such a functional arrangement, and such coordination was based in a shared sense of identity and purpose.

Cities are loci for socially generative practices—participation in political or religious performances and simple daily trading activities would have required interactions with a wide range of urban occupants as well as visiting traders. These circumstances call for practices that help to construct social relations across rather obvious economic and cultural distinctions within a diverse population (Golden and Scherer 2013). Continuous interactions would have facilitated the creation of a shared identity that united people as the residents of this city. This identity was shaped by their common experiences of sharing an urban landscape charged with the architectural identifiers of stratification and densely populated by similar social units with which they interacted in supra-household groups.

An example of this shared identity is the common template for the quadrangle and domestic house-lot group design at Chunchucmil. The basic form of quadrangular arrangement with a pyramid on the east side is repeated at a smaller scale in most residential groups, where a square and relatively tall structure is present in the east side of a patio around which other structures are placed. Excavations in several residential groups have revealed that the eastern building was a ceremonial structure or shrine while the other structures around the patio were residences or auxiliary rooms like kitchens (Ardren 2003a, Hutson, Magnoni, and Stanton 2004; Magnoni et al. 2013).

Artifacts such as pottery, ornaments, and even architecture were the perfect symbolic medium to build a self-evident identity within the imagination of the inhabitants of Chunchucmil. To Benedict Anderson, in largely nonliterate cultures such as the ancient Mediterranean, the "figuring of imagined reality was overwhelmingly visual and aural" (Anderson 1991:23). Although the exact political mechanisms that governed Chunchucmil are still unknown, it is more than likely that a dynastic or generational system of some sort was in place even if it was mediated by the fluctuations of economic negotiations. However, within the social realm, Chunchucmil presented a much more open system where a wide range of options for social identity were known and exploited.

A central component of the creation and maintenance of a shared social imaginary are ritualized daily practices performed by all members of a society (Anderson 1983:35). As we read the newspaper, we are aware of other people doing the same thing, even though we neither meet them nor see them performing this act. Yet in our minds we do not question that this fundamental ritual is a shared one. Maya cities had many shared rituals as well as many private rituals that others did not see—domestic burials, dedication caches, even graffiti scratched in fresh stucco were all very common private rituals shared by the imagined community of Classic Maya society (see Golden and Scherer 2013 for a similar argument applied to the southern lowlands). In many ways these shared domestic rituals are the best indicators of identity as they seem to be arenas less subject to the overt intrusion of the state.

Was there an imagined community created in the material practices evident at the Lool group of Chunchucmil? Undoubtedly there were many shared identities, as the inhabitants of the city shared many daily routines and participated in a common urban experience. However, the selective use of certain stylistic elements during the later end of the Early Classic period that were long identified with areas outside the core of the Maya lowlands can also be understood as the construction of a mutual shared and imaginary identity, one that reached beyond the limits of Chunchucmil to the nearby royal center of Oxkintok, and beyond that to Tikal and other southern lowland cities and then to the Gulf coast and central México. Like the Creoles of Anderson's study, perhaps the midelites of Chunchucmil, deeply invested in the pan-Mesoamerican trend of greater trade and exchange during the Early Classic period but excluded from the royal privilege of dynastic power, sought to build bridges and a shared identity with other non-elites, with whom they shared the experience of mutual exclusion. Mutual exclusion from the core Classic Maya symbols of power such as divine kingship could have been the basis for a shared imagined identity of legitimization through other means, through participation in a different language of power that relied less on dynastic bloodlines and more on an awareness of broad regional trends. From this perspective, the use of talud-tablero architecture, cremation burials, and cylinder tripods by this northern Maya population was a deliberate attempt to reframe the way power and authority were conveyed without completely rejecting local traditions.

Lool and the other residential groups were likely an integral part of the production activities of a trade-intensive site such as Chunchucmil. The spatial linkage of residential groups with the commercial activities of a quadrangle may reflect part of Chunchucmil's social organization of labor and trade. These linked pairs may constitute a Chunchucmil-style sociological "house" or extended network of family members who shared land, resources, and memories (Gillespie 2000, Hendon 2010). If so, the use of a talud-tablero style of architecture is a significant indication of one aspect of the identity of this particular house. Households did not simply constitute areas of domestic activity; they also provided a network of obligation and exchange that invariably affected the political and public arenas of life (Hendon 1996). Residential groups such as Lool or 'Aak may have been important in the social representation and reproduction of the Chunchucmil economy. If they constituted areas of production, then these groups would have had significant power regardless of their relatively modest size. Their daily interactions reflect extended kin networks as well as changes in the political economy that would have bound "farmer, artisan, and kings in larger networks of exchange and obligation" (Ashmore 2004:177).

Because of the unique nature of Chunchucmil's trading economy, the relationship with stylistic trends from farther west may have extended deeper into the supporting levels of society, as demonstrated by the appearance of a talud-tablero structure at the rather modest and private Lool group. Chunchucmil's nearest royal center, Oxkintok, has a series of at least seven public temples with talud-tablero–style architecture in the heart of the ceremonial area. The preponderance of pan-Mesoamerican architectural styles may indicate that the architects of Oxkintok sought to augment traditional Maya claims to royal authority with a set of symbols familiar to those with a broader regional perspective. This choice reflects the historical role of the northern lowlands as a central crossroads of trade within Mesoamerica—a place where many different Mesoamerican peoples stopped for periods of time during trading excursions. This type of economic activity was the lifeblood of Chunchucmil, and thus the adoption of a Mesoamerican style of architecture at the Lool group makes sense as a means to illustrate and perpetuate the importance of those regional connections.

The concept of the social imaginary facilitates understanding how the individualized experiences and expectations of citizens of ancient Chunchucmil created the cooperative mechanisms we see materialized today as raised roads, house-lots, and quadrangle groups through living in the city (Taylor 2002:106). It also encompasses the idea that there was a repertory of possible actions and reactions at the disposal of any citizen, a series of choices based on concrete understandings and norms but adaptable to individualized experience. Benjamin Lee has expanded the discussion of the social imaginary to a consideration of the "urban imaginary," or the enabling matrix within which those that inhabit a city imagine and act as urban-making collective agents (LiPuma and Koelble 2005). The concept of the urban imaginary acknowledges that cities are largely "fictionalized interrelationships among strangers" but also our own reality as urban living citizens (LiPuma and Koelble 2005:156). In this sense the "imaginary" captures the ambiguities of urban life, the sacrifices of crowded and dangerous living counterpoised with the continued willingness of people to participate in urban environments. These characteristics are no less true of ancient urban centers. In many cases the harshest aspects of urban life were more prevalent in ancient societies that had little expectation of public works such as education or sanitation. What then was the motivation, the expectation, for living together in a dense environment for ancient inhabitants of Chunchucmil?

LiPuma and Koelble suggest that one of the characteristics of the urban imaginary is the specific nature of circulations—an overlapping set of experiences of exchange, whether that be of goods, stories, ideas, ways of being, etc., that lead to a unique and specific everyday understanding, an identity of being "from there." Each time a person states that she or he is from Miami, for example, they reassert their position in a shared imaginary urban space and circulate this idea to those around them.

Obviously one of the most important forms of circulation accessible to an archaeologist would be the circulation of goods throughout an urban space and the shared experiences this generated. While we can see the exchange of ceramics and obsidian in the archaeological record of Chunchucmil as specific elements that indicate a regional and supra-regional network, we cannot lose sight of the fact that relations between things are actually relations between persons. The material record of Chunchucmil reflects a high degree of exchange and circulation because in fact many people were involved in these circulations over a vast period of time and participated in a shared culture of trade and commercialism. Furthermore, circulation is performative; as each obsidian core was traded for a bushel of salt, we can be sure elite Maya traders maximized opportunities for the demonstration of their economic connections through ritualized ceremonies of exchange. Examples of the performative rituals of trading parties in Classic Maya culture are portrayed on ceramic vases and murals and indexed in use of the trading god on western Yucatecan ceramic bowls meant for exchange. Clearly trading experiences were shared and circulated experiences, which came to constitute part of the shared urban imaginary of Chunchucmil.

We see another avenue for shared participation and circulation in the movement of people to and from the saltworks on the coast via the wetland savannah. An economy built around control of salt trade necessitated movement from the urban center to the coast by some part of the population. Apparently on an annual basis some large segment of the urban population may have moved out to the salt flats to harvest salt, perhaps also transporting it back to site for warehousing. This annual event must have taken on ritualized significance as the stories and experiences of citizens were told and shared, reinforcing the expectation of future harvests. The hamlet and camp sites identified within the savannah zone certainly played a part in this experience, perhaps as way stations for rest along the journey or as landmarks. In order to walk to the coast, one left the relatively higher ground and dense urban atmosphere of the city, moved through an often wet and grassy savannah filled with freshwater springs and wildlife, and then eventually reached the coastal mangroves and estuaries of the salt flats. Those workers who traveled together must have shared stories of their work and lives, and returned home with stories of the landscape outside the city (Ardren and Lowry 2011b). This circulation of people through contrasting environs, locations of profound economic, political, and cultural significance in the society of ancient Chunchucmil, became part of the shared circulations of stories and knowledge that helped shape the experience of the city.

The expectation of circulation also plays a role in the growth of Chunchucmil into an immense urban center. Given our documentation of the challenges inherent in the local environment, it is necessary to explain why such large numbers of people (thirty-one thousand to forty-three thousand) would choose to live in such a challenging landscape. Part of understanding an urban imaginary is seeing the choices people make given their expectations and understandings of the repertory of possibilities. A pattern of traded items placed in small domestic shrines at Chunchucmil (Hutson, Magnoni, and Stanton 2004; Ardren 2003a) demonstrates that trade items were shared not only among a small or select part of the population but were widely consumed, even by the dead. This pattern also indicates that these items were chosen for deposit in structure dedication ceremonies in part because ritual actors had the expectation of further access to such goods. Thus we can see that traded items as an indicator of wealth were widely available to the population, confirming the expectation of access to such goods that might have drawn people to the city from the surrounding region. By their frequent presence in burial offerings, which by their nature takes such materials out of day-to-day circulation, we can also see that continued access to trade goods was expected. Thus an essential part of the urban imaginary of Chunchucmil was the circulation of goods and the circulation of expectations about wealth in the form of trade goods. Both of these acted to cement the fragile bonds of the urban center and counteracted the very real difficulties of living in a marginal environment.

Hinterland residents certainly recognized Chunchucmil's identity and may have chosen to identify with it in varying degrees (Golden and Scherer 2013, Hutson et al. 2008, Yaeger 2003). Like most cities, ancient and modern alike, Chunchucmil would have provided many attractive options—real or perceived—for rural dwellers. The attraction of city life for rural dwellers provided a continuous flow of newcomers that adapted to and reshaped the identity of urban Chunchucmil: "Greater Chunchucmil was linked with Chunchucmil by economic interactions and by embodied material practices that established imagined communities" (Hutson et al. 2008:20). The lack of satellite centers around Chunchucmil is consistent with this pattern. Although settlement density drops off toward the boundary of the residential periphery, Early Classic–period occupation is relatively continuous for the entire Greater Chunchucmil area (Hutson et al., 2008:30). The draw to live in the conceptual city, even if that meant construction of a household group four kilometers or further from the central area, was so strong that it overcame realistic needs for domestic resources and "commuting time." Despite the aridity and poor soils, and despite the crowding and potential for danger, vast numbers of people wanted to live in Chunchucmil. We can enumerate various specific reasons that are common to all large urban centers such as access to a diversity of goods, a relatively high level of wealth, and the chance to participate in social experiences larger than the individual, but we must also consider in this case the lure of commerce and the dream of a really good deal.

CONCLUSION

This chapter began with a desire to explore the experience of living in an ancient city. Urban lifestyles are distinctive and share many features across space and time. But often archaeological studies of ancient urban life have focused on questions that ignore the personal experiences and challenges of its most compelling aspect—the large human population living in close quarters. While archaeologists have been very successful in documenting the growth of cities over time, their rapid evolution from small settlements into crowded metropolitan environments, and even their decline, we have not often asked why ancient people moved to cities, why they chose to live in places that are well documented as dangerous, unhealthy, and challenging.

Building on the work of Monica Smith (2003) and others, I argue that cities are composed of people who utilize fluid and evolving social networks to manage their place within this particular social context. Cities succeed or fail largely based on the willingness of a large supporting population to remain living together, despite the challenges of difference they face. Social networks provide a way to mediate those differences, and in turn create mutual interdependencies and identities. A sense of shared ideas and practices can help define these social relationships. Recent scholarship has suggested that a disintegration of social relationships is at the heart of the phenomenon known as the Maya collapse (Golden and Scherer 2013).

Ancient Chunchucmil is one of the greatest achievements of Maya urbanism. Over the course of the Early Classic period, a flourishing trade-based economy drew inhabitants together and the city swelled to over thirty thousand people in some of the densest domestic arrangements known for this region of the world. Elite architecture in the form of quadrangles that provided limited access to warehoused trade goods reproduced at a grander scale the commoner domestic arrangement of structures around a simple patio. In both cases ancestral connections were maintained by a ceremonial structure or mausoleum on the eastern edge of the group, while daily living and activity took place around it. Hundreds of domestic groups and a dozen quadrangles at Chunchucmil repeat this arrangement of space and the activities that the space helped to shape. The circulation of so many people who lived at Chunchucmil through similar spaces helped create and perpetuate a sense of shared identity and membership. Despite stone boundary walls that set apart each domestic group, citizens were able to view the same arrangement of structures and activities across the entire city. This cohesion of daily practice overcame the fact that Chunchucmileños did not know most of their fellow citizens and may have immigrated to the city from very different places.

A shared sense of participation in the economic systems that the city provided and its location next to rich saltworks and other coastal resources also contributed to the social imaginary of the city. Lacking other basic resources such as extensive farmland or fresh water, Chunchucmil attracted immigrants who were convinced long-distance trade had the power to transform and sustain their lives. A high level of material wealth at even the most modest residential groups proves them correct in some measure, and the use of imagery that resonated with people from outside the immediate region such as the pervasive use of quadrangles and Gulf coast trade wares as well as the rare but significant example of talud-tablero architecture and cremation burial housed in a cylinder vessel also reinforced a sense of shared participation in something bigger than the local. From this perspective we can read the material culture left behind by Chunchucmileños as part of a deliberate strategy to reach beyond local northern Maya discourses about what the members of cities do and who they are. At Chunchucmil, the social imaginary allowed for and protected a larger conceptualization of connection and interdependence. This sense of being part of something bigger, something moving that provided tangible daily benefits, was the framework within which crowded streets and noisy neighbors were understood and reconciled. Shared participation in economic exchange, whether it be harvesting bushels of salt, producing obsidian blades, or constructing ancestral shrines, created relationships between people that in turn defined these people as part of the same collectivity, sharing membership in a base of knowledge and experience common to everyone in this particular city.

MEMORY, REINVENTION, AND THE SOCIAL IMAGINARY OF LATER YAXUNA

Chapter 3

INTRODUCTION

How did ancient Maya communities adapt to the changes that occurred after the end of the Classic period and how did they choose to remember their past? Were certain places or events commemorated while others were forgotten? How did the population of northern Yucatán remember and reinvent itself during the Postclassic period, when the political, economic, and social systems of the past thousand years unraveled and reunited in new forms? How were the boundaries between the past and present redefined? This chapter examines the material and artistic evidence for the invention of a new social imaginary that helped explain these changes through connection to a selective vision of the past at the city of Yaxuna, a once large and powerful urban center with a long history of occupation. Identity is often linked to a shared perception of the past, and memory can be deployed as a powerful tool in identity maintenance. Social memory, or the construction of a collective notion about the way things were in the past, is commonly used to support a sense of community identity (Van Dyke and Alcock 2003:2). The creation of a sense of place in particular can be intertwined with remembering, forgetting, and the powerful hold memory has over our sense of home. Memory as a layer of social identity is accessible to archaeologists through both tangible monuments and the practices or performances that accompanied such charged places.

Through the record of Postclassic architecture and artifacts from Yaxuna, we can see that despite widespread abandonment of most northern Classic-period urban centers after 1150 CE, at Yaxuna construction and use of certain very specific structures continued perhaps as late as 1450 CE. While modest, these buildings utilize architectural technologies consistent with previous periods and demonstrate a continuity of skills and ideas about how architecture is constructed and exploited. The locations where new structures were built indicate a deliberate choice to reinterpret some of the cultural values from previous periods within the constraints and concerns of the Postclassic, a time of reduced populations and material production. This later period of Classic Maya history is a particularly suitable moment to explore how memory is used to construct social identities and social imaginaries, because of the gap or pause just prior to the appearance of a pan-Mesoamerican style of art and artifacts in the Late Postclassic. Memory studies have proved an excellent tool for understanding social transformation as change, which cannot be understood without reference to how the past was framed in service to the present. As Laurent Olivier observes, "We are able to create meaning between two moments precisely because there are gaps. Better stated, meaning emerges in the field of tension that gaps generate" (Olivier 2011:186). I attempt to show how memory of the past, especially the glorious excesses of architecture and wealth that characterized the dynastic rulers of the Classic period, was manipulated by the Postclassic population of Yaxuna to support territorial claims and cope with a radically shifting political and economic landscape. I conclude with some ideas about how the exploration of the materialization of memory and its partner, forgetting, can be a powerful tool for understanding how social identities are used to deal with change and social transformation.

REMEMBERING THE CITY

The Postclassic inhabitants of Yaxuna, like their contemporaries at many other inland sites of the northern Maya lowlands, remain an enigmatic group. Yaxuna was a large and powerful ancient urban center located in the heart of the Yucatán peninsula. The site was first visited in modern times as a result of interest spurred by Charles Lindbergh's 1929 flight from Belize to Havana (Bennett 1930). Lindbergh's colleague Robert R. Bennett hiked the length of the ancient Maya road that connects Yaxuna to the prehistoric city of Coba, and this in turn attracted the attention of archaeologists working at the nearby site of Chichen Itza under the sponsorship of the Carnegie Institution of Washington. Sylvanus G. Morley and J. Eric S. Thompson both visited Yaxuna at this time and later sent Chichen project staff to the site to create a basic map and collect ceramic samples that were later incorporated into George Brainerd's pioneering study of northern lowland ceramics (Brainerd 1958). Research conducted there from 1986–1996 by the Selz Foundation Yaxuna Archaeological Project, which I codirected from 1992–1996, as well as more recent investigations by archaeologists of the Instituto Nacional de Antropología e

Historia (INAH) from 1996–2000 recovered a small but interesting collection of materials dating to the Postclassic period (1150–1550 CE) (Hernandez A. and Novelo R. 2007, Stanton et al. 2010, Toscano H. and Ortegón Z. 2003). Three small architectural structures generally described as "shrines" in the regional literature, a sample of ceremonial artifacts and ceramics from across the major architectural groups, a modest sample of residential ceramics, and one unique burial constitute the total complement of remains despite fifteen years of research at the site. How can such an unusual pattern be explained? Did the site function without a supporting residential population during this period? Have we missed something? I will show that relevant ethnohistoric documents offer an important conceptual framework for the cultural practices of Late Postclassic Yucatán, and that the shrines built at Yaxuna were a deliberate effort to circulate a new social imaginary based upon a reinvention of select aspects of much earlier dynastic rule.

The analyses and interpretations of ancient Yaxuna presented by members of the Selz Foundation Yaxuna Archaeological Project are based on fieldwork that included an extensive program of regional mapping coupled with excavations in household and monumental groups, and which yielded a large body of data including a burial sample of over forty individuals from royal and commoner contexts (see Stanton et al. 2010 for a summary of this research). The site of Yaxuna is a large urban center of approximately eight square kilometers, occupied throughout the Classic period and beyond, as indicated by the presence of two seventeenth-century colonial haciendas within the ancient settlement (Alexander 1993). There is substantial ceramic evidence to suggest an initial occupation of Yaxuna during the Middle Preclassic period (700–350 BCE), and by the transition to the Late Preclassic (350 BCE–200 CE), monumental architecture and iconography associated with the origins of Maya kingship had been constructed within the urban core (Stanton and Ardren 2005; Suhler, Ardren, and Johnstone 1998). Particularly notable is the presence of public architecture dating to the Late Preclassic period in the form of two dance or performance platforms covered in painted stucco and dedicated with Late Preclassic ceramics and jade ornaments (Suhler 1996). The population continued to expand in the Early Classic period (200–600 CE) and two royal tombs excavated in the early 1990s attest to the presence of dynastic rule at Yaxuna (Freidel, MacLeod, and Suhler 2003; Suhler 1996; Suhler and Freidel 1998). One of these tombs contained the remains of a single king surrounded by offerings and trade goods brought to Yaxuna during his reign in the Early Classic period. The other tomb is a remarkable family crypt that contains the remains of twelve individuals marked as royal through insignia such as a jade diadem. This group was executed in a single episode of dramatic conflict that coincides with the appearance of fortifications around major architecture and a shift from Puuc-affiliated ceramic traditions to materials associated with the eastern lowlands and Coba.

The settlement of Yaxuna reached its maximum extent in the Late Classic period (600–900 CE) when the population was tied economically to the even larger city of Coba, located one hundred kilometers to the east. The relationship between Yaxuna and Coba is most dramatically materialized by a raised road, the longest known within the Maya area, connecting the two cities (Villa Rojas 1934). The two cities' ceramic and architectural connections have been apparent since the Carnegie archaeologists visited the site and noted a radically different material culture than what was excavated at nearby Chichen Itza. It was not until the Instituto Nacional de Antropología e Historia completed a long-term project at Coba during the 1970s that serious attention was focused upon the role of Yaxuna in the history of the northern lowlands. Fernando Robles Castellanos and Antonio Benavides Castillo suggested that the rulers of Coba built Sacbe 1 to Yaxuna in part due to Yaxuna's position as a gateway center along overland trade routes from the southern lowlands into the eastern part of the northern lowlands (Robles 1976, Benavides C. 1976). This hypothesis was developed further by Anthony P. Andrews and Robles, who suggested ceramic evidence showed that Yaxuna was situated on the frontier between separate eastern and western cultural spheres (Andrews and Robles 1985, Robles and Andrews 1986).

Yaxuna is situated only twenty-two kilometers south of the urban metropolis of Chichen Itza, and during the Terminal Classic period (900–1150 CE), when Chichen rose to economic, political, and territorial dominance, Yaxuna was brought forcefully under the control of its dominant neighbor. Late Classic elite architecture was ritually terminated and Chichen-affiliated ceramics and architecture were deposited quickly on the North Acropolis. The residential settlement during this time was smaller and materially impoverished; very few trade items appear in the record and earlier architectural materials were reused in place of new construction. The site was largely depopulated by the end of this period. Perhaps after a period of exile following the territorial expansion of Chichen Itza, people returned to Yaxuna in the Postclassic period (1150–1550 CE) to construct a small number of ceremonial structures and make offerings scattered across the ruins of the Classic city, a process of reinvention and recovery that will be explored in this chapter. Many cities in the northern Maya lowlands show little evidence of occupation during the period from 1150–1250 CE, a time that has come to be described as the interregnum or "dark age" formerly known as the Early Postclassic period (Andrews, Andrews, and Robles 2003). Not all northern cities were completely abandoned during this time, nor were all of them reoccupied in the Late Postclassic, like Yaxuna. This quiet period of perhaps 100–150 years remains an intriguing time with little material indications of the social processes underway.

The Postclassic material culture known from Yaxuna includes primarily ceremonial architecture and artifacts—a very small number of domestic ceramics have been found at two locations within the center of the site. This particular kind of sample could have only two possible explanations. The first and most obvious explanation is that the data result from sampling error and the rest of the residential occupation of Yaxuna in this period has yet to be discovered. The research to date has been comprehensive across the chronological and spatial parameters of the site. The Selz Foundation Yaxuna Archaeological Project excavated or tested sixty-seven residential structures across an area of six square kilometers (roughly equivalent to the urban core and periphery of Yaxuna) and a much larger number of structures were sampled as part of an initial surface collection survey (Freidel, Suhler, and Krochock 1990; Stanton et al. 2010). The body of data on major periods of occupation such as the Early and Terminal Classic periods is substantial, and even poorly known periods such as the Middle Preclassic and Late Preclassic are well represented (Stanton and Ardren 2005). Furthermore, the Postclassic period is generally considered one of the more robust occupational phases in the northern Maya lowlands, and materials from this period are easily accessible close to the ground surface.

If one accepts that research on this period at Yaxuna has been comprehensive enough to have eliminated the most egregious levels of sampling error, then the only other explanation for an archaeological sample of ceremonial architecture and artifacts with a nearly invisible resident population is that it accurately represents the cultural patterns of the time. This chapter will show that while other sites, especially the type site of Mayapan only eighty kilometers west of Yaxuna, had a more diverse or robust occupational history during the Postclassic period, the remains from Yaxuna are consistent with sociopolitical models derived largely from native-language and colonial documents of the sixteenth century. Specific events of the late prehistoric period, such as the rise and dominance of the military state of Chichen Itza, as well as multifaceted responses in the north to the collapse of the southern Classic polities, set the stage for a Postclassic reinvention of elite power and society. This process depended upon (re)membering abandoned cities and structures and drew selectively upon the social but certainly contested memory of Classic political power structures (Stanton and Magnoni 2008). The unique societies of the Postclassic northern Maya lowlands incorporated the remains of their local histories but also generated new responses to environmental and political changes happening throughout broader Mesoamerica (Rivera D. 2000). Ceremonial performances and their material partners circulated a new social imaginary characterized by collective forgiveness of royal excesses and remembrance of monumental architecture as a cultural touchstone. Something both identical and different was created that did not do away with the past but deployed it in order to set boundaries around a new social imaginary (Olivier 2011).

Across the entire six square kilometers of ancient Yaxuna, our research recovered evidence of only three small structures built during the Postclassic period. The architectural design of these three buildings is consistent with the somewhat larger and better-known Postclassic shrines that line the east coast of the peninsula at sites such as Tulum, Xcaret, and Playa del Carmen, although this same type of structure has been found across the northern lowlands during this period (Freidel 1981, Rivera D. 2000). Comparable masonry structures found on Cozumel were designated "Structure Type 1a" and identified as shrines based upon their similarity to shrines described in the ethnohistoric literature of the sixteenth-century east coast (Freidel and Sabloff 1984:44). On Cozumel these small buildings were interpreted as locations for offerings of incense or other sacred perishables and storage of deity images (Freidel and Sabloff 1984:50). Just as at Yaxuna, the east coast shrines of this type are often isolated from residential settlement.

STRUCTURE 7 OF THE XKANHA GROUP

Excavations conducted in 1991 and 1993 as part of my dissertation research focused on the well-preserved remains of an elaborate Postclassic shrine located approximately 1.5 kilometers north of the center of Yaxuna. Structure 7 is a small mound adjacent to the Xkanha Acropolis, a natural bedrock outcropping heavily modified in the Early Classic period as a defensive outpost and midlevel elite residential area (Ardren 1997). The Acropolis and its associated three structures are located on the northern

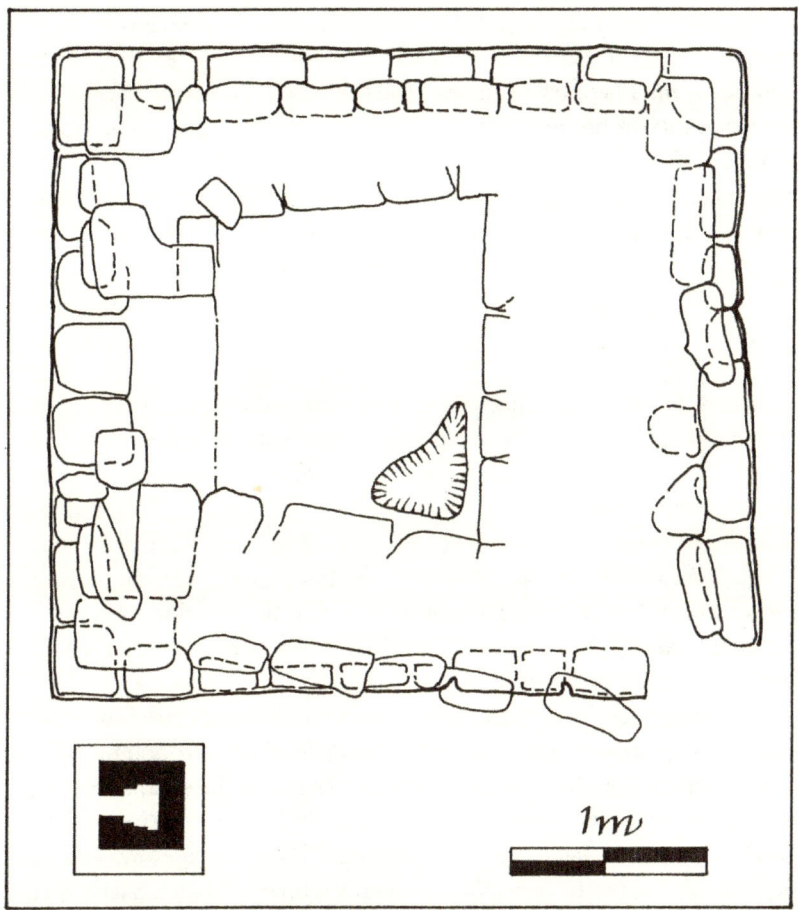

FIGURE 3.1. *Structure 7, Xkanha group, Yaxuna. Illustration by Jack Scott based on Selz Foundation Yaxuna Archaeological Project field drawings.*

edge of the ancient settlement of Yaxuna, at the location of the second-largest freshwater *cenote*, or natural sinkhole, in the area.

Structure 7 is a pyramidal mound 3.75 meters high and located approximately 62 meters to the east of the base of the Xkanha Acropolis. At the summit of Structure 7 is a well-preserved c-shaped shrine facing the Acropolis, a group of structures that were largely abandoned during this period (Figure 3.1). Horizontal excavation and clearing of the shrine confirmed the presence of large quantities of ceremonial ceramic wares but little other artifactual material (Ardren 1992, 1994). Three walls of the c-shaped shrine were preserved to the height of approximately one meter and plastered red on their exterior. The fourth or open side consisted of a step or ledge that separated the interior of the shrine from the plastered floor in front. The interior floor of the shrine was poorly preserved and a large quantity of broken censer fragments, including diagnostic features of Chen Mul Modeled effigy vessels (discussed at more length below), were mixed in with broken plaster fragments. No other artifactual materials were present inside the shrine, although flecks of carbon suggest that organic burned remains may originally have been present.

STRUCTURE 6E-13

Structure 6E-13 is the famously small mound at the terminus of the one-hundred-kilometer *sacbe* that connects Yaxuna with its eastern ally, Coba. This modest mound has an interesting and complex occupational history that appears to begin in the Early Classic period nearly a thousand years prior to the time of its latest use (Ardren 2003b). It may have been chosen as the terminus of the *sacbe* due to its earlier significance, but certainly earlier use and reuse must have contributed to the decision by returning Yaxuneros to reoccupy and resignify this modest but highly charged location during the Postclassic period.

Structure 6E-13 is a platform 3.5 meters high and situated in an open area midway between the massive Eastern and Main Acropoli of Yaxuna. Like other freestanding small pyramidal mounds in the area, it was originally constructed as part of an extensive Early Classic building program. During the Late Classic period, the Early Classic passageways and platform were covered to construct a larger platform to which Sacbe 1 from Coba was connected by means of a gradual ramp. Following the Terminal Classic abandonment of Yaxuna, a small c-shaped shrine was constructed on the summit of the existing platform and ceremonial offerings were placed inside the shrine.

Initial excavation in front of the 6E-13 shrine recovered many broken fragments of Late Postclassic Chen Mul Modeled censer ware, and, as at Structure 7 of the Xkanha group, these fragments included diagnostic effigy elements. Further excavation of the entire shrine area recovered a small *tumbaga* (gold/copper alloy) bell from the interior of the shrine area, in association with additional Chen Mul censer fragments. Metal artifacts are extremely rare in ancient Yucatán, but appear more frequently in the Postclassic period after 1250 CE, when metals from outside the peninsula were reworked by artisans at the ancient center of Mayapan (Paris 2008). Clusters of bells nearly identical to the one discovered at

Yaxuna were found connected by thread at Mayapan, and it is likely that these bells were costume ornaments as well as a form of social currency throughout the Postclassic world (Paris 2008:49). Mayapan is the only place where metal production debris has been discovered in the northern lowlands, and it is clear that *tumbaga* bells were traded widely by the elite artisans and merchants of Mayapan.

Identical in conceptual design to the Structure 7 shrine at Xkanha, the Postclassic shrine at the summit of 6E-13 consisted of a single course of reused Late-Terminal Classic veneer stones set horizontally and vertically into a plaster surface. These well-shaped stones were frequently reused in later periods when construction methods were less precise. No plaster covered the veneer stones, although given its exposure to the elements for approximately eight hundred years, such plaster may have eroded long ago. A single course of wall stones was visible on the northern, eastern, and southern sides of the shrine, and the fourth or open side faced west, toward the Main Acropolis of Yaxuna, a little more than one hundred meters to the west. Inside the shrine, fragments of ceramic censers were mixed with broken plaster floor fragments. Three earlier floors dating to previous construction episodes were found in the fill beneath the shrine interior. In the late 1990s this shrine was consolidated as part of INAH excavations at 6E-13. The shrine as well as earlier elements and associated *sacbe* are visible to visitors today.

Rather than the more substantial double-course masonry of the Xkanha Structure 7 shrine, the architects of the 6E-13 shrine relied upon reused materials probably obtained from nearby structures. Late-Terminal Classic veneer stones were finely made and retained their well-worked edges for many hundreds of years. We should consider the possibility that reused stones carried with them additional significance of equal or greater importance to the Postclassic occupants of Yaxuna than the cleaner lines and red-painted stucco of the Xkanha Structure 7 shrine. In our decipherment of Postclassic cultural patterns, it is significant that both types of architecture are present — new constructions utilizing presumably new materials, and new constructions made of reused materials, especially well-worked and carved stone from Classic architecture.

STRUCTURE 6F-37

I excavated a more unusual Postclassic shrine in an open area just east of the North Acropolis in 1989. Structure 6F-37 is a mound 1.5 meters high with a single course of wall stones that suggest the foundation of a resi-

FIGURE 3.2. *Structure 6F-37, Yaxuna. Photograph by the author.*

dential structure (Ardren 1990). Horizontal excavation exposed a simple but highly unusual c-shaped shrine rather than the residential structure we expected. The western, northern, and eastern structure walls were made of perishable materials set into a single course of reused veneer stones. In the southern wall, an entryway was outlined in similar stone (Figure 3.2). At least one of these veneer stones was carved with warfare-associated imagery and likely originated from the elaborate carved stone façade of structure 6F-68, on the North Acropolis, which was deliberately destroyed in the Terminal Classic period (Ambrosino 2003; Friedel, Suhler, and Cobos 1998).

The wall stones sat upon a well-preserved plaster floor that covered four evenly spaced round depressions in the center of the shrine. Each of these depressions was approximately six centimeters in diameter, and because the plaster surface was continuous across these depressions, it is clear they were integral to the original floor and design of the structure. It is difficult to discern the function of these depressions, although they are the same size as the gourds used to hold offerings in many modern Maya ceremonies where *h'men*, or traditional Yucatec Maya shamans, place four or more gourds filled with liquor or corn gruel in a row across an altar. Fragments of Chen Mul Modeled ceramic censers were found scattered across the floor, but there was no domestic debris or evidence that the structure had been utilized for daily activities. Although plenty of other worked and unworked stone was available in the area, the architects of the 6F-37 shrine chose to incorporate existing carved stone, probably from the nearest monumental architecture. All three Postclassic shrines face the largest adjacent monumental architecture. This is an indication, along with the similar artifactual materials found and the construction materials used, of conceptual cohesiveness centered on reinterpreting the abandoned remains of the Classic period in a new time of transition.

OTHER POSTCLASSIC MATERIALS

The primary material dating to the Postclassic period at Yaxuna are the three c-shaped shrines described above. But two additional material patterns exist that must be integrated into the architectural and artifactual information provided by the shrines in order to understand the complexity of Late Postclassic Yaxuna. One of these is a scatter of Chen Mul Modeled censer ware at monumental architecture near the shrines. For example, broken censer fragments were found on the summit of the largest structure at the Xkanha Acropolis near the Structure 7 shrine (Ardren 1997), on the summit of two structures (6F-2 and 6F-3) at the massive North Acropolis near the 6E-37 shrine, and on the summit of 5E-19, a Preclassic triadic group not far from the 6E-13 shrine. The quantity of ceramic material at these locations is quite small (a handful of sherds in each case) and suggests either human presence for a very limited period of time (one or two visits?) or more regular activity in which nonperishable material like ceramics played only a small role. The locations where these ceramic scatters were detected appear to have been largely abandoned during the Late Postclassic with the possible exception of Structure 6F-2 (see below). The presence of small quantities of censer ceramics at historically important loci may reflect efforts by some Yaxuneros to circulate again through certain historical power centers of the city, visiting them in person and thus in turn reinterpreting these places from a new perspective. We see the same conversation about history and identity demonstrated in the decision by Late Postclassic builders to construct their only shrines on mounds with earlier architectural history. In both cases strategic decisions by actors shaped the culture of the city as they changed it.

The only area at Yaxuna where nonceremonial Late Postclassic ceramics were recovered is within the latest phase of two structures at the center of the site. One location is Structure 6F-9, known locally as *pocoxna* or little house, because it was the site of the only standing vaulted architecture when archaeological research began in 1986. It was also described by Carnegie Institution–era archaeologists (Brainerd 1958:13). Local lore says that this building was used as a refuge and shelter in the Caste Wars, a story corroborated by the discovery of a historic-era burial during the course of excavation (Ardren 2002b). Perhaps the reason this building is still standing is that the interior walls are constructed in typical Puuc veneer stone masonry over a concrete load-bearing core. The exterior stones had fallen, or been removed, from the face of the structure prior to any research by the Selz Foundation Project (Suhler and Freidel 1993:44). Ceramic material from beneath the floor confirms a Late-Terminal Classic date for the original construction of structure 6F-9. However, a Late-Terminal Classic cache was found in an interior corner of 6F-9, and in conjunction with the historic burial mentioned above, it is clear this building was used over many centuries. Part of this evidence is a scatter of Late Postclassic nonceremonial ceramic materials found just above the floor level outside the 6F-9 structure (Shaw 1998). These domestic sherds include a small amount of Navula sin Engobe, Cehec-Hunacti Compuesto, Mama Red, and Papacal Inciso, all types associated with the Hocaba/Tases phase at Mayapan (Ochoa R. 2007, Shaw 1998, Stanton et al. 2010). At two groups adjacent to 6F-9, the Puuc group and the Ballcourt, Lourdes Toscano reports that the INAH project recovered nonceremonial Postclassic ceramic materials including *molcajetes* (grinder bowls) in Xcanchakan Negro sobre Crema and other forms in Cumtun Compuesto (Toscano H. and Ortegon Z. 2003:442). Finally, at the base of the platform where the 6E-13 shrine was built, horizontal excavation of the exterior of the building where it meets the *sacbe* revealed that 10 percent of the ceramic samples were domestic types dating to the Postclassic period such as Mama Red and Yacman Striated (Shaw 1998). While these three samples represent meager evidence of a potential residential population at Yaxuna in the Postclassic, they nonetheless indicate the presence of limited activity beyond ritual offerings. Further analysis of materials recovered during recent road construction that indicated 2.5 percent of the ceramics were from the Hocaba/Tases or Postclassic sphere as well as future excavations may confirm a more substantial residential population.

The final material evidence of Late Postclassic Yaxuna is more unusual and extremely significant to an interpretation of the political geography of the northern lowland interior hinterlands during this period. In the course of excavation of a set of labyrinthine chambers near the summit of 6F-3, the largest pyramid at the North Acropolis of Yaxuna, an unusual burial was encountered that has been interpreted as a high-status elite sacrifice.

Structure 6F-3 is a complex funerary pyramid initiated at least as early as the Early Classic period, and then modified many times during the major occupation of Yaxuna during the Late-Terminal Classic periods (Suhler 1996). A key feature of this structure is a central staircase leading from the plaza floor to the summit, under which there was a passageway intentionally left open at the level of the penultimate terrace. After consolidation conducted by the Selz Foundation Project, visitors to the site today can walk this passageway and enter the chamber leading into the heart of the Early Classic rooms, one of which was ultimately utilized as a royal burial tomb chamber with an associated labyrinth (Suhler, Freidel, and Ardren 1998). The architectural history of the building is sufficiently documented to know that the passageway under the central staircase was left open after the Early Classic period, and was only filled or blocked off in the Late Postclassic period in association with the deposit of a sacrificial victim inside the passageway, directly in front of the chamber threshold (Suhler and Freidel 1994:20).

Burial 19 was excavated and analyzed by Selz Foundation Yaxuna Project osteologist Sharon Bennett (Bennett 1994:91). Found in an oval pit dug into a largely degraded plaster floor, the body of a twenty-five to thirty-five-year-old male was deposited without the benefit of a stone-lined crypt or other mortuary features typical of Terminal Classic and earlier burials in the northern lowlands (Figure 3.3). Fragments of the cranium of this individual were found between two large flat rocks that may indicate his skull was crushed. The skeleton was laid with his ankles together, the tibiae and fibulae bent back sharply at the knees under the femora. The body was then bent over at the hips so the individual was face down in the powdered floor material. The arms were bent at the elbows with the wrists together and the hands crossed under the chin. Bennett believed the wrists and ankles of this individual had been bound, and the

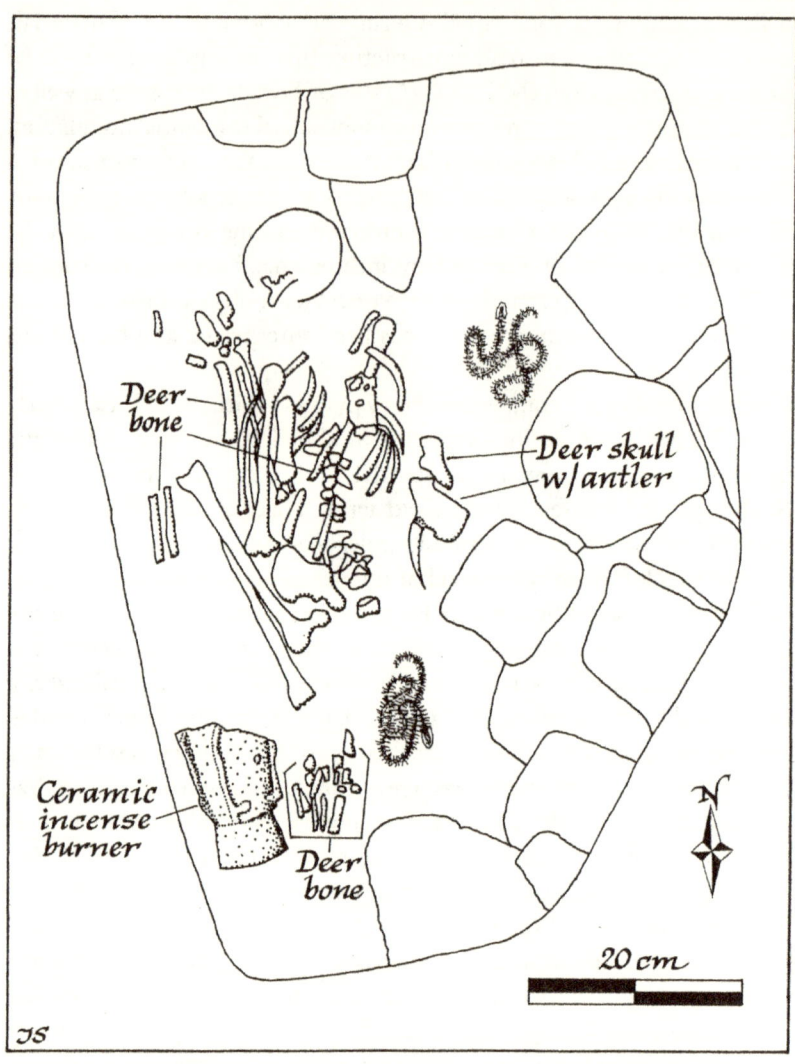

FIGURE 3.3. *Burial 19, Yaxuna. Illustration by Jack Scott based on Selz Foundation Yaxuna Archaeological Project field drawings.*

face-down position of the body is consistent with depictions of Maya captives in the Classic and Postclassic periods.

Although the skull of this individual was too fragmentary to provide much information, thirty-two adult teeth were recovered (Bennett 1994:92). Only one was carious, a much lower-than-average frequency for carious lesions or cavities at Yaxuna, while all of the teeth were covered in a thin layer of calculus, including the articulating surfaces. Bennett suggested the calculus formed just before death, perhaps when this individual was fed only a thin corn gruel or similar substance that would not have provided abrasive material to clean the teeth (Bennett 1994:104). Consistent with the lack of cavities, this individual had no evidence of enamel hypoplasia or other indicators of childhood nutritional stress or trauma (quite common in the Yaxuna burial sample) and only minor arthritis of the spine. Given the relative robusticity of this individual prior to death and the trauma present in his burial position, I am confident that the individual represented in Burial 19 was a higher-status male, captured and held for some time before his particularly brutal execution and subsequent burial at Structure 6F-3.

A number of interesting artifacts were found in association with the Burial 19 individual, including the ubiquitous Chen Mul Modeled censer ware (firmly associating this execution with the Late Postclassic occupants of Yaxuna) and a large number of unusual faunal remains that likely represent a ritual deposit (Suhler 1996). Christopher Götz analyzed this material and reported that 23 different taxa were represented in the 522 bone fragments (Götz 2010:276). While some of the bone was consistent with food offerings, such as the hindquarters of white-tailed deer and turkey, the majority of the faunal remains were from nonculinary species such as the Yucatecan jay (*Cyanocorax yucatanicus*), northern cardinal (*Cardinalis cardinalis*), and jaguarondi (*Puma yagouaroundi*) or were complete enough specimens to suggest that they were not food offerings, such as the nearly complete skeleton of a boa constrictor (*Boa constrictor*) and juvenile deer (probably *Odocoileus virginianus*). Many of the animals represented in Burial 19, such as the iguana, turkey, and deer, are depicted as important ceremonial offerings in Postclassic Maya codices, and given the presence of these remains not just with the burial but in the adjacent room, they may have been sacrificed at the same time that the adult male met his demise.

BORDERS, MEMORY, AND CONTESTED IDENTITIES

Susan Alcock has been a pioneer in the application of the concept of "memory communities" to archaeological cultures (Alcock 2002, Burke 1989). She argued, following the work of Maurice Halbwachs (1992), that landscapes form the material of a memory community, or a shared sense of belonging based in repeated actions and routines carried out in common space. The experience of being part of a memory community is layered and negotiated alongside other social identities that intersect with dominant memory communities of the state (for example) and "counter-memory" communities that challenge master narratives, among others. Archaeology is uniquely suited to recover evidence of counter-memory, especially when compared to ancient written texts with their focus on dominant histories. With its emphasis on how memory can be located in objects or places, archaeological studies offer a unique perspective on the material framework for understanding the past created by an ancient culture. In Alcock's powerful study of Classical Greek society, identity, memory, and landscape are interlocking components of the social negotiations that result in a sense of being and belonging (2002). Provincial elites deliberately invoked the past through building programs, and urban centers such as the Agora became calculatingly memorial spaces (Alcock 2002:177). Different memory communities, elite or commoner, Greek or Roman, viewed and debated these monuments differently, but certain "channels of memory" were nurtured while others were erased (Alcock 2002:178).

Laura Villamil (2007) has explored the memory communities of two ancient Maya cities in Quintana Roo and argued that individuals or groups with the necessary resources could create and manipulate spaces that defined social boundaries and reinforced political strategies. Villamil argues the compact city plan of Lagartera resulted from a single political strategy continuously in use following the origin of statehood in the Maya area, while the multiple elite complexes of Margarita demonstrate the re-invention and restructuring of power after the Late Classic–period sociopolitical challenges. The built environment is a powerful way to communicate group identity, and the long histories of re-use and continuous occupation of urban landscapes are rich examples of how landscape memory is mutable and inherently social.

In a powerful transgression of the artificial border erected between past and present by Western scholarship, archaeologist Laurent Olivier has put forward a suggestion that archaeology as a discipline is "an investigation into archives of memory" (Olivier 2011:xv). The artifacts that we excavate become objects that belong to the present, and as much as we might like them to clearly define the past, or a moment in the past, usually they come to signify an evolving memory of the past, a memory that only takes meaning because it is situated in the present. Olivier wants archaeology to be redefined as a discipline particularly attuned to the symptoms of material memory (Olivier 2011:188). By symptoms, Olivier means signs, or visible manifestations of invisible phenomena, after the medical use of the term. To Olivier, our reconstructions of ancient cultures are symptoms (or signs) of a memory that is still being shaped in the here-and-now, and he argues persuasively that there is no border between past and present. The present, even when viewed as the sum of material elements, is largely composed of residues of the past—either forms still in use or inspired by a rejection of the past—while the past, defined by the sum of material evidence that survives, continues to have a direct and reciprocal effect upon the present. He argues that our rightful intellectual ancestors are Charles Lyell and Charles Darwin, who argued that to reach the past we have to start not in the past, but from the present since information about the past is contained in the present (Olivier 2011:184). The way in which past and present as discrete parts of time are circulated as concepts within modern archaeology illustrates and constructs our modern social imaginary. While most archaeologists would agree these concepts are locked in a reciprocal relationship, Olivier has gone further than many to explore how permeable (rather than discrete) the past and present truly are, in part because the processes of inscribing matter with memory never end. The repetition and reiteration that creates the archaeological record through the inscription of memory into matter is a continuous process because the objects we excavate are given meaning through our understanding and memory of the past. Memory only exists because of the parts of the past that we have lost. History is created by the repeated inscription in matter (materialization) of behaviors and beliefs, the circulation of practices that uphold a discourse about membership and identity. Material objects hold or are inscribed with memories of a given moment, over and over again, until they become what Olivier calls palimpsests of layered meaning.

This same perspective on the way the past defines the present and vice versa must also be applied to our understanding of how ancient cultures understood their history (Van Dyke and Alcock 2003). It is well known that ancient Mesoamerican peoples understood time as broadly cyclical, and they developed a sophisticated means by which to record and predict the repetitive events they observed. The present of an ancient culture such as the Late Postclassic Maya was also constructed from the residue of the past, and the past was understood and shaped in the here-and-now. Late Postclassic people chose to construct shrines in Classic cities after hundreds of years without daily interaction with that material landscape. The process of returning to previously significant locations in the urban center, of choosing stones to remove from early architecture and reset into new shrines, and of working together or at least witnessing this may have been more significant than the end result itself (Pauketat and Alt 2003). As Tim Pauketat argues for later Cahokia, the act of building together was an integrative social process that brought people together around a common goal that required shared knowledge, skills, and time (Pauketat and Alt 2003:152). While monumental architecture was not a form of cultural capital available equally to the whole population in the Classic period, the process of building such structures was still likely a communal one. The architectural knowledge of how to build monumental structures was specialized and restricted to a segment of the population, and the experiential knowledge of what vaulted rooms felt like and contained was limited to an even narrower segment of the populace. The return to this architectural tradition, even in a modest form, after generations of ambivalence is a dramatic and forceful claim to historical authority. We must consider what role memory and forgetting played in this choice, and how it was constructed, because there is no other explanation for why this population chose to return to ancient settlements. The abandoned temples belonged to the Late Postclassic present, and at that moment, based on the layers of memory inscribed on the abandoned urban landscape, Yaxuneros built something new. They contributed to the trajectory of the city by using the past as a reference point. However, in addition to referencing the local landscape, regional dynamics played a role in strategic decisions about which ideas would be circulated in a new sense of shared membership.

Prevailing models of the Late Postclassic political geography of northern Yucatán describe two separate spheres or regions, each with distinctive cultural traditions (Gonzalez de la Mata and Andrews 1998, Kepecs and Masson 2003, Ochoa 2007, Rivera D. 2000, Robles C. and Andrews 1986). The provinces of the west encircled the city of Mayapan, a walled urban center founded by a confederation of relatively autonomous elite families from the northern and western parts of the peninsula known as the League of Mayapan (Kepecs and Masson 2003; Masson and Peraza L. 2010; Masson, Hare, and Peraza L. 2006; Milbrath and Peraza L. 2003). Mayapan has been described as a Postclassic attempt to revive the Classic model of a royal urban capital, in which monumental architecture provided a framework for the demonstration of elite privilege, but with a significant change in the way power was shared. Marilyn Masson, Timothy Hare, and Carlos Peraza see evidence for a large number of powerful merchants and religious specialists who shared influence within the confederacy with members of royal families (Masson, Hare, and Peraza 2006). The architecture of Mayapan has direct ties to earlier structures of the northern lowlands such as the Castillo of Chichen Itza (reproduced at a smaller scale at Mayapan) while the stucco murals that decorate these buildings are clearly part of what is known as the International Style, due to its connections to artistic traditions from across Mesoamerica at this moment in time (Taube 2010, Vail and Hernandez 2010). Artifacts from Mayapan corroborate this tradition, and elite households were filled with storerooms of ceramics imported from the Peten Lakes region of Guatemala and the Gulf coast (Masson, Hare, and Peraza 2006:198).

The provinces of the east, along the Caribbean coast of Quintana Roo, constitute a very different cultural sphere, although still closely interrelated with the peoples of the west. The east coast experienced tremendous population growth, and more than one hundred sites along the coast date to the Late Postclassic period (Gonzalez de la Mata and Andrews 1998:459). These sites range in size and character, but do not appear to have united into a political unit organized under the control of a single urban center such as Mayapan. Certainly Cozumel was the east coast region's largest population center during the Late Postclassic, but Tulum, Conil, El Meco, and Ichpaatun were all significant centers. The independent eastern provinces formed a chain of small but interconnected political entities along the coast, competing with one another for a share of the active maritime trade conducted by Postclassic people throughout Mesoamerica. This trade reached south past the coast of Honduras to Panama and north all the way to New Mexico and Arizona, feeding the huge urban centers of the central Mexican basin.

The western and eastern spheres of the Late Postclassic northern lowlands have been defined partially on the basis of differing historical trajectories of archaeological research. The Carnegie Institution of Washington sponsored four years of investigation at Mayapan in the 1950s, and excavation and stabilization have been carried out intermittently ever since. Most archaeological data from the Caribbean coast is the result of salvage operations conducted over the last twenty years as development threatens to erase all vestiges of ancient cultures in the path of resort construction. The two spheres also have distinctive architectural patterns, ceramic traditions, and ethnohistoric histories. The settlement design of Mayapan is a large central walled city with sprawling settlement, while the coastal centers are characterized by many small settlements each with plazas and shrines. The western sphere of the Tases ceramic macrosphere is dominated by ceremonial censers and a larger percentage of fine paste trade wares, whereas the eastern sphere has fewer censers, fine paste wares, and ceramic types with closer ties to the Postclassic centers of the Peten and Belize (Ochoa 2007). Finally, ethnohistoric documents differ greatly as sources for understanding the lives of Late Postclassic occupants of the peninsula. The League of Mayapan is described in abundant but conflicting detail in many native histories of the early Colonial period, while the polities of the eastern provinces are known primarily from Spanish post-contact accounts. In other words, while research on this period has focused upon two discrete areas of the peninsula with distinct research trajectories, those areas appear to represent actual cultural interaction spheres with interconnected but distinct histories and perhaps social identities.

Late Postclassic settlement is documented at a few centers outside the two main western and eastern spheres. The site of Ek Balam, perhaps on the eastern edge of the Mayapan-dominated interior sphere, has a well-explored record of residential and ceremonial settlement dating to the Postclassic period (Bey, Hanson, and Ringle 1997; Bey et al. 1998). The Chikinchel regional survey documented many sites from this period on the north coast in an area described as independent from the two main geopolitical spheres (Kepecs 1998). But overall the hinterland between the west and east is not well understood, especially the political ties, which likely shifted and changed during the 350 years of the Late Postclassic epoch. The data presented here from excavations at Yaxuna provide a unique window into the cultural dynamics of the rural and largely abandoned areas of the interior.

Yaxuna is located approximately eighty kilometers east of Mayapan, on the political as well as cultural frontier or border between the western sphere of the League of Mayapan and the eastern trading polities. Although poorly documented, occupation was not limited to these two well-known spheres, but was spread sparingly across the interior of the peninsula. But how can we evaluate the political and cultural relationships between Yaxuna and the two dominant spheres? Ethnohistoric documents in conjunction with the archaeological data presented above provide a convincing argument for the participation of Yaxuna in the League of Mayapan. A strategic change to the local identity through participation in the social imaginary of the confederation centered at Mayapan may have provided the best opportunity for the survival of Yaxuna. Given the historical alliance with Coba in earlier periods, a conversation about difference that resulted in an adjustment of the local community identity toward a new nonlocal ally was a familiar form of social discourse at Yaxuna. As Olivier notes, "As it grows, the present is pervaded by the creaking of the past, enlarged by all that growth untiringly brings" (Olivier 2011:180).

Various ethnohistoric documents of the early Colonial period describe the southwestern border of the Cupul province as a disputed area, where "one local ruler readily made war upon another" (Roys 1957:114). Yaxuna is situated along that border, between what Ralph Roys defined as the provinces of Sotuta and Cupul, based on his understanding of various native-language and Spanish colonial sources. Roys's own maps show the area around Yaxuna to have been claimed by both the Cupul families to the east and the Xiu families to the west (Roys 1957:93). Recent reinterpretations of the ethnohistoric literature have deemphasized the existence of actual borders between Contact-era provinces, suggesting instead that polities were more fluidly defined based upon shifting alliances and claims to territory (Okoshi 1995, Quezada 1993, Restall 1997). Where Roys emphasized the province, which he believed to correlate with the native term *cuchcabal*, ethnohistorians Sergio Quezada and Tsubasa Okoshi, and now many other archaeologists working on this period, prefer a model that emphasizes the *batabil* (single central place administered by a lord with dependents) as the central unit, although at certain times *batabils* joined together into the larger administrative unit of the *cuchcabal* (Kepecs and Masson 2003:42, Quezada 1993). Such alliances were formed through marriage, trade, and defense, and were broken often over land disputes or raids. Okoshi and Quezada describe the Cupul area surrounding Yaxuna as composed of several *cuchcabalob*, each of which in turn was composed of alliances of various *batabil* or settlements. Each *cuchcabal* was subject to a separate overlord or *halach uinic* who resided at a certain central place, but the *cuchcabal* did not have to be territorially contiguous to be in alliance (Ringle and Bey 2001:269).

Quezada has described Mayapan as a "true innovation in Maya political history" because ethnohistoric documents relating to Mayapan include claims to legitimacy based on a confederate system of governance among many lords who created a set of alliances and submissions (Quezada 1998:471). William Ringle and George J. Bey note that ethnohistoric sources describing the confederacy at Mayapan are all quite late and hardly impartial (Ringle and Bey 2001:273). They suggest these descriptions reflect a traditional Maya court composed of powerful vassals who retained landholdings and rights, but who were ultimately ruled by leaders from the Cocom and Xiu families (Ringle and Bey 2001:275). In both interpretations of the ethnohistoric narratives, the heads of various historically important lineages moved their residences to the walled city of Mayapan where they received tribute, revived their fortunes after the defeat of Chichen Itza, and redefined Maya urban life after the collapse of the Classic cities and in relation to the changing fortunes of Postclassic Mesoamerica. The documents are clear that from the latter half of the thirteenth century, this confederation based at Mayapan was the dominant force in the political, religious, and economic life of most of the northern lowlands. Such a delicate experimentation did not last very long, and by the fifteenth century a dispute between two of the major lineages of the League caused war to erupt again and the city was destroyed.

What was the effect upon Yaxuna of the founding, rise to dominance, and eventual destruction of Mayapan? As described at the outset of this chapter, the citizens of Yaxuna suffered miserably during the Terminal Classic territorial wars led by their neighbors from Chichen Itza. Quickly subdued, the Yaxuneros likely paid tribute to the rulers of Chichen Itza and may have been captured for slavery or sacrifice, since there is so little evidence of a resident population at the site after the Terminal Classic period. By approximately 1000 CE, when Chichen Itza was fully in control of most of the central northern lowlands, the city of Yaxuna was abandoned, with no evidence of new building or activity until two hundred years later when the Late Postclassic shrines described above appear at very select locations across the deserted landscape.

Many aspects of the Late Postclassic data from Yaxuna suggest that participation in the social imaginary surrounding the League of Mayapan was responsible for the revival of ceremonial activity seen in the material record of the site. While no direct mention of the inhabitants of Yaxuna, or Cetelac as the site was known in colonial records, is made in ethnohistoric documents related to the League, the lands of the Cupul region were highly contested during the contact period, and it would be easy to conclude that certain *batabil* within the area might have sought protection from the occupants of Chichen Itza within the folds of the competing confederacy centered at Mayapan. There are various interpretations of the relationship between Chichen Itza and Mayapan, but most of them acknowledge a serious rivalry and outright hostilities between the rulers of the two important cities (Andrews 1990; Andrews, Andrews, and Robles 2003; Masson, Hare, and Peraza L. 2006; Stanton and Gallareta N. 2001). Since the population of Yaxuna was a target of the leaders of Chichen Itza due to the city's strategic location and earlier alliance to Coba, the remaining Yaxuneros may have chosen to align themselves with the enemies of Chichen Itza for protection, forging a memory of alliance and community through shared enemies. The most notable enemies of Chichen were the ruling families of Mayapan.

Artifactual evidence also suggests participation in the western sphere of Late Postclassic influence, and these items may have been the mechanisms that cemented fragile social bonds during this time of change. The most common Late Postclassic artifact in the Yaxuna assemblage is Chen Mul Modeled censer ware, a ceramic type found at virtually all sites across the peninsula and much more important in the Mayapan ceramic assemblage than on the east coast. Furthermore, the finest effigy censers have been found at Mayapan, and many believe it was home to the production of these pieces and a related religious practice (Lyall 2012, Masson 2000, Milbrath and Peraza 2003, Peraza L. and Milbrath 2010). These censers have been found in front of altars at Mayapan and are depicted in Postclassic Maya codices as part of calendrical rituals (Figure 3.4). All the censers have a cylindrical form in which to burn copal resin incense, and most are decorated with three-dimensional modeled imagery of deities. They are unslipped but the most elaborate are large and well painted, while smaller versions carry much of the same imagery of deities and supernaturals. In the codices they are often shown billowing smoke while religious specialists approach the figural component in conversation. Robert E. Smith and others have demonstrated that the main period of censer manufacture and use at Mayapan was the latter half of the Late Postclassic, and there is relative consensus that Chen Mul Modeled is a good chronological marker (Masson 2000, Ochoa 2007, Robles 1990, Smith 1971:218). Thus the three shrines with associated scatters of Chen Mul Modeled censer wares from Yaxuna likely date to the latter half of the thirteenth century, or after 1250 CE. While specific interpretations vary, architectural, ethnohistoric, and artifactual data suggest a florescence at Mayapan after 1250 CE, when Masson suggests the elite reinvented the city based on their memories of an imagined past (Masson 2000, Milbrath and Peraza L. 2003, Quezada 1998:471).

The lack of many exotic trade goods at Yaxuna during the Late Postclassic period argues against its active participation in the trading networks of the east coast, as does the total absence of stucco murals or iconography in the multiethnic International Style found at many sites like Tulum and Tancah on the Caribbean (Robertson 1970, Taube 2010, Vail and Hernandez 2010). The *tumbaga* bell found in the 6E-13 shrine is the single example from Yaxuna of the trade goods moving throughout the Mesoamerican Postclassic world, and is more indicative of the participation of Yaxuneros in the ideology of offerings and sacrifice than a richly diverse economic life.

Finally, the lack of residential structures at Yaxuna despite the construction of ceremonial structures might be best explained as the result

FIGURE 3.4. *Chen Mul Modeled censer from Mayapan in the form of a female maize deity and Chen Mul Modeled censer fragments from Yaxuna. Censer photograph by Phillip Hofstetter, used with permission of the Instituto Nacional de Antropología e Historia-Proyecto Mayapan, Carlos Peraza Lope, director. Fragments photograph courtesy of Jeanne Randall, Selz Foundation Yaxuna Archaeological Project.*

of the ethnohistorically documented Late Postclassic residence pattern of the region surrounding Mayapan. In this model, the *batabil*, or local lord of Yaxuna, resided at Mayapan as part of the League while he administered the lands of Yaxuna through ceremonial visits or circulations through the landscape. Ethnohistoric documents including firsthand accounts by the grandsons of the lords of Mayapan are quite clear that many lords moved within the city's protective walls after the Itza wars of domination (Ringle and Bey 2001:274, Restall 1998:88). Whatever population survived the termination of Yaxuna by Chichen Itza may have lingered on site for some period of time until the opportunity for a new chance at independence arose in the form of the League confederation or participation in some way in the political life of Mayapan. The materialization of a shared identity through shrine construction and the performance of rituals of inclusion in the form of shrine offerings demonstrate an ideological and political statement of participation in the Mayapan cultural sphere on the part of Yaxuna elite. In addition to these materializations, this social imaginary relied upon a contract of collectively remembering the past, especially certain key expressions of dynastic or royal power such as monumental architecture, ritual authority, and specialized knowledge.

MEMORY AND REINVENTION AT YAXUNA

The Late Postclassic period in Mesoamerica has been described rightly as a period of tremendous social change following the upheaval of the Classic Maya collapse and the push to empire emanating from central México after 1100 CE. In the Maya lowlands this period is often characterized as a time of decline, yet Masson and others have criticized this terminology as limiting and inherently based on comparisons to periods in which very different social conditions prevailed (Masson 2000). One can see the survival of the northern Maya polities into the thirteenth and fourteenth centuries as one of the greatest accomplishments of Maya culture, an episode of profound cultural reinvention and reorganization comparable to the emergence of stratification or statehood centuries earlier. The construction of standardized shrine structures was an integral component of this deliberate reinvention, and their location across the landscape as well as the materials they contain are important clues to the values of Late Postclassic elites struggling to maintain social complexity. The consistency of these structures across the northern lowlands suggests that specialized knowledge circulated among elites and that they shared a social imaginary and memory community where power or legitimacy was expressed through sacred architecture.

Obviously, religious practices and rituals of inclusion centered on censers and shrines were tied closely to this reinvention. Rituals of inclusion circulate ideas about social membership and difference because they are performed with the knowledge that others within the group are performing the same actions. Across the northern lowlands, nearly identical shrines were built almost simultaneously at cities separated by hundreds of kilometers. The act of participating in the construction of such a shrine brought people into a social collectivity that set them apart from their recent ancestors who lived without monumental or civic architecture. The return to the idea of civic architecture, as well as to actual examples of abandoned monumental architecture, created a new layer of meaning and memories that linked past, present, and future—it created Olivier's palimpsest (Olivier 2011, Rowlands 1993, Stanton and Magnoni 2008).

Ringle and Bey argue that Postclassic shrines are culturally consistent with earlier structures used for the collection and display of tribute in the northern Maya lowlands such as thrones (Ringle and Bey 2001:277). They suggest structures described as "ceremonial shrines" or "raised shrines" were places where leaders addressed members of their *cuchcabal* and received modest amounts of tribute as a form of status reinforcement (Ringle and Bey 2001:276, Smith 1971). The artifactual material from the shrines at Yaxuna is consistent with this interpretation, given that many of the tribute goods were highly perishable (cotton, fowl, beeswax) and those that have survived are composed exclusively of censer ware fragments and trade items. While the quantity of these materials is quite small, we do not have a large number of other Late Postclassic shrines from the rural hinterlands with which to compare quantities of offerings. More importantly, the Yaxuna shrine materials are ideologically consistent with what is offered at more elaborate and better-studied Late Postclassic ceremonial architecture at Mayapan and the east coast sites.

Censers are not evenly distributed across all the settlement at Mayapan, and Masson and Peraza have demonstrated that the most important architectural groups in the heart of Mayapan have the largest percentage of these wares, while outlying groups have very few censers (Masson and Peraza L. 2014). Many groups dating to this period at Mayapan have no censer fragments at all, a distributional observation that suggests censers were not uniformly available to the population of the city but were clustered in the hands of the most important elite lineages, a pattern that mirrors how prestige ceramics were distributed across Maya cities of the Classic period. The presence of censer wares at frontier sites such as Yaxuna takes on additional significance given this pattern at Mayapan. Clearly, high-status ceramic wares with ceremonial significance were controlled by a segment of the population and were not available widely to every household, as earlier models of religious life at Mayapan suggested (Pollock 1962, Thompson 1970). The circulation of censers was closely tied to the circulation of elites who controlled production and distribution, and their presence at certain sites but not others suggests not only that the use of censers was performative, but that access constituted a performance of inclusion within elite circles. That these ceramics were so iconographically rich and so closely tied to religious practice suggests the group who had control of their distribution was the same elite who read and used the codices where censer practice is depicted (Graff and Vail 2001).

Earlier authors argued the dispersed shrines characteristic of the Late Postclassic are an indication that religious worship was decentralized at this time, settlements were isolated from one another, and elites vanished (Coe 1962, Thompson 1970). Economic resources were indeed expended differently during the Late Postclassic period, with less investment in large architectural monuments or funerary contexts. But one could argue that within the western sphere, the location of shrines atop previously abandoned monumental architecture rather than in new locations or within domestic areas is a stronger indication of cultural continuity in ceremonial life than of any decentering. The use of reutilized carved stone to build shrines within sight of earlier monumental architecture created an appearance of social continuity where it did not exist. In a context of competing discourses about the future of Maya urbanism, one group chose to define themselves around a reimagined urban past. A sense of place is one of the most powerful elements of social identity, and the two are locked together in a reciprocal relationship in which the experience of circulation within a space reinforces and confirms the identity that derives and constitutes the place. The creation of a sense of place is in turn intertwined with remembering, forgetting, and the powerful hold memory has over our sense of home.

Given the pattern of unequal distribution of censers at Mayapan, the location of shrines atop elite architecture, and the depiction of elaborate ceremonial knowledge in the codices, there does not seem to be reason to think official religious practice was any more democratized in the Late Postclassic world than it had been before. Sixteenth-century ethnohistoric documents clearly depict efforts by certain elite Maya families to maintain their positions of power and privilege, and we should expect that the linkage between authority and dynasty was a continually evolving social contract. The selection of monumental architecture from an earlier time when dynastic power was expressed through construction underscores the efforts by Postclassic elites to maintain symbolic ties to their royal ancestors and perform those claims as part of their identity. Even given all the failures of the Classic political system, in the aftermath of the southern collapse and Terminal Classic wars, the native elite families of the northern lowlands chose to remember and accentuate the glories of Classic elite power as they reinvented local political and ceremonial systems within the Postclassic reality of pan-Mesoamerican integration.

The concepts of civic or social memory are very relevant to the study of Late Postclassic remains from urban Yaxuna. Why were certain northern Maya cities able to recover from the challenges of the Terminal Classic-Early Postclassic "interregnum" while others were not? Many studies have examined the unique characteristics of the confederated rule at Mayapan and its influence on the rest of the Maya area. But Yaxuna is situated on the frontier of this political system and appears to have experienced a sparse reoccupation or reuse unlike what is documented for either Mayapan or the east coast centers, but which may be characteristic of other interior sites such as Ake, Okop, or Xuenkal, where small scatters of Late Postclassic materials have been reported (Andrews 1993). In a study of post–civil war Athens, Andrew Wolpert suggests that the Athenians were able to recover while their neighbors were not in part due to the Athenian ability to reinvent and reimagine their defeat. Key to reimagining defeat is reinterpreting the past, selectively choosing elements to accentuate, while simultaneously ignoring those details that are too painful or too confrontational to allow the inhabitants of a city to carry on. Conflicting or competing images of the past often exist simultaneously, as the destroyed walls of fourth-century Athens coexisted with the remaining population living under the rule of Sparta (Wolpert 2002). Collective memory makes sense of this landscape, often by the erection of monuments that crystallize a particular attitude toward the past. The Postclassic shrines of Yaxuna and other frontier sites in the northern lowlands must be viewed within the social and cultural context of reconciliation and revival characteristic of the time. The blending of remembering and forgetting they represent presents an opportunity for cultural revival after defeat, and also for nascent reinvention by emergent opportunists who wished to define themselves as the inheritors of all that was glorious about the past. What we see materialized is a negotiation with the past and the present in order to recover a collectivity that incorporated stratification and privilege. The historically powerful lineages of the northern lowlands utilized a potent combination of the ancient tradition of ritual architectural performance with the amplification of trade-based power characteristic of the period. This combination allowed the negotiation of a social imaginary that achieved a remembering of their positions at the apex of society. Echoing scholars such as Henrietta Moore in the analysis of social difference, it is not that the material world of Late Postclassic

Yaxuna reflected the natural division of the world into victors and failures, but rather that cultural discourse, including how material culture would be organized and distributed, produced cultural difference (Moore 1994). Shrines served as the perfect locations to reassert authority as part of a discourse about power, tied as they were to past traditions but easily adaptable to current religious practices.

Centers with smaller populations than Mayapan's during the Postclassic period, such as Yaxuna, were probably brought into the reorganized Late Postclassic political landscape and social imaginary through the incorporation of local *batabils* in the Mayapan power structure. This incorporation was accomplished by the circulation of elite ceremonial practice within the abandoned urban landscape, which generated the experience of inclusion and the expectation of social regeneration. The emotional landscape was remade through memories of a celebrated past. The location of Yaxuna on the shifting frontier of the Cupul province, in an area characterized as unstable and disputed in the ethnohistoric literature, accentuated the need for rituals of inclusion and ritualized statements of participation in the greater imaginary of the League of Mayapan. The lands previously occupied by Yaxuneros not only were valuable components of the tribute- and alliance-based politics of the Postclassic world but also were essential to the social imaginary of Mayapan that sought to re-create a community identity of dominance. Far from being peripheral to Late Postclassic life, religious practice in the form of censers, trade goods, and perishable offerings at shrines, coupled with selective memories of state-organized religious practice in the past, were deliberately used by an optimistic society that strove for economic and political glory after many centuries of struggle and conflict. The practice of placing ceramic offerings, and the deities depicted on these censers, were both vehicles for the renegotiation of relationships as well as visual memories that built a shared understanding of the present. A new identity was carried forward, operational only after it was circulated and performed, that eventually laid claim to an identity based in continuity and survival (Olivier 2011).

CONCLUSION

This chapter asks questions about how northern Maya populations reinvented themselves and survived into the Late Postclassic period. Was the Classic period and its institutions something they remembered or forgot? We cannot answer these questions without exploring how memories are used to shape social identities and broader social imaginaries that provide a collective sense of community. The name of the Postclassic period itself encapsulates the way this time was understood initially by academics—it was the absence of the Classic, of the remnants of a greater time. This perspective has provided Maya archaeology with very little explanatory power for how people in certain areas of the Maya world, specifically the northern lowlands and Caribbean coast, continued to build architecture, create innovative artifacts, and engage in flourishing long-distance trade with the other cultures of Mesoamerica. While we can puzzle over this material evidence, it is crucial to explore why people made the decision to persist in northern lowland settlements (when they did not make the same decision in the southern lowlands) despite hundreds of years of experience with the failures of Classic urban life.

Archaeologists have unique access to the archives of human memory, and many have generated rich scholarship into how memory is materialized and deployed over deep periods of time. The time depth available to archaeologists argues that we must consider memory as a key component of ancient cultures and how they defined themselves, especially when societies return to places long abandoned or reshape themselves in the wake of social trauma. The long view available to archaeologists provides a perspective on how often the most exciting social innovations occur after the destruction or disappearance of what was previously understood as a fundamental institution.

The end of the Terminal Classic period is one of those gaps within ancient Maya history, a moment in which previous models of social life had been stretched thin and reworked only to collapse again. Urban settlements ruled by dynastic families had given way to a single dominant urban entity, the mega-city of Chichen Itza. Through pan-Mesoamerican trade and a militaristic outlook, Chichen seized control of weakened northern lowland polities and yet was only able to maintain such control for approximately 250 years. The fall of Chichen left the region without a dominant power for another hundred years until slowly we see material evidence that elite families returned to their previous touchstone of offerings within monumental architecture. The three nearly identical shrines built at Yaxuna in the Late Postclassic period, similar to other shrines built during this time within the hinterlands, and the artifacts from Yaxuna suggest close ties to Mayapan, the final attempt to revive Maya urban life. Building masonry and even monumental architecture (the Xkanha shrine is the best example) required the remembrance of specialized knowledge of architectural skills as well as the history of abandoned Classic-period pyramids. It required that some form of peace be made with the ruined urban past and all it represented, that memories be reshaped to suit the needs of a population that wanted to survive.

Building and using shrines together was an integrative process that required leading families to share resources and knowledge, and the tolerance and understanding of the rest of the population. The artifactual and ethnohistoric record from Mayapan suggests a Late Postclassic social imaginary that included practices supporting the continuation of elite families in positions of privilege—tribute payments continued, although simpler than in Classic times, as did highly specialized calendrical and ceremonial practices. The choice to return to Yaxuna and create new monumental architecture was not one made by a single family, but shows that elite families circulated ideas and information across the peninsula, that they participated in rituals of inclusion at Mayapan and elsewhere that helped cement a new sense of identity as innovators connected to the rest of Mesoamerica. The material wealth of the Late Postclassic outside Mayapan was not as great as at other periods in Classic history, but it was a familiar indicator of success and participation in something larger than local economies. Behaviors and their material partners circulated a new social imaginary characterized by collective forgiveness of the failures of prior dynastic urbanism and the commemoration of many elements of earlier civic life. A new social imaginary that provided for the perpetuation of some of the most fundamental aspects of ancient Maya society within a framework of new pan-regional networks of exchange recalled the past in order to transform the present. Circulating through the urban center of Yaxuna and once again making offerings of material wealth in order to perpetuate the social order shows how remembering and forgetting can be one of the most powerful forms of contingent change.

BURIAL RITUALS AND THE SOCIAL IMAGINARY OF CHILDHOOD

Chapter 4

INTRODUCTION

How did the people who lived in ancient Maya cities and towns understand what we call childhood? How is the identity of a child created and materialized? Is it inherent in the experience of a young body or relational with adults? What does studying childhood reveal about cultural reproduction in ancient Maya society? Were children important, were they socially visible? Could a young child become a revered ancestor? This chapter examines a potent social identity that is often taken for granted as universal or biologically determined. In fact, childhood as an identity does not exist in the same way in all cultures, and we must look carefully at how it was constructed. The anthropological study of childhood has explored all of these questions and found this particular social identity to be one of the most fascinating. An undeniable biological component, one which today in the West we take as determinative of ability and value, is understood in highly diverse ways across cultures and time. Within the West, childhood has evolved only recently from a time of responsibility and work to a time we idealize as carefree and irreplaceable. Elsewhere in the world today work expectations of young people are substantial, and this seems to have been the case as well in many ancient states. This chapter examines how the social identity of the child was reproduced in one particularly charged context, the family burial ritual.

I utilize burial data from three Classic-period Maya sites in the northern lowlands to explore the social identity of a child and how childhood was understood in ancient Maya society. Yaxuna, Xuenkal, and Dzibilchaltun were all important Maya centers during the Late Classic and Terminal Classic periods and shared many cultural features, including ideas about how the dead could be treated. This shared background understanding was communicated through rituals of identity transformation that moved deceased people into the realm of ancestors. I describe the three ways in which child bodies, also described by some scholars as non-adult bodies because the term "child" means many different things to different people, were processed after death. Children were interred in family crypts, treated so their bones could be added to bundles or kept as tokens, and the very young were placed in burial urns. Like the practices we see materialized in the burial record, ideas about children varied, and we cannot expect to recover a singular way in which a child's identity was conveyed. However, we are able to read patterns across these sites that reflect the presence and acceptance of children as uniquely potent members of the collective society. The social imaginary of childhood in ancient Maya times was very distinct from the one we hold in the modern West. I argue that children were not only visible and valued members of society, but held key roles in social networks that cemented and affirmed kin relations. The burial treatment of children conveys a social biography that surpasses the physical lifetime of a child and circulates an idea about how life force was exchanged and social bonds affirmed along highly scripted social relationships. In the repeated emphasis on childhood as an identity more closely connected to the otherworld, materialized in child burials, we can read that the social imaginary of childhood included the power of children to connect corporate groups through the indebtedness of social relations.

As archaeologists utilizing the social imaginary, we must explore how material culture was used by ancient people to naturalize childhood as a social identity. What artifacts and practices helped make childhood as a status self-evident? To many scholars, childhood is by its nature self-evident—the biological realities of small bodies that must learn the basic skills of human interaction determine the reality of childhood. But as research on the social construction of childhood demonstrates, very little about childhood is universal across all cultures and time periods, and how this identity is defined—its duration, its capacities and limitations—varies tremendously (Lally and Moore 2011, Lancy 2008, Montgomery 2009).

LATE AND TERMINAL CLASSIC BURIAL PRACTICES

Burials represent only one of a wide variety of data available for interrogating the nature of childhood in the past. Children in prehistoric cultures performed work and made artifacts that are distinctive, they had child-only spaces within the landscape, and they are portrayed in sacred as well as secular art (Baxter 2005, Bird and Bliege Bird 2000, Crawford 1999, Stavrakopoulou 2004, F. Thomas 2002). But funerary practices, because they reveal both the living and dead (Pearson 1999:3) provide a particularly powerful window into both the cultural conceptions of childhood and the practices or circulations that were performed to enact and solidify those conceptualizations. How to best read such complicated texts will be discussed further, but first I want to introduce the material record of child burials from three Maya centers during a specific moment in time.

The four hundred years that span the Late Classic to Terminal Classic periods in the northern Maya lowlands were a time of intense social activity and transformation. The material record of this time and an exploration of the social motivations behind it have been the subject of concentrated scholarly inquiry since early in the twentieth century (Culbert 1973; Demarest, Rice, and Rice 2004; Sabloff and Andrews V 1986). The particular economic, environmental, and social dynamics of this transition are provided in other works, but as a framework for our discussion of identity creation and maintenance through the funerary rituals of children, I provide the following summary. In the three centers to be discussed in depth below, and across the northern Maya lowlands, the Late Classic period is defined by a cultural florescence that left a rich material record of art, architecture, civic works, and many other manifestations of large urban populations. Many cities in the northern and southern Maya lowlands reached their peak of population around 700 CE, and the textual record is richest from this time period as well. While this florescence was short-lived in the southern lowlands, where the majority of cities were abandoned by around 900 CE, in the north most centers continued to be densely occupied until at least 1100 CE, when the Terminal Classic period ended. Despite this prosperity, social changes are evident in the material record of the north after 900 or so, and while population numbers remained very high, social stress is evident in declining standards of architectural construction, increased standardization of art and artifacts, increased evidence of warfare and conflict, and the rise of a single dominant urban center, Chichen Itza, concurrent with a general decline of all others. Factors such as environmental degradation, large-scale population movements, endemic warfare and conscription, and even foreign invasion have all been suggested as causal factors for this social transition. No single factor was likely responsible, and there is reasonable data to support the notion that the Classic Maya people living in the northern lowlands during this time were challenged to adapt to the unfortunate convergence of nearly all of these factors. This was a time of social accommodation, when old patterns might have been wearing thin and new innovations or remedies were needed. Much of the material culture, including the burials to be discussed, exhibits a cultural conservatism that has long been considered a hallmark of Maya society—certain funerary practices are known to have been practiced more or less consistently for nearly a thousand years—but the social context of the lowlands during this time when resources were becoming scarce and traditional models of power were changing makes this consistency in funerary ritual all the more significant. Despite changes in other social arenas, funerary ritual was one form of circulation that remained largely unchanged, and the social imaginary of childhood was materialized consistently throughout this era.

The forty-one child burials to be discussed here as examples of the performative circulations that helped define the social identity of a child are drawn from three Classic Maya centers: Yaxuna, which was discussed in chapter 3; Xuenkal, where I have directed research since 2004; and Dzibilchaltun, one of the best-documented and most important population centers in the northern lowlands. Common practices can be seen in the samples from across all three sites, which indicate some form of shared ritual and belief at the regional level. There are also clear differences between the sites, as well as a range of funerary practices represented.

Yaxuna was a large urban center located in the heart of the peninsula and connected to the even larger urban center of Coba by a one-hundred-kilometer-long raised road that was likely constructed during the Late Classic period (Stanton et al. 2010; Suhler, Ardren, and Johnstone 1998). During the Late Classic period, the population of Yaxuna gradually recovered from a lull in construction and other activity that occurred at the end of the Early Classic period, reaching a peak population density during the Terminal Classic. Residential structures that date to this four-hundred-year period are located across the entire urban zone and well into the hinterland, even in previously open areas adjacent to monumental architecture or on top of earlier structures that were long abandoned. Excavation of these simple residential structures provided a wealth of burial data, given the long-standing Maya practice of interring the dead beneath the floors of domestic structures (Gillespie 2001, McAnany 1995, Welsh 1988). Overall, the Selz Foundation Yaxuna Archaeological Project recovered the remains of forty-three individuals while I was codirector from 1991 to 1998. Twelve of these remains were of commoner children, and seven of those date to the Late-Terminal Classic period (Table 4.1). Child burials are found most commonly at Yaxuna in primary context within subfloor crypts, but also in a fragmented state as part of secondary contexts such as caches and additions to later primary burials.

Xuenkal was a smaller Maya center located along the trade routes between the northern coast and the urban capital of Chichen Itza, in the

TABLE 4.1. YAXUNA LATE-TERMINAL CLASSIC CHILD BURIAL INVENTORY

Burial	Structure	Period	Age at Death[i]	Primary/ Secondary	Pathologies	Artifacts
1	5E-103	Terminal Classic	5–7	P-crypt	Cranial mod, 3 caries	Sacalum Pizarra vase and platter (?) on pelvis, deer tibia, shell pendant
4	5E-105	Terminal Classic	12–15	P-crypt	Cranial mod, 2 caries, 2 hypoplasia	Muna tripod dish, Ticul incised sherd, shell pendant
5	5E-59	Late Classic	2–4	P-crypt	Cranial mod	Bowl over cranium
9	5E-77	Terminal Classic	4	P-crypt		Ticul bowl, 2 shell pendants, 2 deer bones
15d	5F-49	Terminal Classic	4–6	S-1 small fragment of humerus with other burials		Shell pendant, possible part of shaman's pot of bones
18a	6F-73	Terminal Classic	5–6	P-crypt	Cranial mod	Yokat bowl at feet, plate over skull, shell pendant, deer bones
18b	6F-73	Terminal Classic	4	P-crypt		Shell beads by teeth, shell pendant

[i]Based on tooth development (Bennett 1992:83).

center of the peninsula. I have directed research at Xuenkal since 2004 to better understand how the rise of Chichen Itza affected regional centers within an area that had access to both marine resources and very rich agricultural features (Ardren et al. 2005; Manahan, Ardren, and Alonso 2012; Tiesler et al. 2010). In the Late Classic period, Xuenkal was a growing settlement much like other northern Maya centers of the period. A single palace compound built at this time mimics the design and orientation of Ek Balam, a nearby city ruled by a royal dynasty. But during this period, as Chichen Itza grew in size, population, and economic strength, the city of Xuenkal was absorbed within the influence of the larger nearby center and local elites were conscripted into craft production of shell, chert, and textile goods at levels far beyond their domestic needs (Ardren et al. 2010).

Just prior to this social crisis, at the beginning of the Late Classic period, wealthy occupants of the city built a platform known as 9M-136 to house a series of five family crypts. These five crypts contain the remains of twenty-three individuals, the majority of burials from research to date at the site. Of these twenty-three individuals, nine were children, and they are found most commonly as fragmented remains in secondary contexts (i.e., as additions to the family crypts) in the form of probable bundles or token bone elements, although three of the children from Xuenkal are relatively complete, primary interments in their own crypt (Table 4.2).

Dzibilchaltun was an urban center located in the dry northwestern plains of the peninsula and the first large urban center in the northern Maya lowlands to be systematically investigated by archaeologists. Research at Dzibilchaltun under the direction of E. Wyllys Andrews IV and later E. Wyllys Andrews V documented a long and continuous occupation from the Preclassic through early Colonial periods that saw its greatest growth during the Late Classic period, when the site was an independent polity with royal dynastic leadership (Andrews and Andrews 1980; Maldonado, Gongora, and Voss 2002). Investigations were conducted at the site under the auspices of the Middle American Research Institute of Tulane University from 1955 to 1977, and the exceptional material record recovered from this work has been published in a series of specialized volumes. Although no bioarchaeological analysis of the skeletal material recovered has been conducted since T. Dale Stewart's study in 1967, nonetheless the Dzibilchaltun burial sample of 142 individuals from 110 burials that span the entire occupational sequence is unique in the study of ancient Maya funerary ritual in the northern lowlands (Stewart 1974). Within this sample, there are twenty-five commoner child burials that date from the Late Classic to the Terminal Classic period (Table 4.3).

TABLE 4.2. XUENKAL LATE-TERMINAL CLASSIC CHILD BURIAL INVENTORY

Burial	Structure	Period	Age at Death[i]	Primary/Secondary	Pathologies	Artifacts
16-1-1b	9M-136	Late Classic	12–15	P-cist, disturbed by later burial		Possible ceramics
16-1-2-2	9M-136	Late Classic	Child	S-fragments in fill		Deer scapula
16-1-2b	9M-136	Late Classic	9–13	P-cist	Cranial mod	3 Muna plates, deer mandible
16-2c(4)	9M-136	Late Classic	9–13	S-tooth and humerus fragment, from bundle		Miniature flask
16-1-2d(2)	9M-136	Late Classic	Infant	S-hand bones only, in association with other burial		
16-1-2e(2)	9M-136	Late Classic	Infant	S-phlanges and clavicle only, in association with other burial		
16-1-4c	9M-136	Late Classic	Child 2–3	S-tooth and skull cap only, in association with other burial		
16-1-5a	9M-136	Late Classic	12–16	P-crypt, open after burial		Sacalum bowl, Ticul Thin Slate vase near cranium, 3 shell pendants including mask and plaster beads on chest, deer bone along lower body
16-1-5b	9M-136	Late Classic	6–10	S-incomplete skeleton, in association with 5a	Caries, 2 hypo	

[i] Based on morphology of auricular and pubic surface and dental wear (Tiesler et al. 2010:396).

TABLE 4.3. DZIBILCHALTUN LATE-TERMINAL CLASSIC CHILD BURIAL INVENTORY

Burial	Structure	Period	Age at Death[i]	Primary/ Secondary	Pathologies[ii]	Artifacts
1	14	Late Classic	Child	S?-urn		Large jar covered with sherd lid
1	30	Late Classic	6–12	S-crypt, only a few fragments		
Sub 7	38	Late Classic	2	S?-urn, intrusive		1 imported polychrome rested in large jar, jade bead, *mano*
Sub 8	38	Late Classic	Child	S?-urn		Remains in large jar
Sub 8	38	Late Classic	Infant	S?-urn		Remains in large jar
Sub 2	38	Late-Terminal	7	P-crypt		2 shell pendants, jade necklace, earplug, 22 shell beads
Sub 2	38	Late-Terminal	3	P-crypt		
Sub 2	38	Late-Terminal	3	S-crypt, very few fragments		
Sub 6	38	Late-Terminal	2–3	S-crypt		Bones painted red, plate over cranium, 6 carved shell pendants, 16 shell beads
2	384	Late-Terminal	Child	S, P-urn		Plate over jar
1	385	Late-Terminal	Child	S-crypt, few fragments		Plate over a jar

4	385	Late-Terminal	infant	S?-urn	Jar with infant, 8 jade beads, 1 serpent fang
5	385	Late-Terminal	Child	S?-urn	Jar covered with plate
6	385	Late-Terminal	infant	P-cist	Head covered by bowl, jade bead
7	385	Late-Terminal	Child	S-cist	
8	385	Late-Terminal	Child	P-crypt	Plate over cranium, shell bead painted blue
9	385	Late-Terminal		Urn	Plate over jar
2	1005	Late-Terminal	Sub-adult	S-crypt	With two adults, 3 ceramic vessels, shell pendant
1	3536	Late-Terminal	6–12	S-crypt, teeth only	Teeth only, 1 ceramic vessel
4	38	Terminal Classic	6	P-crypt	2 ceramic vessels, fragments of shell
6	57	Terminal Classic	1	S?-crypt, skull fragments only	2 fragments of cranium with adult male, shell bead
1	96	Terminal Classic	10–12	S?-crypt	Part of cache
2	96	Terminal Classic	6–12	S?-crypt	Part of cache
6	96	Terminal Classic	Sub-adult	P-crypt	2 ceramic vessels
8	96	Terminal Classic	Child		3 ceramic vessels, 2 whistles

[i] Age was estimated by T. Dale Stewart (Andrews and Andrews 1980:320).
[ii] Not available for this collection.

Child burials are found most commonly in primary context family crypts, as at Yaxuna and Xuenkal, although secondary fragments of children are also common. Eight of the twenty-five child burials at Dzibilchaltun are urn burials of infants and very small children, a funerary ritual also found at Xuenkal and known from other nearby excavated Maya centers such as Chichen Itza and Isla Cerritos (Bennett 1990, Perez de Heredia et al. 2004, Ruz 1989).

Nineteen of the forty-one child burials under discussion in this chapter, or nearly half, were recovered from stone crypts built beneath the plaster floor of a simple rectangular domestic structure or platform. Often these crypts were reused as subsequent family members died, and there is evidence for both repeated use of crypts as well as the simultaneous interment of multiple individuals within a crypt. This was the most common burial practice across the northern lowlands throughout the Classic period. Nearly all the child crypt burials from Yaxuna, Xuenkal, and Dzibilchaltun were in primary context, indicating the child had been interred in the crypt relatively soon after death and left relatively undisturbed until excavation.

These children were buried in a manner completely consistent with other members of Classic Maya society. Adults of both genders and all ages were frequently buried under domestic floors and with grave goods such as ceramic vessels or personal ornaments. Fifteen of the nineteen child burials in crypts at these three sites were interred with complete ceramic vessels, usually placed over the cranium or pelvis. These vessels are high-quality domestic serving vessels such as rimmed plates that show little sign of regular domestic use. They are intact and appear to have been relatively unused prior to interment in the burial. Many times they are inverted over the cranium, so they are unlikely to have held offerings of food or other perishables. They were commodities available to nearly every household and are remarkably consistent offerings across the entire burial sample from the northern Maya lowlands. As such, it is unlikely we should interpret them as status markers, since they are present in nearly every burial. A better reading of these domestic vessels understands them as indications of the relationship between the living and dead, a materialization of the social relations that existed between members of a kin network or household. As Annette Weiner demonstrated so persuasively, ceremonialized exchange of domestic goods, especially goods produced by women, at key moments in life cycle events such as marriages or funerals, cements and maintains social relations between kin groups (Weiner 1976, 1992). Weiner was able to show that the circulation of women's crafts at these junctures had profound political consequences rooted in ongoing kinship obligations between siblings and other kin groups. Grave goods are a form of symbolic capital that transcends time, because they are gifted and deposited within a space that surpasses the lifetimes of the craft producers and family members in attendance. The fact that ancient Maya children were interred with these objects in much the same manner as adults indicates the social visibility of children and that they were, in certain cases at least, important actors in the gift exchange networks that we see materialized in these ceramic offerings.

Thirteen of the forty-one child burials in this study, including all the children buried in crypts and some of the secondary burials, also contain shell ornaments as part of their burial goods. The most common form is a shell pendant found in the pelvic region, but small beads are also common. In some cases the pendant is obviously made from *spondylus americanus*, a very important trade item with connections to royal regenerative power, but in most cases the shell is not able to be identified this specifically. There is almost no indication that maritime products such as fish or shellfish were consumed by the populations living at these inland cities, suggesting that the residents of Yaxuna, Xuenkal, and Dzibilchaltun did not travel to the coast on a regular basis, and marine shell for ornaments had to be obtained through trade. Stingray spines are found in some burials at Yaxuna, but like shell, these were a commodity traded very widely throughout the Maya world and are found at even the most land-locked sites many days inland from the coast. Like the ceramic vessels found in child burials, the shell pendants are simple and ubiquitous. They do not represent a significant investment of wealth or effort, and more likely are related to the individual identity of the deceased, as Rosemary Joyce has suggested is common for costume elements in ancient Mesoamerican burials (Joyce 1999).

Spondylus and other marine shells are common offerings in burials throughout the Classic period but are most frequently found in association with the young. In addition to their associations with trade and use as costume ornaments, their ability to represent or connote the power of the sea as a place of origin and wealth is perhaps the most significant aspect of their pervasive presence in child interments. Marine shells, along with stingray spines, corals, sponges, and pearls, are understood to evoke the watery otherworld from which spirits emerge to the world of humans (Joyce 2000a:77, Marcus 1987:149, Zender 2010). *Spondylus* ear flares are diagnostic markers of the Classic-period Rain God Chak, and the standard royal regalia of rulers included a *spondylus* bivalve worn over the pelvis (Joyce 2000a:76, Marcus 1987:149, Miller 1974, Schele and Miller 1986:71). The ocean seems to have been understood as the birthplace of the sun, rainclouds or precipitation, and sustenance. It was also where souls went to rest after death, as the mortuary complexes on the island of Jaina reflect (Cobos 2012). Given this cultural framework for the sea, shell pendants can be seen to be active agents in a dialogue about existence and the sources of life (Freidel, Reese-Taylor, and Mora-Marin 2002). By wearing shell, an idea was circulated that children maintained a closer connection to the otherworld from which they originated. The preference for shell ornaments for children, when ceramic, stone, or bone were readily available, conveys a deliberate connection between children and this particular substance. It may indicate both children and shell were able to transmit or represent, intrinsically, the power of the sea as a source of life. Later in this chapter I will argue that certain children were viewed as appropriate sacrificial offerings precisely because their youth materialized an intrinsic proximity to the otherworld that eroded with age. Shells likewise materialize a close connection to the spirit world, or to the sea as the place of origin, and thus it appears that shells may have been used to materialize a similar conceptualization of children. When children were decorated with shell ornaments, the shared collective imaginary of shell and child as materializations of source was circulated and maintained.

The most common burial pattern in which an individual was buried shortly after death within a family crypt with offerings is exemplified by Burial 16/1/5, one of the many multiple interments from Xuenkal. A Late Classic–period rectangular platform that measured sixteen meters by six meters and was approximately four meters in height, designated Structure 9M-136, held the remains of five separate family crypts that were utilized over a period of two hundred years by the elites of Xuenkal. The platform is located near the only freshwater source at the site and was partially dismantled during the historic period for building materials used to construct an early nineteenth-century hacienda. Burial 16/1/5 was a stone-lined crypt that penetrated the upper surface of the platform and an earlier patio floor to rest on bedrock (Figure 4.1). The crypt was made of rough-hewn stones laid on the bedrock that outlined a rectangular space almost two meters in length. Two individuals were recovered from Burial 16/1/5: a relatively complete young person from twelve to sixteen years of age at death who appears to have been the primary occupant, and the fragmentary remains of a child from six to ten years of age at death (Tiesler et al. 2010:396). The main individual may have been a young male, based on the overall dimensions of the long bones, although this is

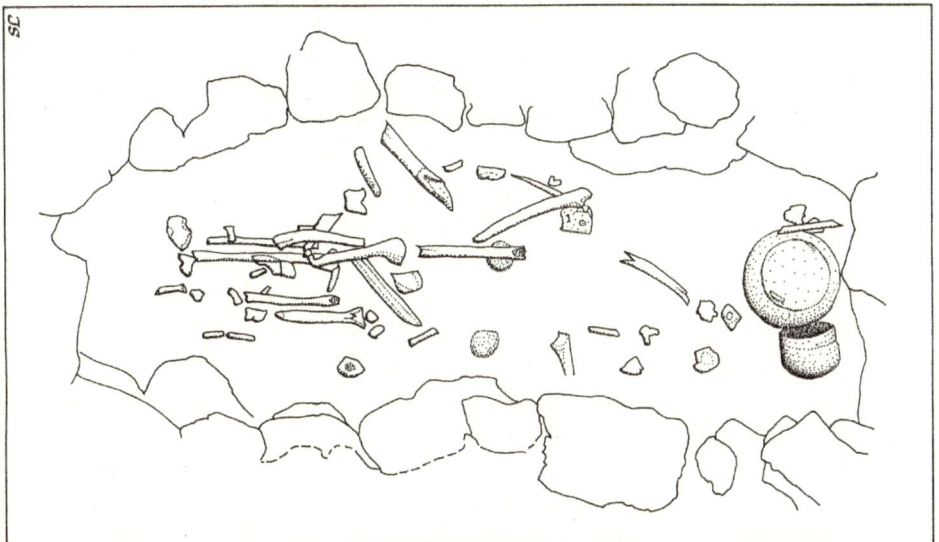

FIGURE 4.1. *Burial 16/1/5, Xuenkal. Illustration by Jack Scott based on Proyecto Arqueológico Xuenkal field drawings.*

a tentative identification and the entire burial was poorly preserved (Cucina et al. 2007). The individual was in an extended position with his head, which was covered with a Sacalum bowl and a Ticul Thin Slate vase, to the east (Manahan and Ardren 2008:261). Vera Tiesler and colleagues have argued that the presence of a patina on the bones of this individual suggests the crypt was left open for a substantial period of time prior to sealing (Tiesler et al. 2010: 400). The incomplete remains of the child were found in an extended position to the right of the main individual, and both occupants were decorated with ornaments including two plaster beads, one of which was painted green to resemble jade, a mother of pearl disc bead, and three shell pendants. One of the shell pendants was carved in the shape of a miniature mask. Fragments of the long bones of a whitetailed deer (*Odocoileus virginianus*) were found alongside the remains of the lower bodies of both individuals.

Fourteen of the forty-one child burials in this study are represented by only a few fragments of long bone, the other important way that Classic Maya bodies, both adult and non-adult, were treated postmortem. Individual elements that exhibit marks of curation, modification, or simply age are found in caches and special deposits across the Maya world at all time periods. Body partibility, explored by Pamela Geller, was a technique by which contact with ancestors was maintained and deployed (Geller

2012). Partibility, in Geller's formulation, is a subcategory of secondary burial practice and refers to the intentional selection and interment of body parts in the absence of the entire body (Geller 2012:5). This practice is known from other cultures, perhaps most famously from the Catholic curation of saints' body parts as a reminder of future resurrection. Within Classic Maya culture, it was one of a variety of ways a dead family member could be transformed into a revered ancestor and thus continue to exercise social potency. As Geller and other scholars have noted, social potency after death is not dependent upon corporeal wholeness, and in fact certain classes of body parts, such as the skull, are emblematic of a social authority much larger than individual identity in many cultures (Geller 2012, Strathern 1988, 2005). This conceptualization has been called "dividual personhood," or an identity that stresses the collective over the individual, the shared and plural aspects of participation in collectivities (Geller 2012, Strathern 1988:13). In Strathern's view, partible bodies reflect the existence of relationships to a variety of kin across multiple contexts, and the way lineage and familial connections can be invoked strategically (Strathern 2005:129). The body is used by communities to both construct and deconstruct social identities that are shared and relational. Treatment of a corpse by kin members reconfigures and solidifies existing networks, and the treatment of a decedent's bones through secondary funerary ritual provides a further opportunity for those same performative circulations. As Geller states eloquently, "Archaeological evidence suggests that the pre-Columbian Maya regarded skeletonized body parts as another substance that flowed between the living and their dead kin" (Geller 2012:12).

An example of this practice from Yaxuna underscores the numinous power of human bone within this collectivity. Structure 5F-49 is a low mound less than two meters high located within the center of urban Yaxuna. During the Late Classic period a family crypt was constructed there that utilized cut stones and a plaster floor from an earlier occupation (Johnstone 1993:133). The crypt was reused several times and grave goods as well as human bone were moved each time the crypt stones were opened, although the crypt was covered by the plaster floor of a domestic structure that also had to be cut and then repaired with each entry (Figure 4.2). Burial 15D, a small fragment of humerus from a child four to six years old, was found in this burial crypt with the remains of three other individuals (Bennett 1993:151). One of those individuals was also represented only through partition; Burial 15C was a small mandible of an adult over thirty years of age at death. The other two occupants were complete

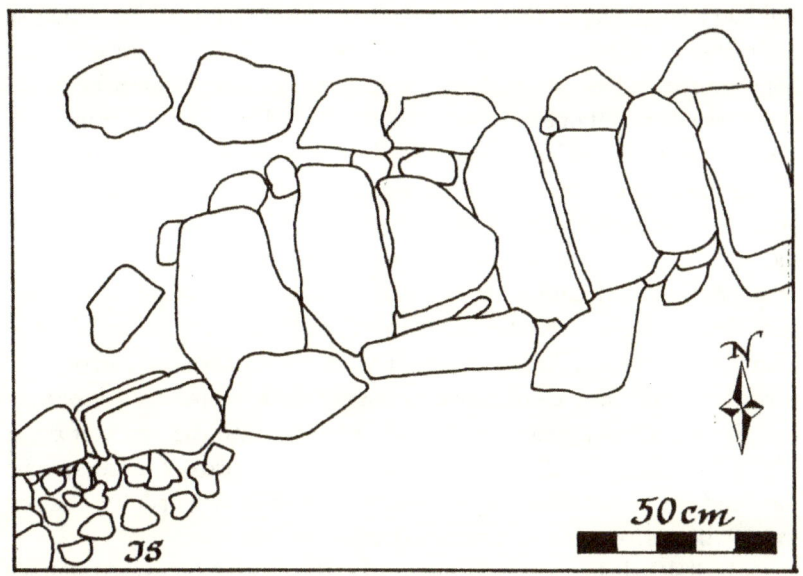

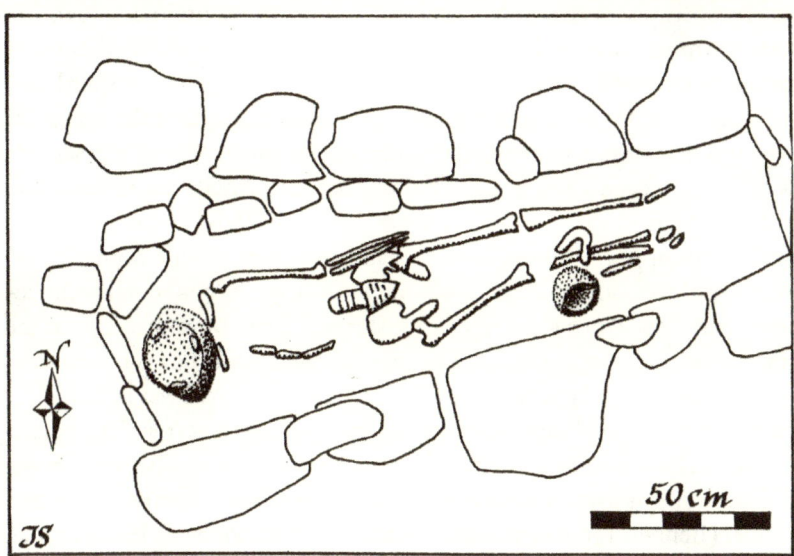

FIGURE 4.2. *Burial 15, Yaxuna. Illustration by Jack Scott based on Selz Foundation Yaxuna Archaeological Project field drawings.*

and had been placed in the crypt sequentially at different times—the last occupant, a healthy adult male over forty when he died, was buried with a bone whistle and awl at his chest, a tripod platter inverted over his head, and a vase that contained a dense mass of crushed human bone fragments placed over his right leg. Prior to his burial, a younger woman twenty-five to thirty-five years old at death had been buried in the crypt with an opposite orientation. Her skull was under the older male's feet and her toes were recovered from under his skull (Bennett 1993:151). Above the crypt, excavators found another vase, carved with the image of a seated man that contained ceramic beads and a mask painted to resemble jade (Johnstone 1993:132, Ardren 2009). The child's humerus may have been part of a textile bundle buried with either of the main individuals or may have been kept as a token of the child curated until the death of these adults. In either case, the bone fragment became a proxy for ideas about the child and social relations between a dead child, dead adults, and the living who performed the funerary ritual.

At Dzibilchaltun, eight urn burials of children were recovered, a practice recently discovered at Xuenkal and known from a limited set of other Late-Terminal Classic sites in the northern lowlands. Typically these urns are large domestic water jars covered with a bowl, plate, or sherd of a different ceramic style serving as a lid. The urns contain the complete skeleton of an infant or very small child, and in two of the eight cases jade beads were placed alongside the human remains. Adults are never found in burial urns in the Classic Maya northern lowlands; this is a funerary option that appears to have been available only for the very young. These deposits are found in the construction fill of larger monumental architecture such as platforms, terraces, and shrines. They were placed into the soil and rock of construction fill during the enlargement of a structure, or in some cases the plaster surface of a terrace or platform was partially removed in order to place a funerary urn into the construction. Urn burials of infants have the same characteristics and contexts at other sites in the northern Maya lowlands such as Chichen Itza, Isla Cerritos, Jaina, and Izamal (Bennett 1990, Gates trans. Landa 1978:85, Perez de Heredia et al. 2004, Ruz L. 1989) and are found in the material record of other sites in Mesoamerica as well (Mountjoy and Sanford 2006, Zeitlin 1993).

Eduardo Perez de Heredia and his colleagues have discussed the depiction of a possible infant urn burial ritual in a carved stone panel from Chichen Itza (Perez de Heredia et al. 2004). In the Edificio de los Falos (Structure 5C14) at the Initial Series group of Chichen, sculptured panels decorate the frieze of the exterior of the building (Osorio 2004). There

FIGURE 4.3. *Carved stone panel showing child urn burial, Structure 5C14 of the Initial Series group, Chichen Itza. Illustration by the author after Osorio 2004.*

are at least sixteen of these panels, and all of them depict deities of the earth known as *pahuatuns*, or royals enacting the role of *pahuatuns*, performing sacrifice rituals. In some scenes they let blood; in others they make offerings of food such as tamales. Most of the panels depict two *pahuatuns* with large ceramic vessels between them like the urns used in infant burials. Jaguars and serpents emerge from some of these urns, but in two instances, children are depicted. In one example the child makes an offering and in another the child is contained within an urn (Figure 4.3) (Perez de Heredia et al. 2004:13). Jaguars, serpents, and other powerful animals of the tropical lowlands have been demonstrated to be the companion spirits for dynasties of rulers and acted as a form of ancestral spirit that was emblematic of certain lineages (Houston and Stuart 1989, Schele and Freidel 1990). The presence of an infant in the same iconographic location as one of these companion spirits suggests that certain infants were understood in a similar manner and may have been ritually tied to ancestral power through urn burial.

Two urn burials were found at Structure 38-sub, a small one-room vaulted shrine located on a platform near the junction of Sacbe 1 and Sacbe 8 in the heart of Dzibilchaltun (Figure 4.4). The 20 x 29 meter platform held a complex of four buildings arranged around a central open patio area in the form of a quadrangle, and Structure 38-sub was on the eastern side of this compound underneath the later temple-pyramid designated Structure 38 (Andrews and Andrews 1980:151, Folan 1969). The

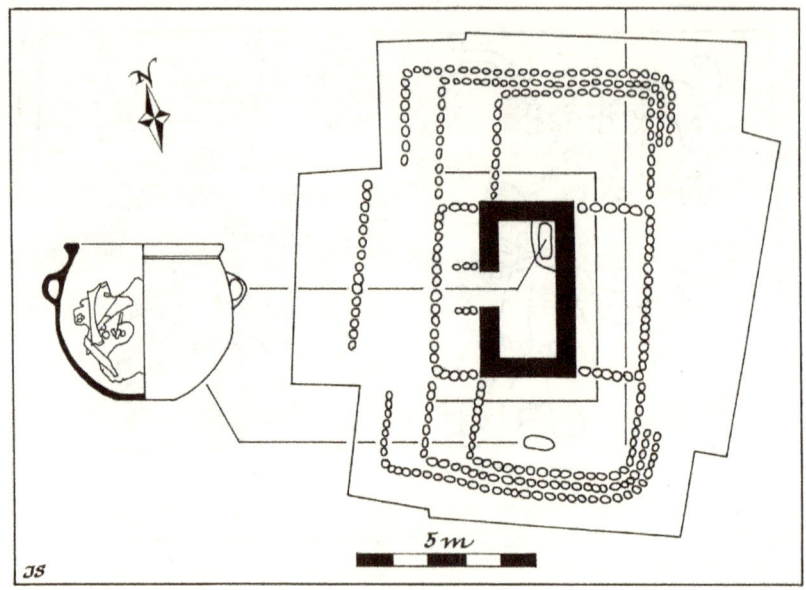

FIGURE 4.4. *Structure 38-sub with location of urn burials, Dzibilchaltun. Illustration by Jack Scott.*

terrace platform, eastern shrine, and domestic structures on the western and southern edges of the platform were all built during the Late Classic period to form an elite residential compound. Twenty-five burials of many different types, including crypts, caches, and urn burials, were found in the compound and reflect an occupation by a kin group or groups preoccupied with maintenance of ongoing relations with their ancestral kin over approximately four hundred years.

Two of the twenty-five burials from the Structure 38 compound are urn burials of infants. One burial (M-631-A) was discovered in the construction fill of the terrace platform on which the eastern shrine rests, approximately 2.5 meters south of the shrine. Another urn burial (M-647-A) was found under the floor of the shrine itself (Andrews and Andrews 1980:167-168). The first burial urn, a Conkal Red jar, held the bones of a two-year-old child and a jade bead, and was covered by an imported polychrome cylinder vase from Belize or southern Quintana Roo. A *mano* or grinding stone was resting in the fill nearby, and the plaster floor of the terrace above the burial showed signs of having been perforated or removed, perhaps to place the urn burial into the construction fill. The second burial urn, found under the intact floor of the shrine just north of the center of the southern wall, was a small Chuburna Brown jar. The jar had been burned and held the remains of two infants, one perhaps a late fetus. Andrews and Andrews suggest the urn was filled with compacted earth before it was placed into the fill of the shrine during construction. A burial crypt with the remains of a child two to three years old at death (M-648-A) was also found beneath the floor of the Structure 38-sub shrine. This child was buried with a Muna Slate tripod dish, a *spondylus americanus* pendant in the pelvic area, and a necklace made of sixteen disk-shaped shell beads interspersed with six bird-shaped shell pendants (Andrews and Andrews 1980:167). The bones of the child had been painted red, which indicates the burial occurred well after the death of the child.

Ceramic urns, like the ones found in the two urn burials described above, are usually repurposed water jars, and are often found in construction contexts containing objects other than human bone. Described as dedicatory caches because of their obvious placement during the construction of a building at Dzibilchaltun and elsewhere during this period, such caches contain shell, jade, obsidian, or stone objects. Often there is evidence to suggest organic materials were present (Andrews and Andrews 1980:323). The durable materials represent valuable prestige items, traded among elites as a result of political and economic alliances. All of these materials were available to a lesser degree to a majority of the urban population, but they were consumed in greater quantities and appear more frequently in the burials of the elite members of society. Likewise, the placement of the burial urns and dedicatory caches are more likely to be in areas restricted to elite families rather than the social majority.

The nature of the objects contained in the dedicatory caches informs us about the nature of urn burials of children. Given an equivalency of all other factors such as context, container, and temporality, it is likely the durable objects in caches and the infant bones in urn burials shared an interpretive meaning or value. In earlier work, I suggested that children constituted appropriate sacrificial offerings because of their liminality and proximity to the spirit world (Ardren 2009, 2011a, 2011b). In a study of the offerings found within the Great Cenote of Chichen Itza, I argued that in addition to a preponderance of human remains of children, the other offerings were items of high intrinsic worth within Maya society such as jade, gold, and incense. These are all substances seen as appropriate for sacrifice due to inherent qualities of sacredness and scarcity. The durable objects found in burial urns such as shell, obsidian, and jade are likewise objects that had intrinsic power and relative scarcity. Given that in ancient Maya society sacrifice was not primarily punitive—rather the practice was utilized to sacralize or make holy—the remains of very young individuals recovered from urn burials in important monumental architecture may represent another example of imbuing a place with sacred power by placing within it the body of a very small child (Stavrakopoulou 2004). Certainly the care and location of these burial urns argue against an interpretation that the very young were seen as expendable or without status. In contrast, the use of very young human bodies in place of, or in addition to, such precious objects as jade or shell suggests a notion that the young carried an intrinsically sacred nature that was recognized and manipulated. Harnessing the numinous power of an infant to an important social space like a shrine prolonged the social biography of that child as well as her social networks.

In fact the young infant placed into an urn burial may have been transformed through this ritual into an idea much larger than her individual identity during a very short life. The sacred liminality of newborns as close to the spirit world, the practice of child sacrifice, and the material equation of infants and other precious substances such as jade in architectural caches suggests these infant burials are better understood as materializations of a shared, collective identity of child-ness. This "dividual personhood" or composite and relational identity carried within its imaginary a numinous quality that was transferable to architecture or other social space (Geller 2012, Strathern 1988:13). Infants, both living and dead, were members of a liminal group that the ancient Maya may have seen as a collectivity with intrinsic sacred worth beyond the meaning ascribed by individual parents or family members. The social persona of their potential, both sacred and familial, is what we see materialized in the urn burials. This perspective explains why certain children were commemorated in urn burials while others were not—the ability to invoke a composite identity of the infant as representative of social networks and sacredness much larger than an individual child may have determined which funerals included such a public commemoration. It is likely that because urn burials are found in monumental architecture, the capacity of elite children to commemorate inalienable social bonds was heightened. But we cannot eliminate the possibility that commoner children also carried this persona of potential, given that juvenile bone was often curated and interred in partible form.

READING BURIALS FOR SOCIAL IDENTITY

In an overview of the archaeology of death and burial, Mike Parker Pearson argues funerary practices reveal as much about the living as the dead, since grave goods and ritual are used strategically by the living. "The clothing [meaning ornaments, artifacts, and dress] of the dead thus constitutes a hall of mirrors, representations of representations, in which things may not be entirely what they seem at first glance" (Pearson 1999:9). Recent anthropological studies of death argue that funerals are political events at which the status of the deceased and survivors are actively negotiated, manipulated, and contested. This is especially true in the case of child burials, where the relational nature of a child's identity is defined in death almost exclusively by members of a different social identity group (adults). We almost never have the opportunity to see children burying themselves (Lucy 1994). Age-based identities are lived relationally, and funerary practices will vary based on the age of the deceased and the age of the mourners (Gowland 2006: 152). As we have seen in the child burials discussed above, certain burial practices were reserved for the very young, and certain grave goods were found nearly universally with the young. Such aspects of funerary rituals seem to construct a social relationship between the mourner and the deceased, and in this particular case a way in which the social identity of a child was defined by adults.

Recently archaeology has shifted the analysis of burials from grave goods as an indication of the inherent status of the deceased to an exploration of grave goods as a materialization of the practices that create a social identity for the deceased. Funerals are arenas for social interactions between actors vested in the identity of the deceased, and these rituals are composed of practices, some of which are repeated over and over again and some of which are unique. From this perspective, grave goods should be read as the result of deliberate actions taken by survivors to express something of their relationship to the deceased, relationships that were tied intrinsically to their social identities. In this sense funerals are excellent examples of performative circulations that maintain the social imaginary. From the decision whether or not to inter a deceased child in the family burial crypt beneath the house floor, to the selection of appropriate shell ornaments and ceramics, to the placement of the body into a reopened crypt, every aspect of this funerary event had to be performed based on prior experience and current expectation. Survivors, surely adults in most cases, both selectively remembered what elements of a funerary ritual were needed as well as enacted those elements for others, to circulate a complex set of ideas. The selection of certain artifacts reinforced a shared notion of childhood, or the social imaginary of childhood—in this case as precious, numinous, bound to kin, and crucial to social relations—by circulating the forms through an interpretive community. The invitation to participate extended selectively to some kin but not to others circulated ideas of indebtedness and inalienability that maintained the corporate group well beyond the lifetime of individuals. The objects given to the dead by guests at the funeral, in a form of gift exchange with a future ancestor, likewise circulated goods but more importantly ideas—ideas about who the person was, who the giver was in the moment, the nature of their relationship in the past, and the expectation for future obligations. Each circulation both maintains and constitutes the imaginary. Even the evaluation or discussion of the funerary ritual after its completion constitutes a mechanism by which the experience is shared in order to explore and reinforce the boundaries of a shared moral order. Henrietta Moore has explored this same perspective in relation to the expression of gendered identities, but it is applicable to the similarly relational identity of childhood:

> It is not that the material world, as a form of cultural discourse, reflects the natural division of the world into women and men, but rather that cultural discourses, including the organization of the material world, actually produce gender difference in and through their workings. (Moore 1994:85)

One advantage of this perspective on the agency of material things is that identities are better able to be viewed as fluid and evolving (Sofaer 2006). Age, even more so than gender, is not static, and age-based identities are by their nature transitory. While there is a biological and material reality to childhood, this reality has been shown to be understood and regulated in culturally and historically specific ways. Over the life course the expression of an age-based identity will evolve and be expressed and experienced through different materializations. We should expect that the way the social identity of a child is marked will involve different materializations when a funeral is conducted by a young mother grieving her first child than by an elderly woman with many offspring. In each case the background understanding, as Charles Taylor describes the foundation of the social imaginary, may be the same, but the practices utilized to enact the background could vary, thereby reinforcing and adjusting the background understanding. People who share a social imaginary possess a common repertory of possible actions as well as the knowledge of how to choose among them and the consequences of an alternative choice.

Susan Gillespie has explored a similar framework for understanding the social identities revealed in ancient burials (2001). Arguing that the integration of society and the individual is the "central problem of modern social theory," Gillespie proposes we utilize a concept of personhood, in order to shift analysis away from the individual and acknowledge the social persona expressed in mortuary rituals (Gillespie 2001:75). Personhood can be held by living beings but also by ancestors and even objects, because each has important social and collective components of their identity that are shaped by membership in social units. Personhood provides a context for reciprocal or recursive relationships between people that are apparent in social interactions and materialized in insignia, regalia, or other indexical artifacts closely linked to social identities. In her discussion of grave goods and funerals, Gillespie explains that grave furniture reflects ritual activity rather than inherent status and might have been used to "distort or mask social relations rather than to reveal or reflect them" (Gillespie 2001:77). This is an important cautionary note and reminds us to read the living in a burial context as much as we read the dead. In the examples discussed in this chapter, we must acknowledge that the relational nature of child identity underscores the importance of reading the burial of a child as a statement by the survivors about the social persona of the deceased—a statement that is constructed to serve the needs of the survivors as much if not more than the needs of the deceased, and a statement or circulation that originates with the survivors rather than with any inherent reality of the deceased. Gillespie's argument for personhood reinforces a focus on the social linkages within a collectivity of the deceased and illuminates how funerary ritual reinforces the obligations and rights that extend beyond biological death. From this perspective, the urn burials of Dzibilchaltun could be read as an example of the absence of social death at the moment of biological death. The utilization or deployment of infant bodies to sacralize civic architecture demonstrates the personhood of certain dead children. Their obligations to the social collectivity extended indefinitely and continued to accrue social capital to their extended kin network. The selective interment of certain infants in this manner circulates a social imaginary of childhood that includes a strict hierarchy of access to the numinous and an important role for children in satisfying social obligations within the collectivity.

Rosemary Joyce has commented on the ability of funerary ritual to transform the dead into members of a social collectivity, such as ancestors (Joyce 1999:17). Joyce argues that since the dead are no longer actively seeking their own advantage, they become significant social leverage for the living (Joyce 1999:17), although we must acknowledge that living individuals are members of social collectivities well before they are transformed into ancestors through mortuary ritual. These social collectivities of the living, whether kin networks or social identities such as child, remain in play during the funerary process and must be negotiated, contested, or defused as part of the transformational process. Following the work of Annette Weiner, Joyce notes that funerals provide a means for the living to reestablish links to one another through their links to the dead and that social linkages to the dead are more permanent than links to the living (Joyce 1999:17). Children were likely at the intersection of various social networks, and given the emphasis on descent and progeny to the virtual exclusion of any mention of matrimony in Classic Maya dynastic inscriptions, it is likely that families were brought closer together through offspring than through marriage. The death of a child may have interrupted this alliance or network, and Joyce suggests that the degree of elaboration of a burial may reflect the degree of social investment on the part of survivors (Joyce 1999:20). From this perspective, a rich child burial may represent an effort by survivors to repair the fabric of a fragile or threatened social alliance.

EXPERIENCING CHILDHOOD

Societies share a social imaginary of childhood that interprets and constructs the ways in which the biological and cultural aspects of young lives will converse. As Heather Montgomery has noted, the term "child" is a relational one, and is used as often to describe interactions between people as to describe a group of individuals at a particular stage of life (Montgomery 2009:55). Often we are described as the "child of" throughout our lives, to reflect ongoing relationships of support and affection within families, and in some societies everyone is considered a "child of" god, the king, or even a forest. Montgomery cites Nurit Bird-David, who in her study of the Nayaka hunter-gatherers of South India found that the Nayaka use the word "child" to describe themselves in relation to their surroundings:

> [They] use the word *makalo* (children) to describe themselves vis-à-vis the forest and vis-à-vis all invisible and previous dwellers in their area, whom they call respectively "big parents," or in some cases "grandpar-

ents." "Children" is a concept that is central to their sense of themselves, their place in the world, and their relationship with their surroundings; it recurs in their moral and ritual discourse. (Bird-David 2005:93)

Obviously for the Nayaka, the interactions of parent and child are a powerful metaphor for human interactions in general, and they share a social imaginary in which the social identity of child is a model for human behavior rather than a transitory status of incompleteness. When Nayaka state they are children of the forest, they are circulating an idea that life within the forest is relational and experienced as a series of interactions based on dependence and reciprocity. Colonial-era Maya mythological texts, such as the Popol Vuh, from the Quiche people of highland Guatemala, also utilize the terms "children" and "grandparents" to frame the relations between humanity and the creator deities. After the first humans are made of corn dough, they thank the Makers and say, "Truly now, double thanks, triple thanks, that we've been formed, we've been given our mouths, our faces . . . thanks to you we've been formed, we've come to be made and modeled, our grandmother, our grandfather" (Tedlock 1985:166). The Hero Twins, the two main avatars of this mythological cycle who through their cunning and skill model correct human behavior, are referred to as "boys" throughout the story, while the Makers tell the recently created animals, "Now name our names, praise us. We are your mother, we are your father" (Tedlock 1985:78). Nearly all the relationships described in the Popol Vuh are described in familial terms, and the dependencies of children and adults upon one another are used as a familiar metaphor for the interdependencies of humanity and the gods.

Childhood is perhaps one of the most relational of social identities and unique in the sense that nearly everyone, in any society, except those who perish as children, holds this identity for a period of their lives and then passes out of it, eventually to participate in its reproduction as an outsider. The ideas of child and childhood held by every adult are based on firsthand experience and thus are circulated through the repetition of behaviors they experienced themselves at an earlier time. This can lead to extremely conservative practices such as rites of passage, which are understood to be performed in a more or less unchanged manner across generations. But less formal daily practices such as the choice of appropriate baby food or sleeping arrangements are based also in deeply familiar memories of one's own experiences or a rejection of those experiences. In this sense the social identity of childhood is contingent to a large degree upon the shared practices and choices made by adults, rather than upon any universal biological experience. While non-children may have a very large role in setting out the theory of childhood, young people themselves will be the ones who enact the practices and behaviors that affirm or deny those ideas. We should expect, therefore, for the social imaginary of childhood to be based on shared memories of past experiences of being a child—selective, fragmented, or manipulated as those may be—in dialogue with the actions of actual children.

The ways in which the social identity of an adult can change in response to interactions with children further demonstrate how childhood is a particularly relational identity. The arrival of a child can signal a change in the social status of its parents through the creation of a family or the satisfaction of familial obligations, and there are many cultures in which biologically mature adults are not considered fully "adult" until they reproduce. In societies where children are viewed as having an economic value, either as laborers or future providers for elderly parents, behaviors are performed by children that were previously performed by their parents when young, such as certain types of labor that are viewed as appropriate for children but not for adults, like fetching water or firewood. These behaviors are circulations that perpetuate a social imaginary or foundation understanding of the young as capable components of a larger economic system, but components that by their identification with certain behaviors define and make possible the social identity of non-child or adult as well. Anytime a certain set of clearly defined behaviors is associated with a particular group of people, those who do not perform these behaviors are likewise defined. Childhood is full of identity-specific behaviors that by their exclusivity in turn define adults. Jane Eva Baxter has written persuasively about this in relation to socialization and the culturally specific ways in which children use space (Baxter 2005:59). Baxter showed that the secret spaces of childhood—the places where children operated outside adult activities—were identifiable in the archaeological record of nineteenth-century American farmhouses (Baxter 2005). These places were defined by their material residue of play and their separation from other normative activities, or in other words, by the materialization of behaviors that were non-adult. Thus even in societies where children are seen as essentially incomplete adults, lacking necessary social skills or knowledge, the social imaginary of childhood is constructed on a relational basis where the circulation of age-specific access to certain spaces becomes a way to order relationships.

Childhood-specific tasks, such as the work of children, are a very good example of the daily rituals that reinforce and naturalize childhood as a social identity. These rituals of inclusion that children perform on a daily basis, such as setting the table and washing up in the modern West, or caring for younger siblings and animals within the household compound in Classic Maya times, circulate and reinforce ideas about their identity. They are aware that other children perform the same tasks, even if they do not know those children or see them doing so, and this awareness helps create a sense of shared membership in what Anderson called a "horizontal fraternity." This sense of shared membership, or participation in a shared social imaginary of childhood, can obscure the very real differences between individual children as easily as it might reinforce their sense of community. Thus we can see the imagined community being constructed by others through discussion of the work appropriate for children, as well as the materialization of these ideas in such things as miniature tools and tokens of domesticated animals. The participation of children in economically productive forms of work is an example of Taylor's macrodecisions, or actions that all members of the imaginary understand and practice. Behaviors are a reflection of the shared understanding of the capabilities of a child. These understandings are operationalized and reproduced by the daily practices of child-specific chores, which leave material traces in the archaeological record evident to us today. A focus on behaviors and associated artifacts as circulations, which create meanings through their performance, shows that childhood is not bounded and stable but rather fluid, evolving, and in need of concretization. The common inclusion of deer bone fragments in the burials of ancient Maya children constructed a social imaginary where children were productive members of a household group and contributed labor to care for animals while it simultaneously reinforced a dependent status as another class of being for whom adult women provide care. This message obscures the reality that some children will be hard-working while others will want to do nothing but play in favor of a shared imaginary where children are understood as social and spiritual wealth within their kin group. It acknowledges the capacity of children to provide productive work, and enforces such an expectation.

The circulation of the expectation that children will provide economic wealth and labor to their kin group is a key component of a broad social identity shared throughout the northern Maya lowlands in the Classic period, based on the consistency of burial goods in child graves. One can see the agency of children at the heart of this social imaginary. While there are many aspects of the relational identity of children that are determined by adults, in societies where children are perceived as needed—whether for labor, demonstrations of fertility, or security—the presence or absence of children is at the heart of assuaging social anxiety. The power of a child to change the lives of a family, especially during pre-Columbian periods when mortality was much higher than today, should not be underestimated in our models of how childhood can be understood.

The standardized funerary treatment of children at Yaxuna, Xuenkal, and Dzibilchaltun, as well as across the northern lowlands, indicates the social visibility of children throughout the region but also the presence of a shared cultural understanding of the child. While burials were undoubtedly a very individual or personal event, shared patterns of material choices are obvious within the forty-one burials examined in this chapter. At each site, children were buried in family crypts, individually in urns, or incorporated into secondary ancestor bundles and deposits. Except for urns, these funerary patterns are also the most common way adults were interred, and this materialization indicates an acknowledgment of existence and status not dependent upon age. In other cultures, child burials are found segregated from the rest of the population due to an inequivalency of existence or a lack of fully human status (Finlay 2000; Lucy 1994; McKerr, Murphy, and Donnelly 2009). This is not the case in the northern Maya lowlands, and the continuity of burial treatment across age groups demonstrates the minimization of age as a qualification of significance for certain children.

Perhaps this is the result of the strong emphasis placed upon close ongoing contact with family ancestors within household groups in Classic Maya culture (Gillespie 2001, McAnany 1995, Welsh 1988). As Patricia McAnany has shown, ancestral contact was deliberately maintained to facilitate territorial claims and spiritual authority. The inclusion of children in family burial crypts located beneath domestic floors is a powerful ritual that brings them forcibly and irrevocably into the kin network of the household. Given the understanding of children as not just potential but actual economic wealth, the death of a child may have indicated not only the loss of that wealth but also an opportunity to commemorate its existence, even if cut short. Family crypts were reopened and reentered, indicating the composition of the kin group was fluid and evolving. The interment of a child meant the kin group had realized or achieved reproduction and thus held the potential to do so again, a key requirement in the perpetuation of social relations. Thus children, even dead children transformed into ancestors, were members of the extended kin network and could exert the moral authority granted to ancestors in Maya society. Their funerals defined group membership and circulated ideas about the moral capital that children could provide to a family.

Age at death was significant for a certain set of children at Dzibilchaltun and some other Classic Maya centers during the Late Classic. The urn burials of infants and children two years of age or less within the construction fill of civic architecture is a practice that accentuates the unique status of the very young. Adults or even older children are never found interred in this way, although rare and precious substances such as shell, obsidian, and jade are often found cached in urns or other ceramic vessels which are then placed carefully and deliberately into the construction ballast of monumental architecture. From hieroglyphic inscriptions, we know that structures were understood as animate; each one had a life cycle of ceremonial events that animated, ensouled, and brought to an end or terminated its existence (Harrison-Buck 2012, Lucero 2010, Stuart 1998). Caches of precious objects were crucial components of these ceremonies, as the intrinsic power of certain materials contributed to the life force of the architecture. This practice existed within a complex cosmology of offering and sacrifice in which art such as stelae, temples, deities, and even households required energetic sacrifice (McAnany 2010, Stuart 1996). Offering rituals were the materialization of a metanarrative at work in the social imaginary of Maya culture, in which energy or life force was a tangible substance to be exchanged and distributed along highly scripted social relationships. The expectation of life force in the form of rain or crop fertility was petitioned and performed through the offering of royal blood on the part of a ruler, and likewise, the expectation of divine presence in a temple or shrine may have been petitioned by the offering of a cache made of highly charged materials such as jade or infant bone.

The qualifications for inclusion of infant bone in a cache may have been related to the perception that infants were in close proximity to the ancestors due to their recent arrival in the world of humans. As Alma Gottlieb has shown in her study of Beng infants, non-Western cultures can hold radically different perceptions of the spiritual potency of infants (Gottlieb 2004). In Beng culture, infants are seen as direct mediators of ancestral guidance, and the sounds they make before they learn to speak adult language are understood and interpreted closely for messages from the spirit realm. Gradually as they assume the behaviors of older children and adults, the Beng understand infants to lose this connection and likewise their spiritual authority. Ethnohistoric accounts written by Spanish priests of Maya and Aztec ritual practices describe both a close emotional connection to infants that were described as "spoiled" as well as the practice of selective child sacrifice. For the Aztec it is particularly clear that children with certain physical characteristics (such as a cowlick) and certain illnesses (chronic infections of the sinuses that produced copious mucus) were uniquely qualified for sacrifice to the Rain Deity Tlaloc (Roman Berrelleza and Chavez Baldera 2006). The mucus coupled with the tears of grieving parents was deployed as sympathetic magic to call rain. Depictions on Classic Maya vases of infant sacrifice appear to relate to a mythological cycle of death and regeneration of the Maize Deity, and the presence of child remains in many sacrificial contexts, such as attendants in rich tombs or the Great Cenote of Chichen Itza, indicates child sacrifice was actively practiced across the Maya area during the Classic period (Ardren 2011b, Geller 2011). In the northern lowlands, the practice persisted well into the Colonial period in response to environmental or political crises (Anda 2007). Rituals of child sacrifice are an attempt to naturalize and make self-evident a social imaginary in which infants are seen as spiritually potent, with spiritual power an intrinsic characteristic that erodes with age. Despite the intense emotional pain that the practice reportedly caused in ancient Maya parents who offered their children for sacrifice, they performed the belief that their child would continue to have existence. As sixteenth-century Bishop Diego de Landa described the practice, "At times they threw the victims alive into the well at Chichen Itza, believing that they would come forth on the third day, even though they never did see them reappear" (Gates trans. Landa 1978:50). The powerful biological reality of death and the cultural anxiety over reproduction of children were both inverted as part of the circulation of the child as a commodity that could be deployed for social and spiritual gain.

The standardized grave goods of many child crypt burials at Yaxuna, Dzibilchaltun, and Xuenkal as well as other northern lowland sites at this time support the interpretation of their social visibility but also demonstrate how material objects have an agency in the production and reproduction of the social imaginary. Those who perform rituals may believe they are enacting a reality that already exists, but the productive contribution of Anderson, Taylor, and LiPuma's theories of circulation is its identification of material objects, especially the commodities of daily life such as newspapers or eating utensils and the practices tied up with these objects, as the mechanism by which social imaginaries are reproduced.

Relationships are created between people and objects that solidify ideas. These ideas are both transferable and inalienable. The value they encode remains with an individual whether or not the objects are still in the possession of that person (Weiner 1992). Thus the movement of objects does not track exactly upon the movement of ideas and relationships, although the objects have often foregrounded the relationship or created connectivity between individuals.

The most common grave goods in the child burials examined here are new ceramic serving vessels, shell ornaments, and deer bone. All three are also the most common grave goods in the burials of non-elite adult women in the northern lowlands (Ardren 2002c). It is not hard to see a connection between domestic productivity or the social wealth of the household in the form of household ceramics, semi-domesticated animals, the fertility of the sea, and the idealized personhood of women and children depicted in burials. Shell ornaments are particularly common in the burials of younger children and are tied to the conceptualization of both the sea and children as the source of life, as well as the perceived proximity of children to the watery otherworld of spirits. Ethnohistoric accounts of shell beads placed on young children and exchanged at significant junctures in the life cycle, such as the shell pendants young women wore over the pelvis, mark or materialize a perception of potency in the young. Unimportant bodies are unmarked in Classic Maya art, and humiliation was indicated by the depiction of bodies stripped of all costume elements including key ornaments and jewels (Johnston 2001). The practice of adorning the very young, in both life and death, circulates an idea that these bodies have significance and are deserving of commemoration. While ornaments worn by an adult during life might be able to be explained as merely the result of personal aesthetic choice, ornaments worn by young children, and especially placed with young children in death, carry significant conceptual capital that engaged with an ongoing dialogue or performance of social values.

From this perspective, the material record is actively employed by individuals or interests and we are able to better understand the wide range of childhoods in the past. And children, as social agents of cultural reproduction, are the perfect lens for understanding how material culture is simultaneously the means, medium, and outcome of social change. Far from unformed or incomplete, the social identity of child within Classic Maya society of the northern lowlands was marked on the bodies and in the graves of the young as both compelling and vital.

CONCLUSION

This chapter began by asking if childhood was a distinct social identity in Classic Maya society and how we might see that in the material record. Childhood is a unique period. Whether prolonged as it is in the modern West or very brief as it was in the Victorian era, childhood is a social category that we all pass through and later help to reproduce based on memories and experiences. Archaeologists have recently spent time discovering the unseen children of many ancient cultures, who are far from invisible once their existence is acknowledged and the correct questions are asked to solicit their contribution to the material record. Within scholarship on the ancient Maya northern lowlands, few studies have tried to find the ways in which children contributed to the daily life of ancient cities or how these young people may have understood their place in society (cf. Hutson 2006).

Why don't we ask more questions about what life was like for children in the ancient world? Demographers have proved that sometimes as much as half the population of an ancient city was younger than eighteen years old, so certainly the young were important from this perspective alone. Perhaps because adults have all passed through the identity of child and left it behind, and our modern social imaginary considers childhood a moment in time rather than an enduring state, scholars find it a less interesting social identity or a less significant one to matters of power and status. However, nothing could be further from the truth, in ancient New World societies at least, as child sacrifice indicates an inherent spiritual potency of the young that is easily manipulated by those seeking moral authority and other related forms of power. The relational nature of age-based identities causes the identity of child to be as much a reflection of the child as of the adults who have left this identity behind. Our studies of what held Classic Maya polities and their constituent communities together would benefit from a better understanding of how kinship networks were created. The wealth and social visibility of child burials within Classic Maya culture indicates the burial of a child was a moment for heightened discourse about the maintenance of corporate groups.

Burials are one of many texts from which we can attempt to understand the ways social identities were constructed and maintained, and the burials of young people from Xuenkal, Yaxuna, and Dzibilchaltun present us with commonalities that illustrate how the social imaginary of childhood was reproduced. At all three ancient cities, children were often interred in family crypts that were reopened in the floors of domestic structures to accommodate a child burial. Those who attended the funeral usually placed offerings of ceramics with the deceased, and sometimes the body was buried with jewelry that spoke to the child but especially to her adult kin. In fact child burials may have been moments in which social networks based in kinship narratives were most profoundly enacted or maintained. Domestic goods like ceramic plates and deer bone placed in child burials circulated a notion that children represented social capital and the ability to bring people together.

The physical remains of children are also found in urn burials and as partible elements of bone that were deposited into burials or offerings after some period of circulation among the living. The other materials that were treated in the same manner, such as jade, incense, or exotic shell, are understood to have carried an inherent preciousness due to their scarcity and intrinsic qualities. By placing infant bone into the same contexts, we can see ancient Maya people engaged in a discourse about the sacred and how it should be deployed. Certain architectural spaces were ensouled with such offerings, which also served to reinforce ancestral networks. The social personhood of the young child was expanded through these burial rituals. It was taken out of the time limitations imposed on the physical body and transferred into the realm of social relationships, where it could exert spiritual authority in an indefinite manner. The selective interment of certain infants in this fashion circulates a social imaginary of childhood that includes a strict hierarchy of access to the numinous and an important role for children in satisfying social obligations within the collectivity.

GENDERED IMAGINARIES AND ARCHITECTURAL SPACE

Chapter 5

INTRODUCTION

How did people grow to understand gendered differences in ancient Maya culture? How did the expression and experience of gender change over the life course? Were there cultural ideals of gendered behavior, and was it possible to resist those ideals? How did interactions with the built environment help shape gendered social identities? How were objects used as partners in the negotiation of gendered social relations between people living in ancient Maya cities? Gender is one of the most profound ways in which people construct identities to differentiate themselves from one another. It is often grounded in ideas about how bodies work, and this translates into how bodies circulate through space. This chapter looks at how spatial arrangements within Classic Maya households, as well as within certain monumental buildings, contributed to a sense of gender difference, and at how gendered ideals in turn contributed to architectural designs.

This chapter will explore the rich data available in the archaeological record of Yaxuna, Chunchucmil, and Dzibilchaltun, which speaks to how gender structured and shaped social relationships and the experience of daily life within Classic-period society. By exploring both architectural remains and material objects, I will look at how gender ordered daily activities, especially collective group tasks, and how gendered identities were constructed and maintained through the use of space. The specific Classic Maya social imaginary of gender can be deciphered through performative circulations that resolved competing discourses about the value of women, men, and those in between, their appropriate relationship to one another, and their unique means for productive contributions to Maya society. I look at how patterns of gender materialize a conversation about certain daily activities and how those activities are tied to broader conceptualizations of difference, value, and worth. These gendered ideals, revealed in discarded tools used repeatedly over time in specific areas or in the design of gender-specific gathering spaces, also contributed to an understanding of how women and men should interact with one another. Architectural spaces that were highly gendered provide data on how certain groups of people cooperated with one another in repeated rituals of inclusion in which the social imaginary of gender was naturalized through regular interactions with people who not only looked somewhat similar, but behaved in similar ways, learned similar gender-specific knowledge, and shared gender-segregated experiences. I argue that commoner domestic compounds were closely associated with an idealized notion of femaleness and the productivity of the family unit. Certain civic architecture was the setting for male behaviors that upheld a conceptualization of dominant masculinity as competitive and hierarchical. Gendered ideals were utilized in Classic Maya society as a means to enforce social reciprocity as well as to make sense of social differences.

Our understanding of how certain architecture was used to create highly gendered spaces, or places where gendered social identities took on heightened social significance, is enhanced by passages from the ethnohistoric literature. Early colonial descriptions of Maya society by Spanish religious officials offer a particular perspective that when used cautiously can reinforce the materializations of behavior solidified in the archaeological record. This chapter includes reference to the writing of Bishop Diego de Landa, a sixteenth-century friar who left a rich description of daily life in the northern Maya lowlands relevant to understanding gendered patterns of behavior and especially the use of space in Late to Terminal Classic Maya society (Ardren 2012b, 2013; Clendinnen 1982; Restall 1995).

GENDERED SPACES IN ETHNOHISTORIC SOURCES AND THE ARCHAEOLOGICAL RECORD

One of the most compelling sources of data on the ordering of Maya daily life activities around gendered categories is the sixteenth-century description of Maya culture left by Bishop Diego de Landa known as the *Relación de las Cosas de Yucatán* (Gates 1978). While ethnohistorians have cautioned archaeologists against an uncritical application of Landa's eyewitness accounts of contact-era Maya life to the material remains of the Classic period and have pointed out why Landa's work should not be read as a coherent narrative, nonetheless the descriptions of gendered patterns in this unique ethnohistoric work are invaluable records of behavior that can enrich our understanding of material evidence (Restall and Chuchiak 2002, Chuchiak 2005). Landa was born in 1524 into a powerful and wealthy Spanish family and worked as chief page at the court of Phillip II, where he was charged with guarding the chastity of royal princesses (Chuchiak personal communication 2012). He became a Franciscan when only seventeen, and left for the New World as a missionary when he was twenty-five years old. The *Relación* was written late in Landa's life when he had returned to Spain to defend himself against accusations of excessive force in the Christianization of Yucatán. The middle-aged friar, like most Spanish ecclesiasticals, had little personal experience with women or children for much of his life. In both sixteenth-century Spanish and Maya society, the daily activities of most women and men were largely segregated along gendered lines that would have allowed Landa very little direct access to the domestic life of Yucatec women, yet his writings are full of exactly this kind of ethnographic detail. There is some evidence that much of this thick description came from his elite Maya scribal assistant, Gaspar Antonio Chi (Ardren 2012b, Chuchiak 2005).

While acknowledging that Landa wrote his text fully four hundred years after the height of the Terminal Classic period and thus recognizing we cannot expect his descriptions to have a one-to-one correlation with the material record under examination here, it is also true that more than four hundred years have elapsed since Landa's writings, and yet certain patterns of gendered behavior described by him remain present in Yucatec Maya society today. Despite the catastrophic effects of Spanish colonialism, the Revolutionary period, and modern shifts toward contract work and tourism, familiar gendered ideals persist in many Maya communities of Yucatán. Women continue to process and prepare food and tend household gardens with domestic animals, while men have primary responsibility for nondomestic economic income in the form of agriculture or wage labor (Elmendorf 1976, Hanks 1990, Kellogg 2005, Martin 2007). Today younger Maya people who migrate to Cancun seeking employment in the tourism industry struggle to maintain certain gendered ideals, and women usually gravitate to the hospitality industry as hotel maids, while men work in construction (Castellanos 2010). These ideals guide daily behavior, which in turn reinforces and naturalizes gendered distinctions (Moore 1994) in a powerful form of cultural circulation. Thus while Landa's writings are flawed in many ways, they remain a valuable source for understanding the complexity of pre-contact Maya culture based on his firsthand experiences living in Yucatán for over twenty years at the cusp of the Colonial period.

Female Gendered Space

There are two main forms of gender-specific architecture described by Landa. Throughout his document, there are multiple references to the activities of women, most of which are centered in the domestic world. From birth through marriage to death, women's lives were situated in a domestic compound that accommodated a multitude of activities. Landa describes the practice of matrilocality after marriage:

> The day of the marriage having arrived, they all gathered at the house of the fiancée's father . . . from that day the son-in-law remained in his father-in-law's house for five or six years, working for him; if he failed in this, he was driven from the house, but the mothers arranged always for the wife to supply her husband with his food, as a mark of marriage. (Gates 1978:42)

Divorce was common, as was remarriage, transitions which again were situated in the domestic sphere and foreground the social relations of marriage as a form of interdependence:

> The marriage of widowers and widows took place without any festival or ceremonies; the man simply went to the woman's house, was admitted and given to eat, and with this it was a marriage. (Gates 1978:42)

The domestic activities of women were clearly highly respected within the Maya society that Landa witnessed. Even without extensive contact with women, he was able to describe in some detail the importance of women's domestic economy:

> [speaking of Maya women] They are great workers and good in all the domestic economies, for on them rest the most, and most important, work of alimentation, housekeeping and education of their children, and the payment of the tributes . . . They raise both Spanish and native fowls for sale, and for eating. They raise birds for their pleasure and for the feathers for adornment on their finer clothes; also raising other domestic animals, among these even offering their breast to the deer, which they have so tame that they never run away into the woods . . . They help each other mutually in their working and spinning, paying for this work in the same way as do their husbands on their farms; and while at this they ever have their jokes and tell their stories. (Gates 1978:55)

Landa noted that men and women did not eat together, but sat apart, and that women were kept very busy with food preparation in their homes:

> Their principle sustenance is maize . . . The Indian women put the maize to soak the night before in lime and water . . . they next grind it on stones, and when half ground make it into great balls and loads for the use of laborers, travelers, and sailors . . . They prepare many kinds of bread, good and healthful, except that it is not good to eat when cold; so that the Indian women are kept busy with making it twice a day. (Gates 1978:34)

The social capital of the domestic world, namely the work women did in this space, was clearly central to the establishment of social networks and relations of indebtedness within Maya culture, as Landa states:

> The Yucatecans are very generous and hospitable; no one enters their houses without being offered food and drink, what drink they may have during the day, or food in the evening. If they have none, they seek it from a neighbor; if they unite together on the roads, all join in sharing even if they have little for their own need. (Gates 1978:40)

The impression Landa conveys of the lives of women in small Yucatecan towns of the early sixteenth century is certainly colored by his own cultural lens on gendered relations, yet he still conveys a uniquely Maya social ideal of domestic activity and productivity. Elsewhere in his writings, Landa bemoans the participation of women in market exchange and the elder women who assumed positions of religious leadership, but in the passages quoted here it is clear that much of women's daily praxis, or embodied intersubjectivity, occurred within the home and domestic compound. While men and children also lived here, the domestic compound was gendered female, and the activities that took place there did not occur against a neutral background, but rather were situated within an arena in which the space defined the people in it. The productive activities of the Maya domestic compound such as food preparation, gardening, and the caretaking of domestic animals constituted circulations that reinforced the potential of female power and productivity (Hendon 1997, Hutson 2010, Pohl and Feldman 1982). The domestic compound and its associated activities was the setting for a social map that structured kin and other interpersonal relationships. Women's production was central to the maintenance of those relations (Weiner 1992).

A RESIDENTIAL COMPOUND AT YAXUNA

The 5E-167 group at Yaxuna is a good example of Terminal Classic-period residential compounds in the northern Maya lowlands. Although not delineated by a boundary wall as at Chunchucmil, these three structures cluster together and share an adjacent open area where gardening or animal husbandry might have been practiced. Given that they were occupied simultaneously, probably by an extended family group, this household group might constitute what Susan Gillespie has termed a "house society," or group of fictive and biological kin (Gillespie 2000). The articulation of these structures and their dimensions is familiar to anyone who has seen contemporary Maya houses in Yucatán, which, while often built of concrete block today, retain the same dimensions and spatial organization. Classic-period compounds provide material evidence of the daily lives of their occupants, in particular the activities of adult women who managed this space and filled it with productive activities. Excavations at the 5E-167 group by David Johnstone as part of the Selz Foundation Yaxuna Archaeological Project in 1992 revealed the construction history of these structures and their associated artifacts. The primary structure of the 5E-167 group is a low rectangular platform less than a meter in height and approximately eight meters long, from which the group gets its name. It runs north-south along the southern side of the group and provided a living and working surface above ground level. At the northern end of this platform is a roughly square-shaped stone foundation brace for a perishable, thatched structure. To the north of this platform are two additional square foundation braces for perishable structures, Structures 5E-82 and 5E-83, each about five meters square and situated directly on bedrock.

Based on ceramic fragments found in the construction fill, it is known that the platform in this group was first constructed in the Terminal Classic period. At the center of the platform, additional materials were added to the construction ballast during the first building episode, and not just the usual trash debris that provides us with such useful chronological indications. On the centerline, fragments of burned human bone and bone beads were placed into the rubble and soil that leveled off the bedrock surface and provided the body of the platform. As discussed in the previous chapter, fragments of human bone that may have been curated for many years were often redeposited in household structures, likely as an offering to ensoul or bring to life the new architecture. At approximately the same time, but certainly while the platform was in its original phase of construction, a stone-lined crypt was placed within the ballast. Unworked tabular stones were set on edge within clean gray soil to create an area 80 x 30 centimeters. A young adult woman was placed into the crypt on her back with her head to the east (Bennett 1993:156–157). Those who performed her funeral placed three ceramic vessels into the crypt, as was so often done in Maya burials of the Classic period. A large domestic cooking vessel (Yokat Striated) was placed upright next to her legs (Stanton et al. 2010:160). Two vessels were placed over her head, one as a lid or cap to the other. The larger of the two was a finely made large water jar with handles for carrying the heavy vessel with a tumpline or rope (Dzibical Black on Red), and the other was a small bowl used as a cap (Sacalum Trickle) (Stanton et al. 2010:159). Also found with the remains of this woman were a small limestone bead painted blue to resemble jade, an obsidian blade fragment, a deer tibia, and a shell pendant. The crypt was sealed with four unworked flat capstones.

When the funerary ritual for this young woman was complete, construction resumed on the platform that provided the most substantial living area of the group. Thick, well-made plaster was applied immediately above the capstones of the crypt and covered the entire rectangular platform surface. Three courses of wall stones were laid into this plaster to create the foundation for a square, thatch-roofed structure that opened to the west. Two additional small structures were constructed to the north. Both were made of perishable materials set into stone foundation braces with a tamped earth floor in one and a thin plaster floor in the other. The walls of Structure 5E-82 included a reused *pila*, or deep ground-stone basin. These modified limestone basins may have been used to grind corn but were more likely used to store water, and were common implements in ancient households. During excavation, other household tools were found in these structures including a broken *mano*, or limestone grinding tool for processing corn, obsidian blade fragments, chert flakes, and an exhausted chert core. A final element of the 5E-167 group was a small feature in the central area enclosed by the three structures just described. This cluster of unworked stone was approximately one meter square and thirty centimeters high and rested on a large tabular stone set flat against ground surface. No cultural material was recovered from excavating this feature, although it clearly represented deliberate human activity and similar features are described, for lack of a better term, as "shrines" in the regional literature.

These living spaces, including the platform with its well-made room, the two smaller structures, and the central shrine, were occupied for perhaps as long as two hundred years. The platform area was replastered at some point during that occupational history with a thinner and inferiorly made surface. Throughout the residential settlement of Yaxuna in the later part of the Terminal Classic period, construction materials were less plentiful and plaster in particular was poorly made. Given the involvement of the city in territorial wars at this time and the dense settlement coupled with droughts and other forms of environmental stress, it appears that the resources for burning limestone and mixing plaster were increasingly difficult to obtain for occupants of modest residential compounds like the 5E-167 group.

A RESIDENTIAL COMPOUND AT CHUNCHUCMIL

As discussed in chapter 2, the research I codirected at the ancient trading site of Chunchucmil was focused on domestic economy and its articulation with trade in salt and other coastal products. My colleagues on this project have produced fine-grained analyses of the material remains of a number of residential groups from the central area of urban Chunchucmil and from the periphery (Hixson 2011; Hutson 2010; Hutson, Magnoni, and Stanton 2004; Magnoni et al. 2014). Scott Hutson has published extensively on a residential compound known as the 'Aak domestic group, which is an excellent example of the gendered patterns of spatial arrangements and activities described by Landa that persist, to some degree, even today (Hutson 2010; Hutson, Magnoni, and Stanton 2004; Hutson et al. 2007).

Like the Lool group discussed in chapter 2, the 'Aak group and most other residential compounds at Chunchucmil are surrounded by stone boundary walls. These simple features provide a wealth of valuable information about the ancient perception of space and social interaction. One particularly valuable aspect of their presence across the site is the way they facilitate understanding household composition. Like at Yaxuna, Xuenkal, and other sites discussed in this text, many simple residential structures cluster together or face one another around a small patio area. At Chunchucmil we have the advantage of seeing not only the structures that ancient people understood to be related, but also the open space associated with those structures that provided a further conceptual framework for family membership and kinship relations. Today, Yucatec Maya villages retain the cultural practice of boundary wall maintenance, and although they are often set up along a grid system, away from the main plaza or paved roads, boundary walls can meander based on social relations in much the same way as the walls of ancient Chunchucmil. Linguist William Hanks describes boundary walls in modern Yucatán as the perimeters that mark the essential division between inside and out, a division which completes the homestead and is affirmed in ceremonies to purify and protect the domestic space (Hanks 1990:324).

The 'Aak group is contemporaneous with much of the construction at Chunchucmil and was occupied for approximately 150 years at the very end of the Early Classic period, from 500–650 CE (Hutson 2010:77). It is located just south of the tallest pyramid at the site, within the urban core. The boundary walls enclose an area of 3,910 square meters with four main structures around a central patio with a fifth structure, a low platform, to the north of the patio area (Hutson 2010:63). The structures were situated around a natural rise in the bedrock and went through many modifications in their short history (Figure 5.1). First a simple house (Structure 23) sat across the patio from a food preparation area, but then a much larger house (Structure 22) with three rooms made of masonry stonework and a beam-supported roof was built to the north of the patio while the original house foundation was covered in a shrine structure, situated on the east of the residential group just like Structure 75 at the Lool group. Soil chemistry analyses that indicate high phosphate levels combined with large quantities of domestic ceramic fragments suggest that food preparation was moved to the southern part of the patio group at this time.

These construction activities were accompanied by burial rituals that further defined or marked the accumulation of meaning and history within the residential group. Two burials, associated offerings, and a simple stone cist were placed below the floor of Structure 23 and covered by a platform that became an ancestral shrine (Hutson 2010:72). Burial 2 was an adult placed into the cist in a flexed or bundled position. The poor preservation of the bones prevented identification of the sex of this individual. The modest burial architecture was contradicted by elaborate jade and shell beads and two ceramic vessels that were buried with this individual (Ardren and Hutson 2001:266, Hutson 2010). One of the vessels was a spherical bowl elaborately carved with an image of the Maize Deity and a hieroglyphic inscription that stated, "the corn gruel drinking vessel of Lord ?" and although the name of this particular lord has not yet been deciphered, the rest of the text uses standard Classic Maya orthography to convey the ownership and purpose of this beautiful vessel. Only fifty centimeters to the north, Burial 3 was placed into the same crypt, perhaps to accompany the occupant of Burial 2, since Burial 3 was clearly the secondary remains of an ancestral bundle. These long bones and scapula were placed inside a large ceramic plate with two other ceramic vessels, jade and marine shell beads, and an obsidian blade. The ritual concluded

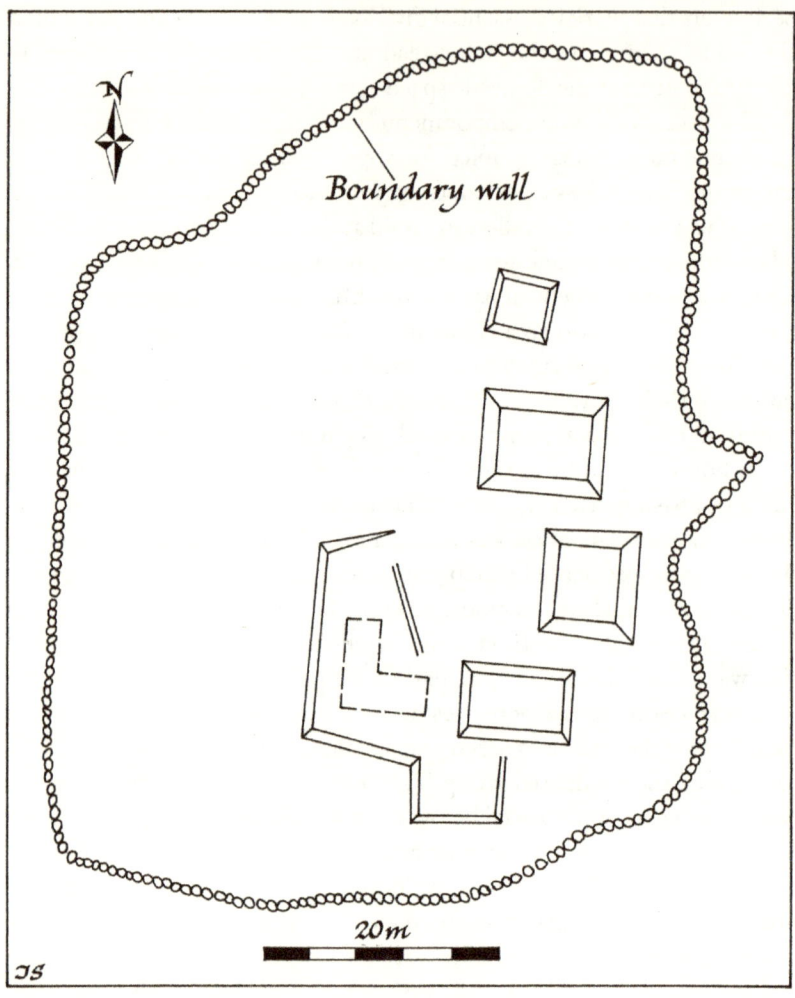

FIGURE 5.1. *'Aak residential group, Chunchucmil. Illustration by Jack Scott based on Pakbeh Regional Economy Program field drawings.*

with specular hematite sprinkled over both bodies before they were encased in the shrine platform (Ardren and Hutson 2001:267).

Not long after this materialization of kin relations and social networks, further construction of new buildings occurred in the 'Aak group. A modest home of stone foundation braces and perishable roofing (Structure 25) was built in the west and another in the south (Structure 24) on top of the area where food had been prepared in the past. Four large grinding stones, originally used for processing corn, were incorporated into this simple structure (Hutson 2010:77). Because they are the only *metates* used in the architecture of the 'Aak group, Hutson argues these stones must have been discarded from earlier food-processing activities in this same location, while a spindle whorl was recovered from under a wall that connected this house to the ancestral shrine (Hutson 2010:77). A new kitchen was built on a low platform (Structure 21) north of the patio group where five grinding stones, abandoned by the occupants of the group before they were worn out, were found in situ. Again, higher-than-average levels of phosphates in the soil near Structure 21, broken obsidian blades, and abundant domestic pottery suggest this was the newest kitchen or food preparation area.

A comprehensive program of soil testing, fine screening, and ethnobotanical assays across the entire 'Aak house-lot revealed not only the areas where food preparation activities might have taken place but also evidence of gardening, trash disposal, and craft production. In modern, historic, and ancient Maya households, the house-lot area is the site of numerous economically and socially important activities, many of them supervised or undertaken by women as part of the shared social imaginary of femaleness. Hutson and colleagues argue, based in part on ethnoarchaeological research within the modern village of Chunchucmil, that debris ringing the patio of the 'Aak group was the result of maintenance activities such as sweeping, which correlates with the clean interior floors of the domestic structures (Hutson et al. 2007:457). The patio also yielded average levels of phosphate and trace elements, perhaps because it was the focus of regular upkeep (Hutson et al. 2007:457). A midden deposit between Structure 23 and Structure 22 had a very high concentration of obsidian blades exhibiting use wear patterns consistent with fiber processing, possibly from agave that was used for commoner clothing or palm fibers used for basketry (Hutson et al. 2007:461). Two areas east of Structure 21 had elevated levels of phosphates, deeper soils, and no other artifactual remains, which led the authors to suggest they may have been areas for household gardening. Fruit tree phytoliths were found in the soil samples from the southern part of the household compound south of the structures (Hutson et al. 2007:464).

Not long after the final structures were built at the 'Aak group, the fortunes of the city declined and Chunchucmil was nearly abandoned. The history of rapid architectural expansion and renovation at the 'Aak group came to an end as trade patterns across Mesoamerica were disrupted during the final decades of the Early Classic period. The unique urban arrangement of closely packed residential compounds separated by boundary walls was modified by later occupants of Chunchucmil, who were smaller in number and less integrated in pan-Mesoamerican systems of trade and exchange.

Male Gendered Space

Landa wrote one specific passage about an architectural space that was explicitly gendered male. After discussion of the general obedience of the population toward their male chiefs [*sic*], the industriousness of men in agriculture and trade, and their customs of war, Landa wrote this in a section on punishments and penalties:

> The young men respected their elders highly, and took their counsels and sought to pass as mature . . . So much was the respect given to the elder men that the youths did not mingle with them, except in cases of necessity, such as marriages. Also they visited little among the married people; so that it was the custom to have in each town a large building, whitewashed and open on all sides, where the young men gathered for their pastimes. They played ball, and a certain game with beans like dice, and many others. Here they nearly always slept, all together, until they were married . . . it was their habit to bring to these places the public women and make use of them; and it is said that among them the poor creatures who took up this mode of life, although they were paid therein, were so beset by the number of youths that they were harassed even to death. (Gates 1978:52)

Like the domestic compounds in which both women and men lived, men's houses were experienced by both women and men, although the space was clearly understood by Landa to reproduce ideals of masculine behavior that included women in only a very narrow and specific way. It is significant that Landa mentions the ball game as a key activity within the men's houses, as iconographic and epigraphic data indicate the ball game provided a preeminent script for hierarchical masculine dominance. There are no known depictions of female ballplayers, and the ball game was used to negotiate social ranking among male members of competing royal dynasties in the Classic period, and thus was an arena for ritualized violence and the performance of hegemonic male ideals (Ardren 2009, Gallegos and Gomez 2006, Gillespie 1991, Joyce 2000b). The men's houses described by Landa were not only gender-restricted space but also, like the domestic compounds, places for the performance of activities that reinforced gendered ideals.

Men's houses are known from other Colonial-period descriptions of the Maya area such as J. Eric S. Thompson's analysis of sixteenth- and seventeenth-century reports on the Chol Maya written by Spanish explorers, but these sources provide little additional data other than that married men were in the habit of sleeping in the men's house from the fifth month of pregnancy until twenty days after birth (Tozzer 1912, Thompson 1938). Thompson also drew parallels between the Colonial-period descriptions of men's houses and the male-only spaces of contemporary Kekchi and Lacandon Maya god houses (Thompson 1938:603).

Archaeologists have attempted with little success to locate examples of the men's houses described by Landa and others in the material record of the Classic period. There are few structures that fit all the specifics of Landa's description: a large structure of plastered architecture, open on all sides, in the center of a settlement. Rosemary Joyce and Stephen Houston have both suggested that men's houses can best be identified by the presence of ancillary information, specifically iconographic decorations of the male body or male body parts (Houston 2009, Joyce 2000b). In Joyce's earliest works on Maya gender, she noted that masculinity was strongly tied to sexuality and display of the male body (Joyce 2000b:264, Joyce 2001) and that architecture decorated with images of male-male social interaction or male body parts might be likely candidates for restricted men's houses.

Both Joyce and Houston have overlooked the fact that imagery of the male body, specifically the penis or the adult male body with visible genitalia, is relatively common in Maya art, and this trope appears in a wide variety of architectural and iconographic settings such as plazas, palaces, and elite domestic compounds. While it may be possible that all of these settings were gendered male or used primarily by men to circulate and cement notions of maleness, it is more likely that women moved through many places that were adorned with imagery taken from the male body, given the frequency with which these images were used. From this perspective, male body parts did not indicate the presence of male bodies as much as the ideological importance of masculine power. The common image of penile bloodletting, which took place in private ceremonies but also in communal performances, is an example of how the idealized male body took on an authority of meaning that subsumed both individual men and women. Penile bloodletting was not about glorification of the male member per se, as much as it was about the dynastic privilege and bloodlines of the ruling class. The way in which images of young, healthy, elite male bodies were used to circulate ideas about a social imaginary in which a certain form of masculinity was representative of the state will be discussed below.

If we no longer restrict the identification of men's houses to those buildings that carry ancillary information, as these decorations were not mentioned by Landa and may in fact be a distraction from the identification of actual men's houses since they were used for other purposes, then the possibilities of male-gendered architecture dramatically increase. The salient characteristics of Landa's description are that the building was "large," "whitewashed" (i.e., plastered, monumental architecture, not just perishable wood and thatch), and "open on all sides." Thinking about how Maya domestic structures are designed, both commoner and elite architecture provides shelter for sleeping in the form of walls and a roof—completely open sleeping platforms are not part of the corpus. Thus we must expect walls and a roof, either perishable or vaulted. Maya domestic architecture often has very restricted access. Commoner homes in the Classic period often had a single entrance, as Landa also describes for the Colonial period, and elite palaces had perhaps two to three entrances, but these were often located along the same wall to limit routes of access. Thus Landa's comment about open on all sides is significant and may suggest doorways on more than a single wall, or a generally freer mode of access than other domestic structures. In the Classic period, we should expect to find these masculine spaces integrated into the civic architectural plan, not isolated from other architectural expressions of power, since Landa mentions them as the only other form of monumental architecture besides a chief's house in the Colonial period. This indicates that the construction of men's houses survived the rejection of all other prior forms of monumental architecture in the social transformations of the Late Postclassic, Contact, and early Colonial periods.

MEN'S HOUSE AT YAXUNA

The 5E-73 group at Yaxuna is an excellent candidate for the male-gendered space for socialization and enculturation of young men that Landa called a men's house. It meets the most salient criteria outlined above and is centrally located in the urban core of the city just 250 meters directly south of the only ball court at Yaxuna, near the juncture of Sacbes 3 and 7. The structures in this group were the focus of excavation and eventual consolidation during the 1989 and 1991 field seasons of the Selz Foundation Yaxuna Archaeological Project.

The 5E-73 group began as two separate platforms across from one another on a natural limestone rise during the Early Classic period (Stan-

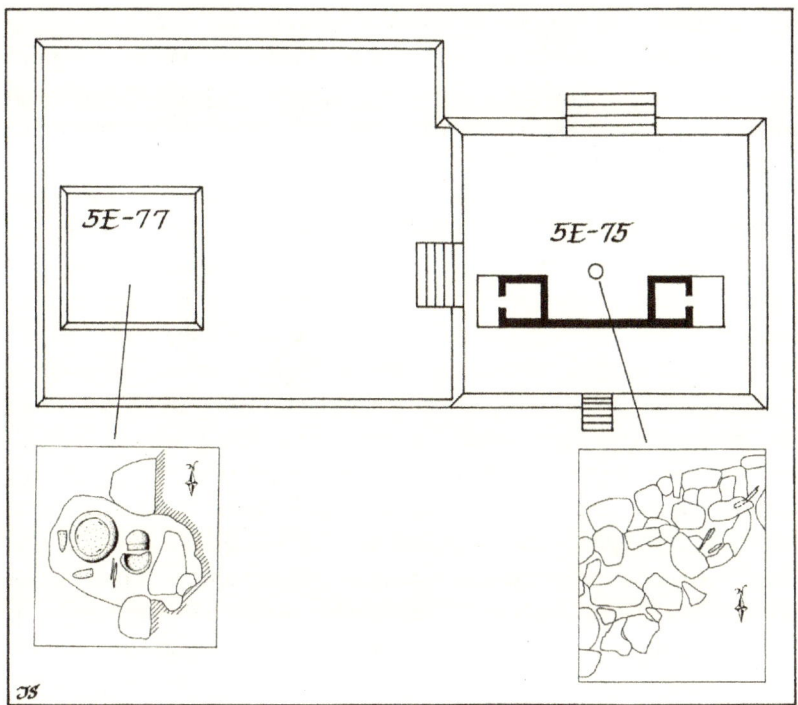

FIGURE 5.2. *5E-73 group with location of burials, Yaxuna. Illustration by Jack Scott based on Selz Foundation Yaxuna Archaeological Project field drawings.*

ton et al. 2010:61). The eastern platform, Structure 5E-75, had a modest superstructure, while the western platform, Structure 5E-77, did not (Figure 5.2). After multiple extensions of these platforms during this period, they were eventually abandoned and let fall into decline. Stucco plaster flaked off the platform walls and some of the wall stones slipped from place. In the Late Classic period this area was reoccupied when the entire central precinct of Yaxuna was renovated during a flurry of construction activity that was perhaps fueled by a new allegiance with the people of Coba, to whom Yaxuna was now connected by Sacbe 1. The previous superstructure on 5E-75 was razed and rebuilt with an orientation to the north rather than the south as originally designed. A very large structure—eighteen meters long by five meters wide—with three large rooms was built atop the platform with a new wide stairway to the north. Of the three rooms, the two smaller ones on either end had a single doorway onto the platform but the middle room was open to the plaza area along its entire length. The area between the two platforms was filled with small stone and plastered over to create a continuous plaza area, and a smaller but still well-built structure was constructed on the summit of the Structure 5E-77 platform. Both buildings and the plaza were covered with a new plaster floor that created a large and highly visible activity area accented by open architecture.

The design of Structure 5E-75, as well as its location in the center of Yaxuna, suggests a possible identification as a men's house. The three large rooms of Structure 5E-75-1 were made of well-worked stone set four to six courses high with a rubble core—an architectural style that provides more stability than a single row of stone and can be easily covered in plaster. These walls would have provided the base for perishable upper walls and a roof made of thatch, although the central room of the structure may not have been thatched since it did not have a northern wall, only a single column along its face. The two large patio areas to the east and west of the structure likewise would not have been thatched. In the course of excavation and consolidation of this building, very little domestic debris was recovered, but a relatively large number of chert flakes (n=5) by Yaxuna standards were found on the plaster floor level as well as a painted limestone ball perhaps used for gaming and a broken chert biface (Stanton et al. 2010:65).

A centerline trench made in Structure 5E-75 to define its construction history recovered the remains of a secondary burial near ground surface to the north of the three-roomed structure (Freidel, Suhler, and Cobos P. 1992:46). Portions of human tibia, fibula, and femur had been placed directly into the limestone fill but above an earlier floor level (Bennett 1992:86). There was no evidence of a crypt or burial goods in association with the human remains, although a single sherd from the vicinity of the burial dates to a much earlier period. Given the lack of associated grave furniture and the consequent inability to date this deposit, we are left with the option that these bones may represent ancestral remains deposited early in the occupational history of the 5E-75 platform, or perhaps the remains of a captive or other low-status individual buried in a desecratory manner during the renovations of the Late Classic period.

Structure 5E-77 across the plaza was not completely excavated so its Late Classic period dimensions are not known precisely, but it was a more modest building that consisted of a stone foundation brace for a perishable structure on a plastered open platform to the west of the main three-roomed building. Four obsidian blade fragments were recovered from the floor level in Structure 5E-77. Three other smaller structures in this group were not investigated.

The 5E-73 group is one of two large architectural complexes that were subjected to a hostile termination event during the Terminal Classic period. Like the higher-status Structure 6F-68, a building decorated with symbols of masculine power including ballplayers, warriors, and shields that was ceremonially terminated and then abandoned, the Structure 5E-73 group appears to have been the focus of a similar attack. Large quantities of ceramic vessels, primarily domestic wares, were smashed along the platform walls and inside the rooms of Structure 5E-75 before it was abandoned. In association with the broken ceramics were broken fragments of greenstone, obsidian, and grinding stones, all of which were burned in situ (Stanton et al. 2010:62). At the same time, the plaster floor in the southwest interior corner of Structure 5E-77 was broken, a wall stone removed, and the remains of a child approximately four years old placed into the subfloor ballast. Two *spondylus* shell pendants and deer bone fragments were found with the human remains, which were covered by three tabular capstones. Terminal Classic ceramic vessels were smashed on top of the capstones.

This termination event was part of a complex of highly focused activities that occurred late in the history of the city when conflict in the region had escalated and resources were stretched. As described in chapter 3, the virtual abandonment of Yaxuna followed these violent terminations of key Terminal Classic locations of civic authority, and the city was only sparsely reoccupied hundreds of years later when memories of these dark times could be reframed and the identity of the city reimagined (see chapter 3).

MEN'S HOUSE AT DZIBILCHALTUN

Structure 44 of the important Classic-period city of Dzibilchaltun has been described as a likely *popol na* (council house), a conceptual model for Classic Maya architecture drawn from Colonial-period ethnohistoric sources (Ambrosino 2003, Fash et al. 1992, Kowalski 2003, Kowalski et al. 2002). Structure 44 is one of the longest range structures of the Classic Maya world, extending for 130 meters along the southern side of the main plaza at Dzibilchaltun (Figure 5.3) (Maldonado C. 2001:67). It was the focus of excavation during 1993–1994, directed by Ruben Maldonado Cardenas, director of Proyecto Arqueológico Dzibilchaltun for the Instituto Nacional de Antropología e Historia. Maldonado suggested the structure must have had a communal, semi-public function given the large number of entrances and the enormous stairway that provides a huge area for public performance (Maldonado C. 1995:74).

FIGURE 5.3. *Structure 44, Dzibilchaltun. Photograph by the author.*

This immense structure has an interesting architectural history, and excavations in the 1990s revealed an earlier and much smaller structure buried inside the long range structure that runs the entire length of the south plaza. Substructure 44 was a small vaulted building that faced east and was built at the beginning of the Late Classic period. It had three entrances leading into three separate rooms, and the exterior of the structure was decorated with brilliant red stucco manufactured with hematite (Maldonado C. 2001:69). Inside the rooms, Maldonado found drawings of elite men executed on the walls in charcoal (Maldonado C. 2001:71). The images depicted men with cranial shaping and elaborate headdresses in a procession, although the preservation of the images was not sufficient to record much detail. No burials were found despite excavation beneath the floors of Substructure 44, and no artifacts were found on the floors. The rooms of Substructure 44 had been filled carefully with rock when it was covered by the much more massive Structure 44. This type of careful preservation of an earlier structure during architectural expansion occurred commonly in the Maya area when the expansion was considered ideologically consistent with the original structure and no break or reorientation with the past was necessary (Freidel and Schele 1989, Mock 1998, Stanton et al. 2008).

Perhaps one hundred years later in the Late Classic period the rooms of Substructure 44 were filled with rock, the southern exterior wall was shaved off, and the entire structure was covered in construction fill to create the basal platform of Structure 44. This new range structure was oriented differently than Substructure 44 and faced north, toward the rest of the central plaza. The Central Plaza is approximately one hundred meters north-south by two hundred meters east-west and is enclosed on all sides by large platforms or vaulted architecture that date primarily to the same moment in time as Structure 44. To the north is a pyramidal platform (Structure 36), to the east is a tall temple structure (Structure 42), and to the west of the Central Plaza is Cenote Xlacah, the primary freshwater source for the central part of the city. The significance of the central plaza was apparent to the Spanish even after maintenance of these structures had been abandoned for hundreds of years, and they chose to construct a Spanish colonial chapel built with stone from the pre-contact buildings in the middle of the plaza.

The latest version of Structure 44 was massive and provided a huge area for both private and public activities with a view of the entire plaza. Approximately four meters above the plastered plaza floor, a set of three long rooms ran the length of the building. Each of the rooms opened onto the plaza via a colonnade of thirty-five doorways along the northern wall. The central room was 17.6 meters long, and was flanked by rooms forty-seven meters long on either end (Maldonado C. 2001:67). Maldonado notes the rooms are so narrow (2.3 meters in width) that they are better considered passageways that open onto a platform nineteen meters wide, which would have provided ample space for a variety of activities (Andrews and Andrews 1980:13, Maldonado C. 2001:67). There was no access into the rooms of Structure 44 from the east or west, although there were passageways between the three long rooms at the summit of the structure and each room had a single doorway to the back or southern side of the structure.

The three immense rooms at the summit of Structure 44 were made with fine masonry stonework, plastered walls, and a vaulted ceiling. The many doorways would have allowed more light to enter into the narrow rooms than in many vaulted Maya structures, which were small and dark, suggesting almost all activity took place outside. Many fragments of modeled and painted stucco were recovered from the excavations at Structure 44 as well as fragments of stone sculpture that Maldonado suggests decorated the façade of the building (Maldonado C. 1995:73). Large quantities of Late Classic–period ceramic fragments and obsidian waste were found in midden deposits to the east and west of the summit platform (Maldonado C. 1995:73). Given that Structure 44 occupies the whole southern side of the central plaza that held thousands of people for festivals or political rituals, and that its enormous stairway for performative space runs along the entire front of the building, it is obvious this particular building had a key role in the civic life of Dzibilchaltun. While such range structures along plazas have often been described as "administrative" in function given their location, dimensions, and lack of fit with materialized patterns of domestic life, the gendered aspect of this space has rarely been considered. In the following section I will discuss how archaeologists can read gendered patterns in architectural designs and how we can apply those theories to what is known about Classic Maya conceptualizations of gender ideals. The gendering of places is a powerful form of cultural reproduction. It can both reflect and help construct the ways in which gender is understood and circulated.

READING SPACE FOR GENDER AND SOCIAL IDENTITIES

In an important early ethnography of the gendered nature of space, Henrietta Moore argues that both physical and social spaces (i.e., domestic structures but also the social life of the domestic world) have gendered qualities (Moore 1986:7). Moore articulates clearly that gendered ideals or the abstract ideas about how women and men should behave are not inherent in the organization of space but must be conveyed or circulated through the repeated activities of the social actors that use the space. In this sense Moore's notion of how gender is reproduced is consistent with Taylor and Anderson's conceptualizations of the social imaginary. Gender, per se, is not a quality that one can know or touch, but rather a set of shared ideas that are transmitted through repeated behaviors, circulated to create a foundation of knowledge from which individuals choose to depart. The organization of space is a key component to these circulations and can be seen to acquire meaning in the same way objects or behaviors accrue gendered significance. The question of how our experiences of a location or a building shape our sense of a gendered identity is an interesting one, and archaeologists have had many responses to it (Baugher and Spencer-Wood 2010, Goldberg 1999, Rodning 2001, Wadley 2000).

Moore notes that attention to the gendered aspects of spatial relations grows out of a long-standing interest in the social dimensions of space within the field of anthropology. Early scholars noted the powerful linkages between kinship and territory and established the principle that spatial relations represent and reproduce social relations. Boundaries and social distinctions are a central component of this observation, and the way boundaries are maintained within a domestic compound or ritual area often is crucially important to how the space is understood. Moore makes clear in her study of Edo domestic space in Kenya that meaning is never inherent in the organization of domestic space "but must be invoked through the activities of social actors" (Moore 1986:8). Social actors and repeated behaviors give space its meaning, just as they are shaped by the spaces in which they circulate. In this sense Moore moves beyond reading the spatial organization of a settlement as a text that reflects cultural values or ideology. Rather she argues that what is apparent is a representation of values that must be maintained, a conversation about beliefs and ideals that is reproduced but also contested in order to produce change. Often dominant social values are maintained by repeated behaviors, but individual interpretation of space can vary and is always both constrained and constructed by previous experience and historical relations (Moore 1986:187). This ensures that some interpretations are repeated, since those who dominate a social environment will ensure a dominant interpretation. But it also predicts change, as those who operate outside the dominant power structures may choose to interpret and utilize social space in a way that creates difference and change. This is Moore's explanation of how architectural space works and comes to convey meaning.

Gender is often a central component to the structure of space, because human cultures rely upon a metaphoric process for the constitution of meaning and the social relations of families who cohabitate are a fundamental metaphor available for explaining social difference. If spatial relations express and construct the power relations between different groups, gender becomes a powerful metaphor for the difference between groups and their stratification. The qualities of maleness and femaleness are a ready value system for organizing space, although the constitution of those qualities is culturally and historically specific. For the Edo, Moore relates that the distinction between maleness and femaleness mediated the distinction between the social and the individual, because men were believed to use extra money for social activities and women were believed to use it for themselves (Moore 1986:110). Maleness and femaleness also became a way to resolve tensions between the household and the patriclan, because household needs were often trumped by lifelong allegiance to the patriclan. Maleness was associated with the values of the patriclan and femaleness expressed the values of the household. Conflicts and tensions between people were understood as between the sexes, and the organization of domestic space presented a representation of these concerns, a representation that was both a product and a producer. Thus the Edo explicitly stated that women were subordinate to men, even though women exercised significant power through their control of production, reproduction, and consumption, because femaleness as a metaphor for individualism was subordinated to the collectivity (maleness). The understanding that gender is used as a metaphor for social values is essential for reading the text of architectural space. As Moore notes, appealing to notions of maleness and femaleness does not necessarily reference what men or women actually do; it is a way of understanding relationships in terms of the qualities around which life is ordered (Moore 1986:111). Thus the qualities of male and female, and additional genders in some cultures, are ways of thinking about the world; they may express and help mediate ideas such as conflict, balance, complementarity, or hierarchy. In societies where gender is a strong organizing principle, like the Edo and the Maya, the ideological categories of male and female "instill the differences which create the social"—they do not prescribe certain behaviors as much as they provide an orientation that precedes thought or action (Joyce 2000a, Moore 1986:167).

In Moore's later work, she even more clearly articulates how gender is one means by which human societies understand difference, with difference being one of the key aspects of identity (Moore 1994). Identity studies must address how identities are constructed and experienced, and how people come to share a sense of belonging. Moore suggests that the bodily experience of social distinctions, or praxis, is crucial to this question. Difference is established and maintained through the negotiation of boundaries, and boundaries are experiential. Both social groups and architectural spaces use boundaries to materialize shared identity, and this is one of the fundamental reasons we must look for social relations in spatial relations. Thresholds are an obvious form of the negotiation of space, but other forms of social negotiation have specific spatial frameworks. Marilyn Goldberg has looked at domestic courtyards in ancient households of Greece as a structured space for the social negotiation and mediation of conflict between gendered ideals and actual behavior (Goldberg 1999). She sees households as places of integration where people separated by difference negotiated social norms within a common shared space. For Goldberg, Athenian households were gendered female by dominant sectors of society such as the literate, even though men spent much of their time in the domestic world and even had specific rooms that were restricted to exclusively male meetings (Goldberg 1999:145). The femaleness of domestic compounds in Classical texts was an Athenian way to order the world; it validated the dominance of civic government by linking the home with qualities of femaleness and the government with qualities of maleness. Thus space, gender, and power are locked together in a powerful arrangement that makes each appear natural and inevitable when they are in fact fluid and reproducing.

Shirley Ardener introduces the dimension of time to an analysis of gendered spatial relationships with her observation that once space has been bounded and shaped, it is no longer a neutral background for social interaction but exerts an influence on the actors and activities that take place within it (Ardener 1993:113). This observation builds upon Moore's idea that values, which may be expressed through the metaphor of gender, "provide an orientation that precedes thought or action," and also resonates with the "macrodecisions" of Charles Taylor, the actions that all members of a shared social imaginary understand and practice. We know intuitively the boundaries of such macrodecisions and the consequences of stepping beyond them, and we share the knowledge that other members of our social imaginary possess this same knowledge base. One way we know such boundaries is through praxis, or the experience of daily shared rituals and behaviors such as preparation of food or the use of common tools. Ardener reminds us that space and time are mutually related spheres of reality and, for some, homologous (Ardener 1993:6). As space defines the people in it and people define a space, experiences accrue and repeat, creating a stratigraphy of understandings that is particularly relevant to settlements occupied for millennia like the Classic Maya cities of the northern lowlands. The text, one might say, of a certain building will have multiple readings. Materiality can suggest a solidity of meaning that obscures the interplay between history and individual experience over time. Thus it is nearly impossible to separate the meaning of a particular space from its meaning through time.

We know that time is a crucial component to consider when reading the meaning of Classic Maya architectural spaces, because we can see in the material record that Maya architects had many choices about building location and materials. Structures could be amplified with additions or modifications; they could be interred reverentially or dismantled. Sometimes building materials were recycled and other times new materials were obtained. Coupled with the emphasis on time as a strong organizing principle in the hieroglyphic inscriptions, it is clear that the life cycle and histories of structures were considered part of their significance. The distinction between maleness and femaleness was a powerful one within Classic Maya society, and there is abundant evidence that many daily activities as well as ritual observances were gender specific (Ardren and Alonso O. 2014, Emery and Aoyama 2007, Gallegos and Gomez 2006, Hendon 1997, Hernandez A. 2011, Sweely 1999, Vail and Stone 2002). These metaphors were used as a means to understand the way the world functioned and the appropriate activities of humans. Space was used and manipulated as a means to reproduce social relations of difference. The most obvious difference was one of power and access. Hierarchical Classic Maya society was ruled by a small segment of self-perpetuating elites who monopolized access to the resources that enabled them to build monumental architecture and live a more lavish lifestyle in palace compounds. But gender was also used to organize difference, and the entire Maya landscape was gendered because the entire Maya worldview was gendered (Gallegos and Gomez 2006, Hendon 1997, Hernandez A. 2011, Joyce 1993, 2001, Kellogg 2005, Knowlton 2010, Restall 1995, Rodriguez-Shadow and Lopez H. 2011, Vail and Stone 2002). Like in many other native New World societies, Classic Maya people saw the qualities of maleness and femaleness as different but equal, not separate but equal (Morrison 1994, Venables 2010). A balance based on reciprocity and complementarity between these gendered ideals is evident in Classic-period creation stories, literary devices, dynastic lineages, burial patterns, occupational specialties, and architectural spaces. How these gendered ideals were used and reproduced as a metaphor for social reciprocity, especially how architectural space defined people's lives and in turn was defined by them, will be explored in the next section.

EXPERIENCING GENDER

As archaeologists utilizing the social imaginary as a way to understand the boundaries people erect to order human difference, we must explore how material culture was used to naturalize gender as a social identity. What artifacts and practices helped make gendered identities self-evident? A wealth of research has shown that the biological differences of adult bodies such as reproduction and sexual dimorphism are by no means the determining factors in how gender is defined or experienced in any society. Very little about gender is universal across cultures, especially the way in which reproduction, which our culture today takes as the biological touchstone of gender, is understood. How the social identity of gender is defined—the capacities and limitations, its permanence or fluidity, and the range of distinct roles—varies extraordinarily across ancient and modern cultures. Each set of data available to modern scholars interested in ancient Maya gender, whether sculptured monument, textual inscription, burial, or artifact, is a material representation of the behavior of a group of people whose lives were shaped by gender, age, community, and status idealizations. Following the work of Rosemary Joyce, I suggest these representations were not a passive reflection of lived experiences but rather materialized conversations about idealized behavior (Joyce 1993, Meskell and Joyce 2003). Read this way, burials, architecture, and texts reveal a great deal about the shared conceptions of ideal femaleness and maleness within Classic culture as well as the ways individuals struggled with such shared conventions. The representational world is not a reflection of typical daily life or the lives of the majority of ancient Maya women; it is instead a form of social dialogue between different constituencies of society about ideas and interpretations, some of which hold a privileged position due to their connection to dominant sectors.

Looking for commonalities of belief while acknowledging the differences in representations or materializations of Maya women and men is consistent with a definition of gender as a social dialogue about membership, normative behavior, and difference (Sørensen 2000:204). Following Mary Louise Sørensen, as an archaeologist I see much of what constitutes a notion of gender is our lived experiences that become materialized in social conventions, what Charles Taylor would call performative circulations. These material conventions are easily recognized by each of us within our own culture, but they can also be defined for another culture through careful analysis of the ways in which material culture is deployed to solidify or prop up the social contract of gendered relations. Following Margaret Conkey and Janet Spector, Sørensen argues gender is a construction that must be continuously confirmed and constructed by society while individuals have the task of obtaining and maintaining such constructions, and often do so through material objects (Conkey and Spector 1984, Sørensen 2000:7). Material culture plays a specific part in social reproduction, and in the case of Classic Maya culture, objects such as personal ornaments, costume, and tools were actively deployed to convey the socially negotiated values of a strictly gendered society (Joyce 2000a, 2001). Thus the evidence that remains for us today—the domestic and civic architecture understood as gender-specific spaces—provides indications of the partnership between material culture and social relations, a dialogue about difference and membership in which the material world played a key role in the perpetuation of social life and social institutions such as gender ideologies. This perspective on gender is inherently flexible, as choices about how gender is represented or materialized reflect choices about inclusion or exclusion that members of society make every day.

The household compounds at Yaxuna and Chunchucmil with evidence of food preparation activities, cloth production, and ancestral veneration and the civic men's houses at Yaxuna and Dzibilchaltun with ample public platforms, gaming artifacts, and evidence of political termination in the case of the Yaxuna Structure 5E-75 group are examples of gendered spaces that shaped the lives of almost all residents within these ancient cities. The domestic compounds were largely private places where intense productivity took place—the raising of children, domestic animals, and comestibles, the transformation of raw foodstuffs into culturally appropriate meals, and the maintenance of ties to lineages and ancestors that ensured the continuation of families are all productive activities demonstrated in the material record of household groups. Women, especially adult commoner women, spent much of their time in these spaces, although they also traveled outside them to gather water or market wares. Men spent much time in residential compounds as well, although their activities are muted because women's productive activities were marked as part of a social dialogue about the value of productivity.

Men's houses were located centrally and in highly visible areas that emphasized the public nature of male-male social interaction and reproduction. The wide platforms and stairways of this form of civic architecture were places where intense socialization took place, and where competitive activities such as military and athletic training, gaming, subjugation of captives, and ritualized violence are demonstrated in the material record or ethnohistoric accounts of such gender-restricted spaces. Men spent time in these places in the presence of other men as part of transitional rituals that solidified their identities as adult men and in activities that maintained a masculine identity. Men also hunted, farmed, and traded goods and they slept in domestic spaces, but none of those activities had the same sort of architectural context or framework for the reinforcement of social values. Some women spent time in the men's houses as well, in service to the activities conducted there, but their presence as well as the other daily activities of men are muted in favor of an emphasis on competition and solidarity.

The analysis I present should not be taken to indicate that I am arguing for an essentialized equation of women with the private sphere versus men with the public. The use of gender as a metaphor for social values in Classic Maya culture was much more complex than this oversimplified generality, although as I have stated, the domestic world was entwined with ideal femaleness. However, in my analysis, idealized femaleness was a metaphor for the productivity of the family unit, and while productivity happened intensely in the domestic context, it also occurred when women went to market, produced ceramic vessels in pottery workshops, fetched water from wells, and facilitated politically important feasts and other state visits (McAnany and Plank 2001). These activities are depicted regularly in representational media as well as in the material record associated with women. Likewise, while the majority of civic gatherings depicted in elite representational media are filled with men as the central actors, there are important exceptions to this pattern that show individual women were often able to negotiate gendered ideals and step into roles associated with idealized maleness. The use of idealized maleness as a way to converse about competition obscures the other masculinities that existed in the Classic period, as is the nature of hegemonic masculinity. Alternative masculinities of male artists, doting fathers, or elderly men are rarely depicted in elite representational media, and while such intersubjectivities likely were common, they did not get marked with specific public architectural spaces because they existed outside of the way maleness was used to reproduce Classic Maya ideological values (Gallegos and Gomez 2006). Many other architectural settings existed in Classic Maya cities that were not as strongly gendered as the domestic compounds and men's houses. In the funerary temples, raised roads, plazas, and markets there is less evidence that gender-specific activities took place, or that these spaces were understood as reproducing gendered experiences and identities.

This use of space as a representation of ideas (i.e., that ideal femaleness is associated with the productivity of domestic space and ideal maleness is associated with competitive solidarity performed in certain public-civic space) is a product of an underlying shared ideology. As Henrietta Moore states about architectural spaces read as texts, "What the text signifies is not real/objective historical relations, but the same historical relations construed in terms of an ideological production, produced by the text's agents" (Moore 1986:87). The men's houses and domestic structures of women we see in the archaeological record were products of a conversation about maleness and femaleness as metaphors for social reciprocity. These spaces evolved within a culture that used gender as a metaphor for difference, and for how activities should be ordered and valued (Hutson 2010, Joyce 2000a, McAnany 2010). This ideology both provided a framework for such gendered architectural space and contributed to the reproduction of gender as a meaningful form of social difference. The cultural text or, in this case, architectural space is also the means by which people produce interactions and experiences that uphold and reproduce certain ideologies. Thus the existence of gender-specific architecture is evidence that gender was a strong organizing principle of Classic Maya society.

Let us consider one important aspect of Maya gender-specific space, the repeated performance of daily activities with people who are culturally defined as similar based on their gender. Food preparation in the domestic compounds is one potent example that is well materialized in the archaeological record, but we could also focus on cloth production, agricultural planting, or ball-game training, all activities that were gender specific and spatially contained during the Classic period. Gendered tasks such as food preparation were rituals of inclusion that circulated ideas of shared membership (Figure 5.4). Artifacts such as grinding stones and discarded domestic pottery materialize repeated behaviors that women often performed together. At an early age young girls were taught to grind corn or fetch water, tasks that were easily performed in small groups of peers. Transformation of corn into *masa*, tamales, and other culturally appropriate food was accomplished by women every day, in the same areas of the household compound, likely with the same family members. These private daily rituals were performed with the knowledge that women next door, across the city, and at the distant capital conducted the same tasks on the same rhythmic schedule. Accompanying the tasks were ideas shared between sisters-in-law and passed from grandmothers to granddaughters about the inherent or natural ability of women to cook, to produce food and sustenance, and through these daily rituals membership in a shared identity, or the imagined community of women, was configured and contested. Artifacts such as grinding stones, cooking fires, and water jugs were the partners that helped underline and communicate the naturalness of gender-specific tasks. Domestic pottery that became familiar through frequent use and retained the same style for generations both reinforced and helped construct a natural and endless equation between femaleness and food preparation. Household tools that only adult women could manipulate, such as the cooking grill in modern Yucatec households, further emphasized an inevitable equation of femaleness with food; by their exclusive use by those who shared a mutual identity, such artifacts performed the boundaries of the adult female social identity.

The spatial distribution of these artifacts within ancient household groups shows us that space was also used as an instrument for materializing the idea that people who shared gender also shared work. Movements throughout a household compound, from the structure used for storage to outside areas where corn was ground and an herb garden planted, were

FIGURE 5.4. *Northern lowlands Classic-period plate showing a woman grinding corn while she converses with a companion. Photograph K1272 © Justin Kerr, used with permission.*

a circulation performed much more often by women in the presence of other women than by men in the presence of other men. Certainly men moved through such domestic areas, but in Classic Maya society they did so with the understanding that the activities taking place there were largely, though not exclusively, ones in which women excelled due to the expectation of expertise and gender-specific skill. Thus as young girls learned to weave from their elder female relatives on the domestic patio, or sisters-in-law ground corn together, they shared these gender-specific tasks within a familiar shared space tailored to such activities. From the soil chemistry conducted at Chunchucmil we know that members of the 'Aak household group shared an understanding of where to dispose of organic waste and where to dispose of artifactual debris (Hutson 2010). The organization of production along gendered lines was reproduced through the provision of gender-specific space and, most importantly, the mutual experience of that common space by members of a shared social imaginary.

Ideas about gender were further naturalized in Classic Maya society through rituals of inclusion timed to coincide with significant moments within the life cycle and set within specific architectural settings. Following Joyce's observation that indoctrination in gender-specific tasks started at a very young age for Aztec children, when they were presented with miniature weaving tools and weapons, it appears that the use of artifacts and space to mark the development of female and male bodies is a particularly effective metaphoric process for explaining difference (Joyce 2000c). The process of training young Maya men in the art of war as well as competitive sports took place in the company of other men and in a unique physical space. This process began when youth were at the transition to adulthood, a status described in hieroglyphic texts as *ch'ok* or young sprout, which seems to indicate younger than twenty years of age (Houston 2009:163). According to Landa, these youths were removed from their families for extended group training in the men's houses (Gates 1978:52). Among the Aztec, *telpochcalli* men's houses are well documented as places where young men were segregated from the rest of the population in order to learn the arts of war from accomplished veterans (Soustelle 1961, Townsend 2000). In both cases, the transition from adolescent youth to adult man was made as part of a collectivity of other men who experienced the same bodily and social changes. Referencing Taylor's theory of how the social imaginary functions, if the understanding of maleness made the practice of men's house sociality possible, then it is also true that the practice of male sociality within the men's house conveyed the understanding of maleness.

Idealized femaleness was associated with the productivity of the household, and the transition to the identity of adult woman was also staged in a specific architectural setting. For women, the productivity of the household and their understanding of their innate ability in this realm was uninterrupted by the transition to adulthood. According to Landa, a married couple resided with the parents of the bride for five to six years while the groom provided bride-service to his new in-laws (Gates 1978:42). A young woman was not uprooted from her daily routine or familiar setting but continued to circulate within the domestic setting into which she was born. This continuity in spatial practice reinforced qualities of idealized femaleness such as consistency, reliability, and privacy. When young men and women married, the young man joined the household of his wife because the value of consistent household production was paramount within Maya society. Rather than a transition marked by spatial change, this was a transition marked by spatial accommodation and persistence. If spatial relations express and construct the power relations between different groups, then gender becomes a powerful metaphor for the difference between groups and their stratification. The qualities of maleness and femaleness existed in a reciprocal balance through the privileging of visible male space against the persistence of domestic habits, although the experience of a gendered identity evolved for both women and men as they became adults and their gender was solidified.

Within Classic Maya society people who shared gender also shared similar access to power. The gendered activities that were performed publicly in men's houses circulated a notion that ideal maleness was closer to authority and dominance than any other social identity. The gendered experiences of gathering publicly on the steps or open platforms of centrally located civic architecture to game, train for athletic competitions, or perform heteronormative sexual behaviors solidified the shared membership in an imagined community of men. These rituals of inclusion, while not as private as food preparation or Anderson's reading of the newspaper, were places where the social imaginary was encountered and reproduced. Landa suggests that young boys were brought to men's houses, and Classic-period hieroglyphic inscriptions record coming-of-age ceremonies for men as young as twelve (Houston 2009, Schele 1984). The social relocation of identity from household to monumental civic architecture was likely a formative and impressive one for young men, one which helped cement a sense of solidarity with those who likewise were uprooted from their childhood spaces in order to inhabit and define the socially dominant status of adult maleness.

On stelae, murals, and portable ceramics, the male body was naturalized as a metaphor for political authority. These elite artistic media were produced by small groups of artisans attached to royal compounds. Messages carried by this art were controlled by dominant groups, especially by ruling dynastic lineages whose members were the most common subjects. By choosing the male body, usually dressed in royal insignia and engaged in rituals of state, as one of the most common artistic images, the dominant social group of young royal men ensured the perpetuation of their privilege. The frequency with which such images appeared in elite media as well as the placement of such images in prominent public locations throughout Classic Maya civic centers materialized the ability of royal masculinity to control the official texts, and thus much of the official rhetoric, of the state. Spatial expressions of power through the metaphor of gender help to naturalize power and make it appear inevitable. Other scholars have begun to explore the nature of Classic Maya masculinity and linkages to men's houses, but have not argued for the same explicit linkage between hegemonic masculinity, civic architecture, and privilege that I make here (Gallegos and Gomez 2006; Hernandez 2011; Houston 2009; Joyce 2000b, 2001).

In addition to the elite painted ceramics mentioned previously, other artifacts were deployed to concretize the use of virile, youthful maleness as a metaphor for the authority of the state, especially within the broader population of Classic cities. During the Late to Terminal Classic period in the northern lowlands, this equation of the youthful male body with political authority was materialized in freestanding stone phalli, often over two meters in height. Approximately 140 examples of carved stone phalli are known from the northern lowlands, with the greatest concentration found in sites around the Puuc hills (Amrhein 2001, Ardren 2011c). In an earlier work I drew a connection between the appearance of these images and the increase in violence and social stress during this time period (Ardren 2012a). The phalli stones were created during a period of greater competition for territory as a result of environmental stress from drought and deforestation coupled with high population pressure (Demarest et al. 2004). Warfare was endemic, and as Sanimir Resic points out, in many complex cultures, both modern and premodern, to become a warrior is to become a man (Resic 2006:423). Processes by which a soldier's identity is formed are often identical to the way masculine identity is formulated. Warrior values are often synonymous with manliness or idealized maleness. Resic notes that many cultures explicitly link genitals, manliness, aggressiveness, and courage (Resic 2006:424), and the mutual performance of idealized masculinity within a male-male space of heightened danger or cultural value often contributes to a sense of shared identity. Given that there is little evidence for standing military orders in Classic Maya society prior to the Terminal Classic period, the shift to territorial wars of expansion would have required the recruitment of much larger numbers of soldiers. The phalli stones may have been a social mechanism for reinforcing the critical role of warrior masculinity in the maintenance of state interests. The spatial distribution of these images within civic plazas, near monumental architecture, and at the entrance to spiritually potent locations such as caves shows the conspiracy of space, gender, and power to make each appear natural and inevitable when they are in fact in need of constant reinforcement.

The presence of gender-specific architectural spaces, and gender-specific behaviors linked to those spaces, is a representation of concern with social indebtedness or reciprocity. Through the design of these spaces and the performance of specific acts with unique props within them, Classic Maya people engaged in a conversation about the importance of reciprocity. Just as we should not assume all married couples lived with the family of the bride even though this was the expectation, some individuals undoubtedly read the text of these buildings and spaces differently than the dominant groups and used these spaces for other purposes. The presence of ideological conflict is a demonstration of the ability of social actors to enact change or to contest the dominant imaginary. As Robert Venables observed in his analysis of gendered landscapes and tasks within Haudenosaunee (Iroquois) society, an emphasis on the larger reciprocal nature of gendered relations rather than a rigid separation of men and women allowed for individual men and women to perform each other's gendered tasks on occasion (Venables 2010). Gendered spatial arrangements of Maya architecture signified a social imaginary in which maleness and femaleness were significant forms of difference, but yet were complementary and related in a way that impacted deeply the actions and lives of individual women and men.

CONCLUSION

In this chapter we explored how Classic Maya people used gender to explain social differences. I posed a set of questions at the start that asked how the experience of gender was constructed and how it changed over the life course. Gendered ideals can structure many daily activities, including the way we circulate through the spatial environments where we work, socialize, and experience community. Many archaeologists have explored the role of gender in shaping the daily lives of ancient people over the past decade, and some very strong research has been done within the Maya area. These studies have explored the myriad ways that gender shaped craft production within Classic Maya society, how diet and burial practices were affected, and how monumental media were used to instill a sense of complementarity among the genders. Fewer archaeologists working in the northern Maya lowlands have been interested in gender or how it structured the architectural record. We have not asked how space shaped gendered ideals or was shaped by these same ideals, so we have not explored in much depth how individuals learned gender or engaged in dialogue with the gendered ideals of their neighbors.

Drawing from Henrietta Moore's groundbreaking theories about the ways gender, power, and space are locked together in a powerful arrangement that acts to naturalize each and obscure their interdependence, I argued that certain key spaces within Classic Maya cities were understood to contain and reveal important social values that were described in gendered terms. Moore argued that both physical and social spaces have gendered qualities, and that these qualities must be maintained through repeated behaviors that circulate shared ideas. The organization of space is a powerful means by which to shape ideas and behaviors. Gender-segregated space in particular both communicates and reinforces the usefulness of gender as a metaphorical basis for social difference.

Architecture at the ancient northern Maya centers of Yaxuna, Chunchucmil, and Dzibilchaltun demonstrates a regional pattern of shared ideas about how gender could be used as a powerful means of organizing social life. Contact-era Spanish descriptions of gender-specific behaviors that were situated within particular architectural settings corroborate the gendered patterns of material artifacts, burials, and architecture we know from Late-Terminal Classic Yucatán. At each of these sites as well as hundreds of others in the northern lowlands, domestic architecture within walled compounds is filled with the material residue of food production, animal husbandry, and family life. From a variety of sources including elite representational media, burials, ethnohistoric accounts, and modern ethnographic parallels, we know the activities of the domestic compound were associated with idealized femaleness. The quality of productivity, especially the productivity of the extended family domestic unit, was closely intertwined with the notion of femaleness in Maya society. This intersection was reproduced through an association between the activities that took place within domestic space and the adult women who possessed expert knowledge of those activities. Men circulated through the domestic compound just as women did, but they did not participate in activities within the compound that contributed to, and derived from, their gendered identity to the same degree as women. At both Yaxuna and Dzibilchaltun we looked at examples of monumental civic architecture that likely were used for gender-specific social activities which reinforced bonds among young men and led them to perform an understanding of idealized male activities such as competitive gaming and ritualized violence. Artifacts, mural art, and ethnohistoric accounts describe a variety of activities that men performed in the company of other men during the Classic period, and some of these actions, such as the ball game, had very specific architectural settings. The quality of competition, and especially competitive social behaviors such as sport, war, and gaming, were upheld by the dominant masculinity of Maya society. While I would no more argue that all ancient Maya men were aggressive gamers than I would argue all ancient Maya women were expert gardeners, male-specific behaviors such as warfare and the ball game were a means by which Maya people engaged in a conversation about what maleness meant within their society. Maleness was not inherent; it was not a tangible quality that all men possessed. It was cultivated and maintained, and the concept of maleness allowed for a conversation about certain social values that had a long history within Maya culture. Gender idealizations were a set of shared ideas that were sometimes contested, and that obscured variation in order for certain values to remain dominant. Circulations through space were an important part of how such ideas were circulated and reproduced.

The domestic and civic architecture of Classic Maya cities, understood as gender-specific spaces, are indications of the partnership between material culture and social relations, a dialogue about difference and membership in which the material world played a key role in the perpetuation of social life and social institutions such as gender ideologies. The repeated performance of daily activities with people who are culturally defined as similar based on their gender constitutes a performative circulation that generates shared understanding. Gender-specific tasks such as food preparation or hunting not only are constituted by the social imaginary but also help to construct it. Women prepared tortillas believing that all the women who lived within their city performed the same task each day, and through this knowledge a sense of collectivity was experienced. Ideas about gender were further naturalized in Classic Maya society through rituals of inclusion timed to coincide with significant moments within the life cycle and set within specific architectural settings. Young men were removed from their domestic childhood homes for some period of extended socialization within an all-male setting, where they learned idealized male behaviors and performed them as part of the negotiation of their new role as adults. In broader terms, a concern with social indebtedness or reciprocity is evident in the social imaginary of Classic Maya gender. Shared work organized along gendered lines, shared space where gender differences were accentuated, and a system of power sharing in which male privilege was often contingent upon male-female partnership all convey a notion of gender as a powerful way in which social reciprocity was ensured.

WHY SOCIAL IDENTITIES? | *Chapter 6*

ARCHAEOLOGY AND THE SOCIAL IMAGINARY

Early in his broadly read volume on the rise of modern nationalism, Benedict Anderson states, "In the modern world everyone can, should, will 'have' a nationality, as he or she 'has' a gender" (Anderson 1991:5). Anderson's analogy between two social identities that both assert powerful influence over our daily lives was made as part of his effort to define the concept of nation and the paradoxes that emerge in its study. Theorists of nationalism, Anderson explains, have been perplexed by the "formal universality" of nationalism in modern societies and its perception of antiquity, despite historical evidence of the relatively recent and deliberate construction of national sentiment through invented symbols, reimagined history, and other social productions. It is significant that Anderson uses gender as his touchstone to explain the self-evident and compulsory aspects of nationalism—gender is perhaps the social identity that is most often perceived as inevitable and enduring due to the ways in which the human body can be entangled in the construction of gendered ideals. Yet decades of scholarship on the social construction of gender have shown that like nationalism, gender is easily manipulated and highly changeable to observers, but participants experience the opposite—their social identities are lasting and predictable. Anderson speaks of the power of nationalisms versus their near philosophical incoherence (Anderson 1991:5). His ability to provide an explanation for the ironies of communal life through exploration of the bonds created by daily rituals proved highly significant to social historians and other scholars seeking to explain how social identities were generated and maintained. The social imaginary, by shifting the analytical focus away from neo-evolutionary frameworks and toward the reproduction of identities through social interactions, returns to us the individual as a meaningful agent and in fact is the only means by which we can understand cultural phenomena such as communities, the division of labor, social reproduction, and many other practices of human society. As Charles Taylor has said, "The social imaginary is not a set of ideas; rather it is what enables, through making sense of, the practices of a society" (Taylor 2002:91).

This is not to argue that archaeologists and other social scientists should abandon the search for broad patterns of behavior and focus instead on the actions of a single individual person or object. The framework for understanding social identities such as age, gender, or nation provided by the concept of the social imaginary relies upon the identification of meaningful communities, large collectivities of people who may not know one another yet share a sense of membership and connection (Anderson 1991:6). Anderson was focused on the emergence of a shared national identity among previously discrete groups of Creoles within a colonial setting, but his argument that collectivities exist in the mind and are created through shared praxis is a powerful one for archaeologists. The nature of the discipline of archaeology is to recover evidence of practices shared by many people, either over a great period of time or across space in a single moment in time. Archaeologists are uniquely positioned to test Anderson's theory of imagined communities and to identify the specific materializations of identity construction, maintenance, and resistance. Anderson even anticipates this, in a brief discussion of the imagined reality of the "ancient world," which he proposes must have been "overwhelmingly visual and aural" (Anderson 1991:23).

The addition of the imagined community conceptualization can make a significant contribution to the analysis of ancient social identities within archaeology. The archaeology of identity has grown over the past twenty years to become a rich and diverse field of inquiry that insists on the active role of the individual in strategic decisions about social identities which intersect and evolve (Bernardini 2005, Cuddy 2007, Gardner 2007, Janusek 2004, Orser 2001, Varien and Potter 2008). While the choices of an individual are constrained in certain ways, both by the entanglements of certain identities with our bodies and by the shared perception of social boundaries, members of a social identity share a repertory of acceptable actions and consequences that they may choose to perform or resist in varying degrees. As individual needs and historical contexts change, strategic decisions can be made about which identity to emphasize and collective practices can be adjusted accordingly. As William Isbell argues, this allows archaeologists (and I would suggest all social historians) to identify alternative discourses of community as well as change that is contingent and calculated (Isbell 2000:250).

Such a perspective is important in archaeology now as we move away from earlier traditions of analysis that viewed identities such as status and gender as inherent and the relationship between material culture and identity as unproblematic. The processual paradigm that dominated much of archaeological research in the latter part of the twentieth century moved the field of archaeology away from an antiquarian fascination with tombs and toward questions of far-reaching significance to social science overall. However, within this paradigm there was little room left for analysis of the role of the individual in social structures and, indeed, entire cultures were treated more or less as the agents of social change. Statements such as this one made in the middle of the twentieth century are familiar: "There is, then, some indication that the Postclassic Maya of northern Yucatán were urbanized and that the concept of the city or town as a fortified position had come into vogue" (Willey 1966:133). The neo-evolutionary approach was concerned with change on such a large scale that variation within communities was obscured and the processes by which social collectivities formed were modeled as natural, inevitable, and empirical. Of tremendous use to the comparative study of cultural evolution, these rigid 'cultures' were ascribed the ability to emerge, coalesce, stratify, and collapse, despite the fact that scholars always understood it was the actions of humans, individuals acting as part of social networks and collectivities, that truly caused any of these significant social phenomena to come to pass.

Margarita Díaz-Andreu and Sam Lucy summarize the shift that has occurred within archaeology toward the analysis of social identities as contingent, critical components of social interaction by focusing on the role of material culture in solidifying a shared imaginary: "While people are reproducing the material conditions of their lives, they are both reproducing their society and their personal and group identities" (Díaz-Andreu et al. 2005:6). Archaeology is uniquely positioned to contribute to the emerging field of Identity Studies by theorizing how objects have agency in social interactions. Our entire discipline is premised upon the material world as an active participant in human culture, and, following Bruno Latour, we have now come to refine our earlier tendencies to see pottery types evolve into other pottery types as the misperception of the significant agency objects have within networks of actors. Latour urges us not to erect an artificial boundary between human and nonhuman actors, but to see both as actors (Johnson 1988, Latour 1993, 1999). Some would say archaeology has spent too much time thinking about objects and not enough about humans, but the importance of Latour's argument is neither the objects nor the humans but his emphasis on the ideas that connect them into a relational network of associations. Like the biographical approach to objects, contemporary approaches to the archaeological study of social identities question simple or naturalized associations between objects and bodies or objects and structures, instead looking for layers of meaning and intentional choice.

THE ROLE OF ARCHAEOLOGY WITHIN IDENTITY STUDIES

As a field with an emergent set of questions that transgress historical boundaries of anthropology, philosophy, or other disciplines concerned with the human experience, Identity Studies needs contributions that explore the materialization of social identities in order to provide a deeper context for understanding the evolution of social categories. Whether the focus is on identities as oppressive and imposed or as the inescapable result of social experiences, a contextual perspective on social identities is essential. Philosopher Linda Martin Alcoff, in her recent argument against the dismissal of identities as inherently unjust (specifically the perception of identity politics as exclusivist, imposed, and self-interested), argues we need a better accounting of the lived experience of identity in order to counter such criticisms (Alcoff 2006:41). Citing sociologist Manuel Castells's work on identity-based movements (Castells 1997), Alcoff argues social identities can operate as special interest groups, but that is not what they are. She notes the necessarily collective nature of social identities and their function as a "generative source of meaning" (Alcoff 2006:41). She calls for contextual analyses that explore the operation of concepts *within contexts* (emphasis added) rather than assuming that concepts such as gender, race, and other "visible identities" operate in a similar manner across specific historical or cultural contexts:

> Identities are best understood as ways in which we and others around us represent our material ties to historical events and social structures. Those events may be traumatic and those structures may be oppressive, but this indicates that the events need to be carefully understood and analyzed and that the structures need to be transformed, not that the identities themselves need to be left behind. (Alcoff 2006:287)

One method to understand better the relationship between identities and oppression is to interrogate the origin of the identity or its development over time. Archaeologists of gender have done exactly this through their exploration of how gender idealizations were manipulated to serve the expansionist demands of early states (Ardren et al. 2010; Brumfiel 1991; Costin 1996, 1998; Joyce 2000a; Wright 1996). At Xuenkal, excavations showed a dramatic increase in the quantity of tools used to produce cloth at the same moment in time when tribute demands fueled the growth of Chichen Itza as a regional capital (Ardren et al. 2010). Spinning tools were found in domestic contexts alongside the remains of other craft production, which suggests entire families produced goods at unprecedented levels. Historical expectations of a woman's skill in cloth production, which throughout the Classic period was directed primarily to the needs of her family, were manipulated to generate a greater surplus than ever before. In this situation, the gendered social identity of women became oppressive because the tribute-based regional economy relied upon a naturalized understanding of women as the only textile producers. Some women may have resisted this distortion of their habitual ritual of inclusion enacted through spinning and weaving, but our excavated sample only shows the place in which the demands were attempted to be met. The performance of the social imaginary of femaleness in Terminal Classic Xuenkal changed, but not through natural evolution or devolution— far from it. The political climate of the moment facilitated the ability of individual elites to expand the boundaries of expected performance through a coercive dialogue about appropriate work, artisanship, and the social networks that bound Xuenkal to Chichen Itza. In this case, archaeology illuminates what Alcoff calls the "material ties to historical events" and contextualizes the heavy burden of women's craft work within a historical moment of shifting political boundaries with associated economic obligations.

In her blistering indictment of the ways in which women and blacks are denied the presumption of privacy that modern America holds as a fundamental aspect of personhood, bioethicist Karla F. C. Holloway documents the ways public (or visible) aspects of race and gender make bodies vulnerable to violation. From medical experimentation to interracial marriage and reproduction, identity has played a major role in the development of medicine within the United States. Holloway argues that black and female bodies have been considered available for a certain kind of public scrutiny that did not extend to white males (Holloway 2011:25). She relies primarily upon case law but supplements these documents with selections from literature: "The complex landscapes from which fictional characters emerge might stand in for the texts of fuller narratives *that do not often (or appropriately) make it into case law* (emphasis added) or case narratives" (Holloway 2011:10). Holloway appreciates the way literature does not patrol its own boundaries in the same rigorous manner as medicine and law, but the same could be said of the material record. A fundamental precept of the discipline of archaeology is that the lives and actions of those excluded from the written record (for whatever reason) are recorded in the same detail as those who controlled the production of historical documents. Archaeologists working on recovering the 'invisible' history of marginalized groups, or those for whom no written records exist, often discover a rich narrative of their lives in the material remains, no matter how modest, which these groups left behind.

Archaeologists of childhood have long grappled with the perception that data on ancient children does not exist since children so rarely produced texts of their own (Baxter 2005, 2008; Kamp 2002; Lally and Moore 2011). When I began research on *The Social Experience of Childhood in Ancient Mesoamerica* (Ardren and Hutson 2006), a number of colleagues expressed their frustration that they could not contribute since they were unaware of any archaeological data on ancient Maya children. Yet of course young people were ubiquitous in ancient cultures, and as our analytical frameworks have matured, we now ask better questions of the archaeological record to solicit information about their lives. We may not have many hieroglyphic passages that describe Maya children, but hundreds of ancient households have been excavated by archaeologists, and the vast majority of them were filled with children, their activities, and the material residue of such behaviors.

In his analysis of the Maya Classic-period households unusually well preserved by the Laguna Caldera volcanic eruption, archaeologist Payson Sheets has been particularly attuned to the ways households were designed to accommodate the presence of children (Sheets 2002, 2006). Sheets notes artifact disposal patterns that are best explained through a consideration of the presence of young people, such as the practice of caching obsidian blades in roof thatch where they would be out of reach of children and the absence of artifacts or debris found on interior floors where such materials would be dangerous to crawlers (Sheets 2006:44–46). Evidence for the role of a child in creating the material record of her household compound was also recovered by Sheets in the form of a small deposit of twenty ceramic sherds collected from different pots in association with a rudimentary miniature ceramic pot that retained a child's fingerprints (Sheets 2006:44). Sheets sees this deposit, found on the front porch of a domestic structure abandoned due to the eruption, as the play area of a child, someone who was perhaps learning to work with clay in order to take on pottery production for her family and perhaps learning the base twenty numerical system of the Maya. A gendered activity in many Maya communities today, pottery production may have been an activity in which this young girl spent time with her mother both learning the art of pottery and learning her gender. Her visible identities of child and female are recorded in the material record of this modest household that would never have been the focus of Maya written records or public art.

In the northern lowlands, Scott Hutson identified a similar type of deposit that he suggested represented objects left by a child, although in this case the context was a child-only space, hidden from adult view in abandoned structures (Hutson 2006). Structures in two adjacent residential groups, the 'Aak and Muuch groups, had a single shell fragment left in the middle of the otherwise clean floors during the time when these structures were abandoned (Hutson 2006:118). Noting that deserted places and especially abandoned structures are common areas for children's play in many cultures, and that small, unusual items are often picked up by children to be redeposited outside their normal context, Hutson helps us to understand how children experienced the urban landscape of ancient Chunchucmil (Hutson 2006:120). These shells in empty rooms might be evidence of the culture of childhood with its secret places and unusual souvenirs, key components of how children learn, explore, and grow. Ancient Maya writing, tightly controlled by the dominant sectors of elite culture, did not concern itself with the lives of children except in the rare moments when child kings took the throne. The northern lowlands was much less literate than other Maya areas, and as in so many places, archaeology is the only way we can consider, as Holloway asks us to, the complications of a richly textured rendering of certain vulnerable subjects. Through Hutson's work we see that children in ancient Maya society had time to themselves, free from adult supervision or family responsibilities, and that they interacted with the city on their own terms. While many scholars interested in Identity Studies will continue to work with documentary resources, the set of questions that defines this field call into question the reliance on these typically hegemonic sources only. Thus archaeology is uniquely positioned to contribute to such conversations by theorizing how objects have agency in social imaginaries and especially by making visible those who are not represented or are under-represented in dominant textual sources.

SOCIAL IDENTITIES OF ANCIENT MAYA SOCIETY

In this book I have argued that social identities, or the communities we build to facilitate social relations and understand difference, were not only a crucial component of ancient Maya culture, but that these shared communities structured much of life in the Classic period, just as they structure much of our lives today. While identities are of interest to us today, given our ability to choose and shift between various social selves, I do not assume that these questions that are so important in the present were also and always important in the past. A shared understanding of how people fit into communities, their expectations and notions, shaped how labor was organized in ancient Maya society; these ideas structured the use and design of space, how memory was deployed to make sense of time, who had responsibility for ceremonies and rites of passage, how people dressed, and what they ate. Each of these shared imagined communities evolved, and while certain elements remained the same for a very long time indeed, with some features that continue today in a form related to the past, other components have disappeared. Historical conditions cause change in the social imaginary as individuals make choices about how to perpetuate or reject elements of shared practice. While attachment to the *cah*, or town of origin, remains a powerful element of modern Maya identity, it has also evolved over time to accommodate modern travel habits. Today people who are born in Oxkutzcab, Yucatán, but emigrate to San Francisco or Dallas remain Oxkutzcabeños long after they leave México and circulate this identity through strong social and economic ties to Yucatán, perhaps as pre-Columbian Maya may have retained a sense of identification with their *cah* when they relocated to Mayapan in the Postclassic period (Adler 2004, Fortuny Loret de Mola 2009, Restall 1997). I argue that social identities are important to many modern scholars, but that they were also a fundamental way in which life was ordered and culture reproduced within Classic Maya society, based on the strong patterning of material evidence discussed in earlier chapters.

Certain social imaginaries that exert profound influence in the lives of Mayan-speaking people today are related to the social imaginaries I have attempted to reconstruct for the Classic period. Elements of the gendered order of work described in this book for ancient times remain part of the social imaginary of gender in Yucatán today, although with the incorporation of strategic changes in response to the modern social moment. M. Bianet Castellanos explores how state policies, ethnopolitics, racial hierarchies, and the global economy have influenced local conceptualizations of gender within Yucatec Maya families (Castellanos 2010). Focusing on the extended families of a small village where the majority of young unmarried adults travel to Cancun for wage labor, Castellanos argues the *maquiladora* (factory) and tourism industries target native women for positions with the least public interaction and opportunities for social mobility because local gender idealizations encourage women to excel only in the domestic realm (Castellanos 2010:80). "As guardians of tradition, girls were expected to leave Kuchmil upon marriage, but not before," and the community approved of girls helping other family members, even outside the home, but it was not appropriate for women to work outside the household because they could not be protected from harm, either sexual or physical (Castellanos 2010:89). Domestic work is preferred by these Maya women because it is perceived as less risky (to themselves, their safety, and their reputations) than hotel work where they are likely to come into contact with strangers. It would be an oversimplification to claim any enduring or natural association between Maya women and the domestic arts, but yet the social imaginary of modern Maya femaleness still circulates ideas that women should excel in this realm, that they are rewarded when they do so, and that transgressing this realm is fraught with uncertainty. Specific behaviors such as highly gendered household duties and the practice of teaching food preparation to primarily female children maintain and reinforce this imaginary today.

Other elements of the gendered social imaginary have changed dramatically since the Classic period. Ideas about the gendered complementarity of divine forces such as the creator couple Itzamna and Chak Chel are no longer part of the discourse circulated by Mayan-speaking people about their gods (Vail and Stone 2002, Knowlton 2010). The names of Maya deities recovered by scholars and published in popular media are once again a component and marker of Maya identity, such as the use of an early twentieth-century scholarly drawing of Ix Chel as the emblem of the Playa del Carmen, Quintana Roo taxi drivers union (Ardren 2006). But the overwhelming majority of Yucatec speakers identifies today as Christian and expresses a gendered ideology that privileges a single, masculine creator god. Throughout the New World, the effect of forced Christianization on indigenous conceptualizations of divine authority was profound and lasting. It was certainly strategic for Maya speakers who lived during the Colonial period to find ways to conceal native religious practice, an effort that served to alter the social imaginary of gender in countless ways (Knowlton 2010). The Spanish struggled to prevent elder women from participating in ritual roles within Yucatec society and eventually resorted to violent suppression of all forms of indigenous ritual, although John Chuchiak and other ethnohistorians have revealed the clandestine perpetuation of highly distinctive Maya practices such as penile bloodletting and child sacrifice well into the seventeenth and eighteenth centuries (Anda, Tiesler, and Zabala 2004; Chuchiak 2000, 2001, 2007; Sigal 2000). As Pete Sigal states, "Catholicism colonized women through a new understanding of gender" (Sigal 2000:126).

Perhaps more influential than the banning of certain practices (which moved from public to private venues but did not disappear for centuries) was the indoctrination of Maya people into a social imaginary in which women did not circulate their connection to divine power through public ritual but rather through individual piety and the much more limited avenues available within the Spanish American Catholic paradigm. Sigal argues a Mayanized Virgin Mary who incorporated some aspects of the pre-Columbian Moon Goddess bridged a gap between Catholicism and certain elements of pre-Columbian gendered power (Sigal 2000:126). Although changes wrought in the social imaginary of gender during the Colonial period are far beyond the scope of this volume, it is clear that choices made at that time about daily practices changed the way in which the social imaginary was circulated and thus perpetuated. While some elements of the background understanding about idealized gender such as the work appropriate for each gender were maintained under colonialism, other elements such as the parallelism or complementarity of creator gods and their religious specialists were largely abandoned. By focusing on practices and material culture as discourse, the social imaginary allows us to see processes of contingent change that do not imply either a total rejection or wholesale replacement of earlier identities.

Other scholars of pre-Columbian Mesoamerica have also found social identities to be meaningful components of the communities they study. As part of a general movement within archaeology to recover the individual and her relationship to the collective as a meaningful unit of analysis, and to correct an earlier vision of identity as inherent, such an approach is particularly welcome within Maya studies. Despite the ability to read the individual names of rulers and their retinue, Maya studies remains a field preoccupied with the study of broad cultural processes that leave little room for understanding how ancient Maya people experienced daily life or the challenges they encountered, an emerging paradigm known as the archaeology of the human experience (Hegmon 2013). To offer only one example, Mayanist scholars continue to debate the role of environmental change, endemic warfare, and overpopulation in the social transformation that led thousands of people to abandon the royal urban centers of the southern lowlands at the end of the Classic period, a social transformation known popularly as the Maya Collapse. But there has yet to be inquiry into how such a profound change in daily life was understood by those who undertook the radical decision to move out of their urban homes and adopt a new way of life. Too often our interpretations close off the role of strategic actors who, as a group, made the choice that their social identities were not dependent upon living in an urban context under semi-divine authorities. Attention to how social identities were maintained and perpetuated in the past fosters the ability to see both individual actors and their collectivities. This volume is part of an evolving conversation about the materialization of ancient Maya social identities grounded in the rich data available to archaeologists. Attention to the archaeology of human experience can help us understand the choices ancient people made and how they decided to create better ways of living together.

In a recent study of three ancient societies within modern-day Honduras, Julia Hendon looks at processes of remembering and forgetting in order to explore how ancient people created meaning in their daily lives and how the material world around them was an active part of that process (Hendon 2010). Using multiple lines of evidence, but grounded in her extensive archaeological excavations of households at the seventh- through eleventh-century sites of Cerro Palenque, Copan, and within the region of Cuyumapa, Hendon utilizes a relational approach to identity and explores how memory communities were generated. Memory is closely bundled with identity for Hendon, who sees both as practice-based, generated through relationships and historical contexts, and materialized in the archaeological record. Hendon focuses on how the ancient inhabitants at these sites formed themselves into enduring social groups through practices such as crafting and the ball game. As identities were created, they were perpetuated through memory—memories of practices, encounters, collective experiences—a process Hendon describes as bringing the past into the present (Hendon 2010:14). By looking at the agency of objects as tools in helping people to remember, Hendon opens up her analysis to include characteristics of ancient Mesoamerican thought, including a sense of many objects such as houses or sculpture, as animate and sentient. Learning and making objects is important to the constitution of identity communities for Hendon, but so is the circulation of certain objects through spaces and practices that "enchant" them with social significance as icons of meaning. While she does not use the language of the social imaginary, Hendon illuminates the material record of three very distinct archaeological areas by exploring both the relational and generative practices that created multiple memory communities and considering how those practices allow us to approach a unique historical consciousness.

In her recent synthetic treatment of ancient Maya economies, Patricia McAnany finds that the multiple social identities of artisans and craft producers are a key element to consider in our attempts to comprehend the many ways economic processes were enmeshed within Maya society (McAnany 2010). Production of textiles, stone or shell tools, pottery, and nearly every other commodity occurred within a ritualized practice that "imbued production with profound meaning and contoured the social identity of those undertaking production activities" (McAnany 2010:xvi). McAnany found it was not possible to carve out the economic sector from other aspects of ancient Maya society, especially from the producers themselves, who were locked in a relational circulation of producing and being produced by the objects they made. Her analysis notes the use of craft production as a metaphor for the generation of human life in the Popol Vuh origin cycle, as she argues that the crafting of goods circulated profoundly significant information about shared values that were involved in propping up the identities of producers and consumers. Artisanship was part of both elite and commoner social identities, although it also served to reinforce social hierarchies that defined the difference between these two communities. This study opens up the exploration of how Maya society was materially reproduced for millennia—we have described the materialization of this history for more than a century, but we have only begun to ask questions about how this culture maintained production through such dramatic social changes and, indeed, how it contributed to those changes. Understanding the social identities of artisan production and their intersections with gender- or community-based social imaginaries promises to illuminate the active role of individual choices in Maya cultural reproduction.

Returning to the geographical heart of this book, Scott Hutson's recent study of relational identities as evidenced in the material record of the northern Maya lowland urban city of Chunchucmil also contributes to the emerging dialogue in Mayanist archaeology regarding Identity Studies (Hutson 2010). Hutson uses a relational perspective grounded in his detailed excavations of various household groups and extensive interactions with the modern Yucatec Maya inhabitants of the agricultural land also known as the ancient city of Chunchucmil. Like the authors discussed above, he sees identity as derived from the interplay of objects, activities, and the social relations in which they are entangled (Hutson 2010:2). Noting that the individualized self as understood within Western modernity may be a wholly inappropriate construction for understanding ancient societies, Hutson looks at the materialization of daily, embodied practices, especially what he refers to as "dwelling." What I might call rituals of inclusion, or the situated practices that constitute key components of the social imaginary, Hutson describes with the concept of "dwelling" as a way to approach and reveal social relationships. Dwelling is the bridge between archaeology and subjectivity for Hutson, a concept that allows him to look at daily practices and their material residues as the result of individual agency as well as social expectation. Hutson uses the term "subjectification" to describe the dialogue between these two aspects of human existence through which humans become members of social identities or communities. Activities recorded in household groups such as fiber processing, food preparation, and ritual were all quintessential relational activities that circulated ideas about membership and what Hutson calls personhood. Appreciating who performed these activities and how they understood them opens up our ability to see larger processes of social reproduction and change.

Social Identities in the Classic Maya Northern Lowlands is situated within this emergent conversation about social categories and how they illuminate our ability to see evidence for contingent change and dynamic actors in ancient Maya society. Emerging from my understanding of gender as a constantly evolving social framework for making sense of difference, I approach social identities as collectivities that are both essential to human society and restrictive. Most importantly, they are constructed, often through repeated behaviors that leave a material residue accessible through archeological methodologies. This interplay of objects and practices occurs within a network of ideas that I have called the social imaginary, after the work of Benedict Anderson, Charles Taylor, and others. The concept of the social imaginary moves the focus of analysis from innate or unproblematized identities to fluid collectivities that need constant reinforcement. Like Hendon, who argues that identity is closely interconnected with memory and that both were generated through social practices, I have suggested that daily practices, or rituals of inclusion such as food preparation or shrine construction, were fundamental to the creation and maintenance of layered social identities. I have built upon the analysis of McAnany, who suggested producers of crafts and the products they made were locked in a relational exchange of identity creation by arguing that the background social imaginary shared by members of an identity group, such as artisans, provided them with a repertoire of possible options for what to create and how to create. By noting how children are the most obviously relational identity group, given that so much of what it means to be a child is determined by adults who stand outside the collectivity of the young, I have attempted to show that all social identities are relational and often reinforced by social hierarchies. Like Hutson and the other authors mentioned here, I have looked for daily, embodied practices in order to understand social relationships. The nature of Classic Maya urban life is particularly compelling, and I hope to have contributed to our analyses of the circulations that perpetuated urban life in Chunchucmil for hundreds of years. Along with Hutson and others, I am interested in how the past contributes to contemporary Maya identities, and my thinking on this matter has evolved to recognize the relational manner in which the archaeological record is deployed by modern Mayan-speaking people in the northern lowlands.

A DASH OF ARCHAEOLOGY IN MODERN MAYANESS

As an archaeologist interested in social identities, in the course of long days excavating I have shared many conversations with Maya friends and workers about their social imaginaries—what it means to be a woman in a traditional village in Yucatán, what it means to be a college student in Mérida whose family lives in a rural village, what it means to live in a landscape that tourists want to visit. The people I have come to know well in Yaxunah, Espita, Chunchucmil, and Kochol choose among their social identities given the situational context in which they find themselves, and their choices have structured our interactions. When the time is right, an adult woman with children from these villages can choose to inhabit the social imaginary of motherhood, an imaginary we share, and for a time we will understand ourselves to be part of a collective of people who share the same hopes and fears, who conduct the same daily rituals of caring for children or taking them to school. That same woman, on another day or in another situation, can emphasize our differences and her Maya or Mexican identity in opposition to my foreigner or *dzul* (Yucatec for white person) identity. On both days, a set of actions with associated material objects would partner with those identities, and a set of spaces and memories would be experienced as the discourse about membership proceeded. Neither day would be more real or authentic. Each of us engages multiple social identities and social imaginaries—we make strategic decisions about inclusion all day long, and given the particular social context we may choose to embrace or resist an identity in order to facilitate relationships. The social imaginary we share provides the mutual background understanding that makes such choices possible. The competing discourses about what an identity means, or how to practice it, are the way in which we create community and set its boundaries.

I return to the ways the social imaginary facilitates our social interactions in order to frame a discussion of the role of archaeological materials and Maya identity in Yucatán today. My intention is not to review the vast literature debating the presence or absence of an authentic Maya identity in Yucatán—this is an important intellectual conversation that has been well summarized recently by others (Hutson 2010; Magnoni, Ardren, and Hutson 2007; Reyes-Cortes and Rodriguez 2007). I hope to add to this conversation the observation that the modern social imaginary of Mayaness in Yucatán draws upon the archaeological record, but it does so in a selective and strategic manner that responds to a variety of sociopolitical factors. This perspective helps resolve some of the confusion and debate about why certain people will self-proclaim a Maya identity while many others do not, why speaking the Yucatec Maya language does not always correlate with Maya identity, and why the friends and colleagues of archaeologists are often more likely to embrace, or inhabit, a self-description as Maya.

Araceli Cab Cumi is a distinguished politician who was born and lived her entire life in Maxcanu, Yucatán, the county seat for the modern village of Chunchucmil. She is a longtime Maya politician, a grassroots leader and political activist since 1960. She served two terms in the Yucatecan State Congress, once in the mid-1970s and the second in the early 1990s (Martin 2007:1). Cab Cumi is also a poet, and her work has been published widely in Yucatán following a biography by the ethnographer Kathleen Rock Martin. Interviewing Cab Cumi in her congressional office in Mérida as well as in her home in Maxcanu, Martin found her a gracious and fascinating individual, filled with pride in her Maya heritage. A natural politician, Cab Cumi could shift between Spanish and Yucatec Maya depending on her audience, and her political activism was rooted in her lived experience as a Maya woman. Throughout her career she worked for socioeconomic equity, enhanced professional and educational opportunities for women, and recognition of the humanity and wisdom of the Maya people (Martin 2007:9). As part of her arguments for the inclusion of Maya people in public policy decision making, Cab Cumi emphasized the role of Maya people in Yucatec history and culture, with special emphasis on the contributions of women to the construction of México as a nation. She also made frequent reference to the archaeological sites of Yucatán, especially the Puuc sites near her hometown, and deliberately drew upon their presence as an indication of the longevity and strength of Maya culture:

> I HAVE HERE (My ruins speak)
> Stop, . . . and listen to me
> I want you to relive
> our passionate history
> and . . . while you listen to my voice
> telling our life, make
> echoes in your memory
> relive with me
> with a common remembrance
> I am . . . the voice of your memory!
> [. . .] I am Oxkintok, I am Entsil
> And in X-pukil-Tun is my echo . . .
>
> ARACELI CAB CUMI, TRANSLATION BY
> KATHLEEN R. MARTIN 2007:151

Cab Cumi is an extraordinary woman and someone who has chosen to embrace the identity of Maya despite the often pejorative and always complex terrain that accompanies this social identity in modern Yucatán. Focusing primarily on the relationships of the archaeological past to this identity, we can see that the imagery of archaeological ruins is often deployed or circulated to create a sense of communion with others, those whom the author does not know but expects will recognize the mention of Oxkintok as a meaningful element of shared identity. (Entsil is the local Maya name for the largest pyramid at the ancient city of Oxkintok [Martin 2007:291]. X-pukil-Tun is a cave near Oxkintok and Maxcanu [Martin 2007:291].) In this way she connects with all Yucatecans who maintain a fierce interest in many aspects of history as a key element of their collective identity. But Cab Cumi goes further than this and claims she is the beautiful ruined city on a hilltop, she is Oxkintok and Entsil. This is an intellectual territory reserved for Maya speakers because the ruins are widely understood by modern Yucatecans to be related to Maya people. The nature of that relationship is contested under constant discussion in Yucatán, as various descendant communities intersect with the apparatus of the nation-state and tourism industries. But what is significant here is that Araceli has made a claim to a certain part of the landscape that few would dispute is hers to claim and that she perceives as a meaningful connection. Her mention of this site in a poem that calls for the world to listen to what she has to say circulates the archaeological past as part of her social imaginary of Mayaness. She is calling on the powerful way in which memory and identity are interlocked with the landscape. Even though very few of her listeners would have memories of direct personal experience of Oxkintok, Cab Cumi calls on them to remember and reproduce her as an inheritor of ancient Maya ruins. We must understand this as a strategic emphasis given Cab Cumi's somewhat unusual position as an outsider-insider within the state government. Like dressing in a *huipil*, or traditional Maya female clothing, while attending congressional sessions or speaking Yucatec Maya to the waiters at the congressional cafeteria, claims to the archaeological heritage of Yucatán by Araceli were not inevitable or obvious; they were materializations of deliberate choices that invoked certain aspects of her social imaginary. Mayaness was not an inescapable or natural identity for Araceli; it was constructed, relational, and deliberate.

Archaeological sites and their iconic elements such as hieroglyphic inscriptions or carved stone façades appear in the poetry of additional modern Yucatec Maya writers such as Briceida Cuevas Cob and Feliciano Sánchez Chan, where they intersect with other social identities such as femaleness or *campesino* (agriculturalist). These ancient elements of the landscape also appear in community histories written by local schoolteachers or part-time historians, such as the work *Breves datos historicos y culturales del municipio de Hunucma*, a history of Hunucma, Yucatán. Described in a recent study of the enduring relationship between *el pueblo* (the town) and Yucatec Maya identity, Paul Eiss discusses *Breves datos* and its author Anacleto Cetina Aguilar (Cetina Aguilar 1996, Eiss 2010). Cetina Aguilar was born in Hunucma, a town to the west of Mérida not far from Chunchucmil with a long occupational history from the pre-Columbian period to the present. Ancient house mounds are found next to the sixteenth-century church in Hunucma and throughout many of the surrounding villages, and an ancient raised road or *sacbe* runs through the middle of the town (Eiss 2010:257). Cetina Aguilar describes his grandparents as slaves on a nearby hacienda. His sons-in-law are a fisherman and a taxi driver, and he was the first in his family to learn to read and the first to complete primary school (Eiss 2010:246). Significantly, prior to his current position as a schoolteacher in Hunucma, Cetina worked for a time in a Mérida bookstore and then as a cultural agent for the Instituto Nacional de Indigenista. While in this position he lived in the most remote Maya villages in the state of Yucatán and was charged with the "Castilianization" of Yucatec Mayan–speaking children through instruction in Spanish (Eiss 2010:247). He grew disillusioned with this position and returned to his hometown in the 1980s.

Cetina is proud of Hunucma and describes it as a Maya town with Yucatecan history. In addition to an illustrated book of poetry, Cetina's life work has been the *Breve datos*, which he published in 1996 with funding from a federal grant competition (Eiss 2010:255). In his history of the town, which begins in the Paleolithic era with rising sea levels that leave Hunucma at the northernmost tip of the peninsula, Cetina describes the town's pre-Columbian demography and weaves the ancient occupation of the area into the better-known modern and colonial histories. The ancient Maya cities are given as much attention as eighteenth-century invasions by pirates and a nineteenth-century visit by Empress Carlota of México, who stopped to bathe in Hunucma on her way to Mérida. *Breves datos* is part of a tradition of local histories written by proud inhabitants of the many villages and towns long excluded from the dominant written history of México and Yucatán. Gualberto Mena, longtime schoolteacher in the village of Chunchucmil, has written a personal history of his hometown, and similar documents were shared with me in Yaxunah and Yaxcaba. In each of these overlooked sources, while the term "Maya" appears infrequently, the ubiquitous archaeological ruins that spread across the northern lowlands figure significantly in local identity construction. The authors chronicle and explain these features in different ways, but it is always with a possessive and protective attitude that clearly conveys a close tie between a sense of place and local identity. As we saw in chapter 5, space and identity are locked in a generative relationship just as memory and identity serve to define one another. When connections between the three are intentionally invoked, the interdependency between understanding and practice is circulated, and the social imaginary reinforced. Land ownership and practices that perform this value have been noted by many scholars as an important touchstone to a relational transmission of identity in the northern Maya lowlands today (Brown 1999, Hostettler 2001, Hutson 2010).

While the writing of modern authors such as Cab Cumi, Cetina, and others uses the landscape, including archaeological features of the northern Maya lowlands, to help circulate the idea that Mayaness is tied in a unique and enduring way to the history of place, we must acknowledge that pre-Columbian elements feature as a relatively small part of how these writers portray or circulate their social imaginary of Mayaness. It does not diminish the significance of archaeology to recognize that culinary heritage, language, and the natural world all figure more prominently than the ancient past in how this social imaginary is conveyed. This may be the result of strategic actions taken over the hundreds of years of the colonial and historic periods, and certainly it is a predictable outcome of colonized educational practices that emphasized the history of the Mexican nation over regional histories such as the Classic Maya. Modern Maya identity construction is a complex net of interchanges, set within a historical and rapidly globalizing context. The point that is most salient is that while archaeologists have often assumed a connection between modern Mayan-speaking people and the ancient remains, the nature of this connection is evolving and contingent, not inevitable (Castañeda 2004, Hervik 2003, Hutson 2010, Restall 2004). As Mayan-speaking people increase their contact with the material remains of pre-Columbian people known as Maya, they may grow to see a connection or they may grow to resist an affiliation some feel has been imposed upon them by the scholarly community (Breglia 2006). At the risk of repetition, material culture provides a way for people to engage in discourse about identity. That discourse can center on difference or on continuity; it provides and reproduces the background understanding that enables members to make decisions and understand their consequences. When writers such as Cab Cumi and Cetina use the materialized remains of what academics have called their ancestors, an attribution that is by no means uncontested, they are choosing to invoke a connection to the past and the moral authority of history. When a teenager from Yaxunah chooses not to speak Yucatec at home, despite the overwhelming consensus of his elder relatives that this is a crucial element of cultural performance, he is likewise engaged in a discourse about modern Mayaness. Pablo, the son of my close friend Deysi Tamay Yam, understands his options and the consequences of crossing certain boundaries precisely because he shares a social imaginary of Mayaness with his family and village.

Deysi and her family live in Yaxunah, the modern village adjacent to the archaeological ruins of the same name (a silent h is added to the name of the contemporary settlement). I met Deysi in 1989, when I first arrived in Yaxunah and we were both young—we are separated in age by only five years. Although she married much earlier than I, we have children the same age and have shared many experiences over the years. Deysi and her husband, Valentin, live on the edge of Yaxunah in a compound of homes connected by shared patrilineal descent. Her father-in-law assists the local *h'men* (shaman) with traditional Maya ceremonies such as the *hetzmek* and *cha chaak*, the family maintains a *milpa* and carves wooden sculptures for sale in the nearby tourist market, and Pablo is involved in the "Jaguares" program run by the Yaxunah Cultural Center for high school students. This program targets promising young adults for additional educational opportunities and supports families who shoulder the cost of sending their children to the nearby county seat to complete high school. In a recent conversation with Deysi and Valentin, I learned that they had been interviewed recently by *National Geographic* on the subject of traditional Maya ritual, and we discussed their concern over how little Yucatec their son chooses to speak. Deysi and Valentin are more interested in language preservation than some other members of Yaxunah, just as they are more involved in traditional Maya rituals than many other members of the village who are primarily Catholic and Pentecostal. Deysi and Valentin will talk at great length about the ruins or rituals because my interest in these subjects has been proved and I express appreciation for their insight. I have seen them avoid these topics in other social situations, such as when interacting with the (non Mayan-speaking) local elementary schoolteacher or when shopping in nearby larger towns. The shared ideas and practices that constitute the social imaginary of Mayaness for Deysi and Valentin, and I would argue for nearly everyone in Yaxunah, are deployed or reserved based on the social relationships in play. Identification with the archaeological ruins, such as replication of designs from the site, can facilitate the sale of wooden carvings in certain contexts while aggravating the hegemonic control of national patrimony by agents of the state in others. It has been fascinating and illuminating to observe how Deysi negotiates quotidian practice. Activities and associated objects such as the daily grinding of corn for her family are sometimes used by her to connect to enduring values of Mayaness. The performance of gendered physical labor reproduces quintessential Maya food. At other times these same actions circulate a connection to modern dietary and sanitation concerns that are part of the social imaginary of motherhood across México. These discourses are not in competition as much as they are complementary depending upon the agendas and reciprocal relationships invoked.

The relatively minor and contingent role that the archaeological past plays in the modern social imaginary of Yaxunah Mayaness is also materialized in the local Cultural Center. Inaugurated in 2010 after many years of conversations within the village about what type of facility would best serve their needs, the center is staffed by Yaxuneros and funded by a board of directors that includes community members as well as interested parties

FIGURE 6.1. *Maya heritage mural chosen by Yaxunah community members for the Yaxunah Cultural Center. Nubia Montserrat Alvarez López, artist. Photograph by Grace Bascope, used with permission.*

with nonprofit organizational experience from Mérida and the United States. During the Selz Foundation Yaxuna Archaeological Project, conversations between the archaeologists and community members about the possibility of retaining control of artifacts within the village evolved into discussion of museums, laboratories, and research libraries. While these were interesting exchanges, none of the facilities provided what the community needed other than the opportunity to attract tourism.

After many years of conversation, my colleague Grace Bascope, an anthropologist with more than twenty years of experience in the village of Yaxunah, opened the Cultural Center in collaboration with leaders of the village and other interested parties. The facility has two buildings set within a botanical garden. One building, decorated with a mural entitled "Maya Heritage" that was chosen by the community from various submissions, houses a library and provides classroom space for a wide variety of instructional programs identified as useful by the village (Figure 6.1). These include computer skills for teens, alternative energy and agriculture programs, and English language instruction. The other building houses the community museum, which was designed by the board of directors. Current artistic programs of the village and modern Maya rituals such as the *hetzmek* dominate the exhibits, with one corner of the room dedicated to the nearby archaeological ruins. Two replicas of tombs excavated as part of the Selz Foundation Archaeological Project are on display, although these have been included mostly to attract tourists who visit the archaeological site. While national laws that control the curation and display of archaeological materials played a role in how this museum was designed, my argument is that archaeological materializations of Classic Maya culture were not deemed the central component of Mayaness by the modern inhabitants of Yaxunah. Exhibits that convey the nature of local rituals, art, and *milpa* practices were the subjects they wanted to share with visitors and preserve for their own educational purposes. Like the writers discussed above, the Yaxunah Cultural Center references the archeological materials within the local landscape and makes a fierce argument for control of that landscape. But this statement is part of a conversation that has been evolving since the excavations began and is aimed at a particular touristic audience. Objects that are more salient to the contemporary community identity are those that encode a visual memory of ceremonies they have performed collectively and of artistic work folded into the rhythm of everyday life.

CONCLUSION

This chapter has returned us to the broader questions of how an investigation into the daily experiences and choices of ancient Maya people is situated within the new field known as Identity Studies and an emerging paradigm within archaeology of interest in the human experience. I suggested in the introduction to this volume that the exploration of social identities was a means by which we could transgress the artificial boundaries between past and present cultures and even acknowledge how information about the past is contained in the present, as Laurent Olivier would suggest. I wanted to bring the social relationships that form such an important part of human society to the forefront of the conversation about Classic Maya culture in the northern lowlands because I am convinced that the rich data available in the material record allows us to do this, and that the ways humans create, maintain, resist, and alter social relationships will reveal a new and valuable perspective on ancient Maya history.

By suggesting archaeologists explore the social imaginary as a powerful tool for understanding how social identities and collectivities are maintained, I hope to have added an additional perspective to a growing group of voices interested in the relational nature of social networks and their associated daily practices that we see materialized in the archaeological record. Defining the membership of a social identity group is always a complex exercise, but the social imaginary facilitates understanding that identities are both evolving and transitory, meaning individuals make a series of choices on a daily basis about the degree to which they will continue to practice membership in a given collectivity, challenge the boundaries of the collectivity, or step beyond those boundaries to alter or disavow membership. While I have not succeeded as well as I would have liked in identifying materialized evidence for alternative discourses of community, I am confident such stories will emerge with sustained use of the social imaginary perspective. We are asking better questions of the material record that help us come closer to revealing the individuals acting as part of social networks in the past. Individuals and their social collectivities were responsible for the extraordinary accomplishments of the past societies we study today.

The discipline of archaeology has a vital role to play in the broader field of Identity Studies by bringing our sophisticated understanding of how objects have agency within social interactions to scholars less familiar with nontextual material evidence. Relational archaeology holds the promise of making more visible the dynamic interplay between humans and the material world. If the material traces we recover are thought of as agitated, it no longer becomes possible to view the use of certain ornaments or tools as "natural," obvious, or unproblematic. The patterns of material evidence we find are real, and they are the result of deliberate choices. This is where archaeologists have a powerful voice to contribute to Identity Studies overall. We traffic in understanding "material ties to historical events," the phrase philosopher Linda Alcoff uses to describe the origin of social identities. In chapter 3 I argued that the revival of ceremonial architecture in the Late Postclassic period of Yaxuna was crucial to the identity of elites who wished to return to a position of privilege after centuries of domination and defeat. Local elite families, bolstered by the rise of Mayapan and a pan-Mesoamerican economy, drew populations back to the long-abandoned civic architecture of the Classic period. The collective practice of construction and ritual at these new/old shrines facilitated a forgetting of past excesses or failures and a re-imagination of authority. Long-distance trade goods and ritual paraphernalia were once again circulated to reinforce the ability of certain individuals to create connections and provide leadership after a dark period in Maya history. The artifactual residue of the Late Postclassic is best understood as the material correlate of a powerful reinvention. Maya elite families continued to exert significant social influence during the Colonial period and pointed to Mayapan as their origin, while the material record of Mayapan points to even earlier periods of Classic history. The present is always made from the residue of the past, just as the past is understood—remembered or forgotten—in the present. The Late Postclassic shrines of Yaxuna provide a powerful example of how a small but interconnected group of individuals leveraged the memory of a traumatic past to reassert themselves as a particular social identity group within a familiar hierarchy.

The richness of the archaeological record, with its reservoir of objects, structures, residues, bodies, and landscapes, provides a unique data set for the type of deeply textured descriptions that are needed to understand social identities and especially how some are made more vulnerable than others. Rather than relying upon the textual or dominant media of elite culture to understand the lives of children in ancient Maya culture, or how childhood was conceptualized, I used the variety of ways in which commoner children were buried to argue for a multilayered notion of childhood. Young bodies were buried in a socially visible way and with objects identical to those of many adults, suggesting their burial rituals reinforced an understanding of children as members of society with value and connections. I argued the networks between families created by shared offspring may have been more culturally salient given the absence of evidence for elaborate marriage ceremonies. The special vulnerability of this population, as indicated by the presence of large numbers of young individuals in sacrificial contexts like the Great Cenote at Chichen Itza, was connected to a desire to obtain and control the unique spiritual authority of the young as mediators of the ancestral world. The social personhood of certain children was expanded to satisfy the needs of social collectivities, and their visibility, inalienable worth as the glue for social networks, and spiritual authority were deployed for gain by those outside their social identity.

The rich data that I have had the privilege of gathering from the archaeological sites of the northern Maya lowlands speaks powerfully to the ways in which social collectivities shape our daily lives. Our identification with a sense of home or settlement, our remembering and forgetting, and our experience of age and gender are all means by which we make sense of our differences. In ancient Maya culture the material world was actively involved in social interactions and the experiences that generated a sense of belonging. The examples presented in this volume show that Maya people negotiated their choices of community and identity in ways that are recoverable, recognizable, and compelling. The gap between the Classic Maya and our lives today will never go away, nor can it be closed, since it is the gap that provides us the opportunity and motivation to explore the Classic period. But if we acknowledge that our memory of the past is shaped in the here-and-now, we can blur the arbitrary line demarcating ancient from present and perhaps be better able to see information about the past that is part of our lives today.

REFERENCES CITED

Adler, Rachel H.
2004 *Yucatecans in Dallas, Texas: Breaching the Border, Bridging the Distance.* Boston: Pearson.

Alcock, Susan
2002 *Archaeologies of the Greek Past: Landscape, Monuments, and Memories.* Cambridge: Cambridge University Press.

Alcoff, Linda Martin
2006 *Visible Identities: Race, Gender, and the Self.* Oxford: Oxford University Press.

Alexander, Bryant Keith
2006 *Performing Black Masculinity: Race, Culture, and Queer Identity.* Walnut Creek: AltaMira Press.

Alexander, Rani
1993 Colonial Period Archaeology of the Parróquia de Yaxcabá, Yucatan, Mexico: An Ethnohistorical and Site Structural Analysis. PhD diss., University of New Mexico.

Ambrosino, James
2003 The Function of a Maya Palace at Yaxuna: A Contextual Approach. In *Maya Palaces and Elite Residences: An Interdisciplinary Approach,* ed. J. J. Christie, 253-273. Austin: University of Texas Press.

Amrhein, Laura
2001 An Iconographic and Historic Analysis of Terminal Classic Maya Phallic Imagery. PhD diss., Virginia Commonwealth University.

Anda, A. G.
2007 Sacrifice and Ritual Body Mutilation in Postclassical Maya Society: Taphonomy of the Human Remains from Chichen Itza's Cenote Sagrado. In *New Perspectives on Human Sacrifice and Ritual Body Treatments in Ancient Maya Society,* eds. Vera Tiesler and Andrea Cucina, 190-208. New York: Springer.

Anda, A. G., V. Tielser, and P. Zabala
2004 Cenotes, espacios sagrados y la practica del sacrificio humano en Yucatán. *Los Investigadores de la Cultura Maya* 12, tomo 2. Campeche: Universidad Autónoma de Campeche.

Anderson, Benedict
1991   *Imagined Communities: Reflections on the Origin and Spread of Nationalism.* London: Verso.

Anderson, Patricia K.
1983   Maya Cosmology: Quadripartite or Dualistic? Master's thesis, Western Illinois University.

Andrews, Anthony P.
1983   *Maya Salt Production and Trade.* Tucson: University of Arizona Press.
1990   The Fall of Chichen Itza: A Preliminary Hypothesis. *Latin American Antiquity* 1(3):258-267.
1993   Late Postclassic Lowland Maya Archaeology. *Journal of World Prehistory* 7(1):35-69.

Andrews, Anthony P., E. Wyllys Andrews, and Fernando Robles Castellanos
2003   The Northern Maya Collapse and Its Aftermath. *Ancient Mesoamerica* 14:151-156.

Andrews, Anthony P., and Fernando Robles Castellanos
1985   Chichen Itza and Coba: An Itza-Maya Standoff in Early Postclassic Yucatan. In *The Lowland Maya Postclassic*, eds. A. Chase and P. Rice, 62-72. Austin: University of Texas Press.

Andrews IV, E. Wyllys, and E. W. Andrews V
1980   Excavations at Dzibilchaltun, Yucatan, Mexico. *Middle American Research Institute* 48. New Orleans: Tulane University.

Appadurai, Arjun (ed.)
1986   *The Social Life of Things: Commodities in Cultural Perspective.* Cambridge: Cambridge University Press.

Ardener, Shirley
1993   Ground Rules and Social Maps for Women: An Introduction. In *Women and Space: Ground Rules and Social Maps*, ed. Shirley Ardener, 1-30. Oxford: Berg.

Ardren, Traci
1990   Operation 4. In *Yaxuna Archaeological Survey: A Report of the 1989 Field Season and Final Report of Phase One.* Dallas: Department of Anthropology, Southern Methodist University.
1992   The Xkanha Excavations: Sub-Operation 16-E. In *The Selz Foundation Yaxuna Project: Final Report of the 1991 Field Season.* Dallas: Department of Anthropology, Southern Methodist University.
1994   The Xkanha Excavations: Sub-Operation 72-B. In *The Selz Foundation Yaxuna Project: Final Report of the 1993 Field Season.* Dallas: Department of Anthropology, Southern Methodist University.
1996   The Chochola Ceramic Style of Northern Yucatan: An Iconographic and Archaeological Study. In *Eighth Palenque Round Table*, eds. M. Macri and J. McHargue, 237-246. San Francisco: Pre-Columbian Art Research Institute.

1997 The Politics of Place: Architecture and Social Change at the Xkanha Group, Yaxuna, Yucatan, Mexico. PhD diss., Yale University.
2002a (ed.) *Ancient Maya Women*. Walnut Creek: AltaMira Press.
2002b Conversations about the Production of Archaeological Knowledge and Community Museums at Chunchucmil and Kochol, Yucatan, Mexico. *World Archaeology* 34(2):379–400.
2002c Death Became Her: Images of Female Power from Yaxuna Burials. In *Ancient Maya Women*, ed. Traci Ardren, 68–88. Walnut Creek: AltaMira Press.
2003a Excavations in the Lool Group. In *Pakbeh Regional Economy Program: Report of the 2002 Field Season*, eds. B. Dahlin and D. Mazeau. Washington, DC: Sociology and Anthropology Department, Howard University.
2003b Memoria y la historia arquitectonica en la estructura 6E-13 de Yaxuna. *Temas Antropologicos* 25(1,2):129–145.
2006 Mending the Past: Ixchel and the Invention of a Modern Pop Goddess. *Antiquity* 79(306):25–37.
2009 Masculinity in Classic Maya Culture. In *Que(e)rying Archaeology: The 15th Anniversary Gender Conference*, eds. Susan Terendy, Natasha Lyons, and Michelle Janse-Smekal, 50–58. Calgary, Alberta: Department of Archaeology, University of Calgary.
2011a Ofrendas de infantes e identidad en la arquitectura maya del Clásico. In *Estudios sobre identidades y cultura material en la región maya*, eds. Hector Hernandez A. and Marcos Pool C., 47–57. Mérida, México: Universidad Autonoma de Yucatan Press.
2011b Empowered Children in Classic Maya Sacrificial Rites. *Childhood in the Past* 4:133–145.
2011c Esculturas fálicas de la cultura maya de las tierras bajas del norte: articulación de la masculinidad e identidad regional. In *Localidad y globalidad en el mundo maya prehispánico e indígena contemporáneo: Estudios de espacio y genero*, ed. Miriam Judith Gallegos Gomera, 159–166. México, D.F.: Instituto Nacional de Antropología e Historia.
2012a The Phalli Stones of the Classic Maya Northern Lowlands: Masculine Anxiety and Regional Identity. In *Power and Identity in Archaeological Theory and Practice: Case Studies from Ancient Mesoamerica*, ed. Eleanor Harrison-Buck, 53–62. Salt Lake City: University of Utah Press.
2012b "They Raise Birds for Their Pleasure": Women, Children, Longing, and Desire in Landa's Relación de las Cosas de Yucatan. Paper presented at the 54th International Congress of Americanists, Vienna, Austria.
2013 "For on Them Rest the Most, and Most Important, Work": The Domestic Lives of Women and Children in Landa's Relación de las Cosas de Yucatán and the Archaeology of Tecoh. Paper presented at the American Society for Ethnohistory Annual Meeting, New Orleans.

Ardren, Traci, and Alejandra Alonso Olvera
2014 Domestic Multi-Crafting and Female Gendered Space: Seeking an Engendered Perspective on Classic Maya Shell Artifact Production. In *Género y arqueología en mesoamérica: Homenaje a Rosemary A. Joyce*, eds. María J. Rodríguez-Shadow and Susan Kellogg, 87-102. México: Centro de Estudios de Antropología de la Mujer.

Ardren, Traci, and C. Blackmore
2002 Social Landscape in a Market Economy: Archaeological Investigations of the Pich and Lool Groups at Chunchucmil, Yucatan. Paper presented at the 67th Annual Meeting of the Society for American Archaeology, Denver.

Ardren, Traci, Raphael Burgos, T. Kam Manahan, Sara Dzul Gongora, and Jose Estrada Faisal
2005 Recent Investigations at Xuenkal, Yucatan. *Mexicon* 27: 92-97.

Ardren, Traci, and Scott Hutson
2001 Ancient Maya Religious Practices: Evidence from Excavation, Epigraphy, and Art. In *Religious Texts and Material Contexts*, eds. Jacob Neusner and James Strange, 251-274. Lanham: University Press of America.
2006 *The Social Experience of Childhood in Ancient Mesoamerica*. Boulder: University Press of Colorado.

Ardren, Traci, and Justin Lowry
2011a Long Distance Trade and Identity Maintenance at Early Classic Chunchucmil. Paper presented at the Tercero Congreso Internacional de Cultura Maya, Mérida, Yucatán, México.
2011b The Travels of Maya Merchants in the Ninth-Tenth Centuries: Investigations at Xuenkal and the Greater Cupul Province, Yucatan, Mexico. *World Archaeology* 43(3):428-443.

Ardren, Traci, T. Kam Manahan, Julie Wesp, and Alejandra Alonso Olvera
2010 Cloth Production and Economic Intensification in the Area Surrounding Chichen Itza. *Latin American Antiquity* 21(3):274-289.

Ashmore, Wendy
1991 Site-Planning Principles and Concepts of Directionality among the Ancient Maya. *Latin American Antiquity* 2(3):199-226.
2004 Classic Maya Landscapes and Settlement. In *Mesoamerican Archaeology: Theory and Practice*, eds. J. Hendon and R. A. Joyce, 169-191. Malden: Blackwell.

Ashmore, Wendy, and Richard Wilk
1988 Household and Community in the Mesoamerican Past. In *Household and Community in the Mesoamerican Past*, eds. R. Wilk and W. Ashmore, 1-27. Albuquerque: University of New Mexico Press.

Ball, Joseph
1983 Teotihuacan, the Maya, and Ceramic Interchange: A Contextual Per-

spective. In *Highland-Lowland Interaction in Mesoamerica: Interdisciplinary Approaches*, ed. A. Miller, 125-145. Washington, DC: Dumbarton Oaks.

Baugher, Sherene, and Suzanne Spencer-Wood (eds.)
2010 *Archaeology and Preservation of Gendered Landscapes*. New York: Springer.

Baxter, Jane Eva
2005 *The Archaeology of Childhood: Children, Gender and Material Culture*. Walnut Creek: AltaMira Press.
2008 The Archaeology of Childhood. *Annual Review of Anthropology* 37: 159-175.

Beach, Timothy
1998 Soil Constraints on Northwest Yucatan, Mexico: Pedoarchaeology and Maya Subsistence at Chunchucmil. *Geoarchaeology* 13(8):759-791.

Becker, Marshall J.
1991 Plaza Plans at Tikal, Guatemala, and at Other Lowland Maya Sites: Evidence for Patterns of Culture Change. *Cuadernos de Arquitectura Mesoamericana* 14:11-26.
1999 *Excavations in Residential Areas of Tikal: Groups with Shrines*. Tikal Report 21. Philadelphia: University Museum, University of Pennsylvania.

Benavides Castillo, Antonio
1976 Coba: Un sitio maya en Quintana Roo. *Cuadernos de los Centros*, no. 26. México, D.F.: Instituto Nacional de Antropologia e Historia.
1981 Cobá y Tulum: Adaptación al medio ambiente y contról del medio social. *Estudios de Cultura Maya* 13:205-222.

Bennett, Robert R.
1930 The Ancient Maya Causeway in Yucatan. *Indian Notes* (7):3.

Bennett, Sharon
1990 The Human Skeletal Remains of Isla Cerritos, Yucatan. Manuscript in possession of the author.
1992 Burials at Yaxuna 1991. In *The Selz Foundation Yaxuna Project: Final Report of the 1991 Field Season*, eds. David Freidel, Charles Suhler, and Rafael Cobos P., 82-91. Dallas: Department of Anthropology, Southern Methodist University.
1993 Burials from Yaxuna, Yucatan. In *The Selz Foundation Yaxuna Project: Final Report of the 1992 Field Season*, eds. Charles Suhler and David Freidel, 144-165. Dallas: Department of Anthropology, Southern Methodist University.
1994 The Burial Excavations at Yaxuna in 1993. In *The Selz Foundation Yaxuna Project: Final Report of the 1993 Field Season*. Dallas: Department of Anthropology, Southern Methodist University.

Bernardini, Wesley
2005 *Hopi Oral Tradition and the Archaeology of Identity*. Tucson: University of Arizona Press.

Bey, George J. III, Tara M. Bond, William M. Ringle, Craig A. Hanson, Charles W. Houck, and Carlos Peraza L.
1998   The Ceramic Chronology of Ek Balam, Yucatan, Mexico. *Ancient Mesoamerica* 9(1):101–120.

Bey, George J. III, Craig Hanson, and William M. Ringle
1997   Classic to Postclassic at Ek Balam, Yucatan: Architectural and Ceramic Evidence for Defining the Transition. *Latin American Antiquity* 8(3): 237–254.

Bird, D. W., and R. L. Bliege Bird
2000   The Ethnoarchaeology of Juvenile Foragers: Shellfishing Strategies among Meriam Children. *Journal of Anthropological Archaeology* 19(4): 461–476.

Bird-David, Nurit
2005   Studying Children in "Hunter-Gatherer" Societies: Reflections from a Nayaka Perspective. In *Hunter-Gatherer Childhoods: Evolutionary, Developmental, and Cultural Perspectives*, eds. Michael E. Lamb and Barry S. Hewlett, 92–101. Chicago: Aldine Transaction.

Blackmore, Chelsea, and Traci Ardren
2002   Excavations at the Pich Group. In *The Pakbeh Regional Economy Program: Report of the 2001 Field Season*, eds. Bruce Dahlin and Dan Mazeau, 58–68. Washington, DC: Sociology/Anthropology Department, Howard University.

Blanton, Richard
1981   The Rise of Cities. In *Handbook of Middle American Indians, Supplement I Archaeology*, ed. R. C. West, 392–400. Austin: University of Texas Press.

Bond, Tara M., and Eugenia Brown Mansell
2001   Preliminary Ceramic Analysis for the Pakbeh Regional Economy Program. Paper presented at the Congreso Internacional de Cultura Maya, Mérida.

Bourdieu, Pierre
1977   *Outline of a Theory of Practice*. Cambridge: Cambridge University Press.

Brainerd, George W.
1958   *The Archaeological Ceramics of Yucatan*. Anthropological Records 19. Berkeley: University of California Press.

Braswell, Geoffrey E. (ed.)
2003   *The Maya and Teotihuacan*. Austin: University of Texas Press.

Breglia, Lisa
2006   *Monumental Ambivalence: The Politics of Heritage*. Austin: University of Texas Press.

Brown, Denise F.
1999   Mayas and Tourists in the Maya World. *Human Organization* 58(3): 295–304.

Brumfiel, Elizabeth M.
1991   Weaving and Cooking: Women's Production in Aztec Mexico. In *Engendering Archaeology: Women and Prehistory*, eds. Joan Gero and Margaret Conkey, 224–251. Oxford: Basil Blackwell.

Bullard, William R. Jr.
1952   Residential Property Walls at Mayapan. *Current Reports* 3. Washington, DC: Department of Archaeology, Carnegie Institution of Washington.
1954   Boundary Walls and House Lots at Mayapan. *Current Reports* 1(13): 234–253. Washington, DC: Carnegie Institution of Washington.

Burke, Peter
1989   History as Social Memory. In *Memory: History, Culture and the Mind*, ed. T. Butler, 97–113. Oxford: Oxford University Press.

Castañeda, Quetzil
2004   We Are *Not* Indigenous! An Introduction to the Maya Identity of Yucatan. *Journal of Latin American Anthropology* 9(1):36–63.

Castellanos, M. Bianet
2010   *A Return to Servitude: Maya Migration and the Tourist Trade in Cancún*. Minneapolis: University of Minnesota Press.

Castells, Manuel
1997   *The Power of Identity*. Vol. 2 of *The Information Age: Economy, Society, and Culture*. Oxford: Blackwell.

Castoriadis, Cornelius
1987 [1975]   *The Imaginary Institution of Society*. Cambridge: MIT Press.

Cetina Aguilar, Anacleto
1996   *Breves datos historicos y culturales del municipio de Hunucma*. Hunucma, Yucatán: s.n.

Chase, Arlen F., and Diane Z. Chase
1998   Scale and Intensity in Classic Period Maya Agriculture: Terracing and Settlement at the "Garden City" of Caracol, Belize. *Culture and Agriculture* 20(2–3):60–77.

Chase, Arlen F., Diane Z. Chase, and Christine D. White
2001   El paisaje urbano maya: La integración de los espacios construidos y la estructura social en Caracol, Belice. In *Reconstruyendo la Ciudad Maya: El Urbanismo en Las Sociedades Antiguas*, eds. Andrés Ciudad Ruiz, Maria Josefa Iglesias Ponce de León, and Maria del Carmen Martínez Martínez, 95–122. Madrid: Sociedad Española de Estudios Mayas.

Childe, V. Gordon
1950   The Urban Revolution. *Town Planning Review* 21(1):3–17.

Chuchiak IV, John F.
2000   The Indian Inquisition and the Extirpation of Idolatry: The Process of Punishment in the Provisorato de Indios of the Diocese of Yucatán, 1563–1812. PhD diss., Tulane University.

2001 Pre-Conquest *Ah Kinob* in a Colonial World: The Extirpation of Idolatry and the Survival of the Maya Priesthood in Colonial Yucatan, 1563-1697. In *Maya Survivalism. Acta MesoAmericana* 12, eds. Ueli Hostettler and Matthew Restall, 135-157. Germany: Verlag Anton Sauerwein.

2005 *In Servitio Dei*: Fray Diego de Landa, the Franciscan Order, and the Return of the Extirpation of Idolatry in the Colonial Diocese of Yucatan, 1573-1579. *The Americas* 61(4):611-646.

2007 The Sins of the Fathers: Franciscan Friars, Parish Priests, and the Sexual Conquest of the Yucatec Maya, 1545-1808. *Ethnohistory* 54(1):69-127.

Claassen, Cheryl, and Rosemary Joyce (eds.)

1997 *Women in Prehistory: North America and Mesoamerica*. Philadelphia: University of Pennsylvania Press.

Clendinnen, Inga

1982 Yucatec Maya Women and the Spanish Conquest: Role and Ritual in Historical Reconstruction. *Journal of Social History* 15(3):427-442.

Cobos, Rafael

2001 El centro de Yucatán: De area periférica a la integración de la comunidad urbana en Chichen Itzá. In *Reconstruyendo la Ciudad Maya: El Urbanismo en Las Sociedades Antiguas*, eds. Andrés Ciudad Ruiz, Maria Josefa Iglesias Ponce de León, and Maria del Carmen Martínez Martínez, 253-276. Madrid: Sociedad Española de Estudios Mayas.

2012 *Arqueología de la costa de Campeche: La época prehispanica*. Mérida: Universidad Autonoma de Yucatán.

Coe, Michael D.

1973 *The Maya Scribe and His World*. New York: Grolier Club.

Coe, William R.

1962 A Summary of Excavation and Research at Tikal, Guatemala: 1956-61. *American Antiquity* 27(4):479-507.

Conkey, Margaret, and Janet Spector

1984 Archaeology and the Study of Gender. *Advances in Archaeological Method and Theory* 7:1-38.

Costin, Cathy Lynn

1996 Exploring the Relationship between Gender and Craft in Complex Societies: Methodological and Theoretical Issues of Gender Attribution. In *Gender and Archaeology*, ed. Rita Wright, 111-142. Philadelphia: University of Pennsylvania Press.

1998 Housewives, Chosen Women, Skilled Men: Cloth Production and Social Identity in the Late Prehispanic Andes. In *Craft and Social Identity*, eds. Cathy L. Costin and Rita P. Wright, 123-144. Washington, DC: Archaeological Papers of the American Anthropological Association, no. 8.

Crawford, Sally E.

1999 *Childhood in Anglo-Saxon England*. Stroud: Tempus.

Cucina, Andrea, Vera Tiesler, Araceli Hurtado Cen, Daniel Frohlich Sol, Mayra Maldonado Lux, Mirna Sanchez Vargas, and Shintaro Suzuki
2007   Excavacion de restos humanos en Xuenkal, Yucatan. In *Informe Final, Proyecto Arqueológico Xuenkal Temporada del Campo 2006*, eds. T. Kam Manahan and Traci Ardren, 111–150. Kent: Department of Anthropology, Kent State University.

Cuddy, Thomas W.
2007   *Political Identity and Archaeology in Northeast Honduras*. Boulder: University Press of Colorado.

Culbert, T. Patrick (ed.)
1973   *The Classic Maya Collapse*. Santa Fe: School of American Research.

Dahlin, Bruce H., Anthony P. Andrews, Timothy Beach, Clara I. Bezanilla, Patrice Farrell, Sheryl Luzzadder-Beach, and Valerie McCormick
1998   Punta Canbalam in Context: A Peripatetic Coastal Site in Northwest Campeche, Mexico. *Ancient Mesoamerica* 9(1):1–16.

Dahlin, Bruce H., and Traci Ardren
2002   Modes of Exchange and Regional Patterns: Chunchucmil, Yucatan, Mexico. In *Ancient Maya Political Economies*, eds. Marilyn Masson and David Freidel, 249–284. Walnut Creek: AltaMira Press.

Dahlin, Bruce H., Timothy Beach, Sheryl Luzzader-Beach, David Hixson, Scott R. Hutson, Aline Magnoni, Eugenia B. Mansell, and Daniel Mazeau
2005   Reconstructing Agricultural Self-Sufficiency at Chunchucmil, Yucatan, Mexico. *Ancient Mesoamerica* 16(2):229–247.

Demarest, Arthur, Prudence Rice, and Don S. Rice (ed.)
2004   *The Terminal Classic in the Maya Lowlands: Collapse, Transition, and Transformation*. Boulder: University Press of Colorado.

Díaz-Andreu, Margarita, Sam Lucy, Staša Babić, and David N. Edwards
2005   *The Archaeology of Identity: Approaches to Gender, Age, Status, Ethnicity, and Religion*. London: Routledge.

Drennan, Robert D.
1988   Household Location and Compact versus Dispersed Settlement in Prehispanic Mesoamerica. In *Household and Community in the Mesoamerican Past*, eds. Richard Wilk and Wendy Ashmore, 273–293. Albuquerque: University of New Mexico Press.

Dreyfus, Hubert L.
1991   *Being-In-the-World: A Commentary on Heidegger's* Being and Time, *Division I*. Cambridge: MIT Press.

Dunning, Nicholas P.
1992   *Lords of the Hills: Ancient Maya Settlement in the Puuc Region, Yucatán, Mexico*. Monographs in World Archaeology, no. 15. Madison: Prehistory Press.

Dyos, Henry James, and David Reeder
1973 Slums and Suburbs. In *The Victorian City: Images and Realities*, eds. Henry J. Dyos and M. Wolff, 359–386. London: Routledge.

Eiss, Paul K.
2010 *In the Name of El Pueblo: Place, Community, and the Politics of History in Yucatán*. Durham: Duke University Press.

Elmendorf, Mary
1976 *Nine Mayan Women: A Village Faces Change*. Cambridge: Schenkman.

Emery, Kitty, F., and Kazuo Aoyama
2007 Bone, Shell, and Lithic Evidence for Crafting in Elite Maya Households at Aguateca, Guatemala. *Ancient Mesoamerica* 18:69–89.

Fash, Barbara, Wiliam Fash, Sheree Lane, Rudy Larios, Linda Schele, Jeffrey Stomper, and David Stuart
1992 Investigations of a Classic Maya Council House at Copan, Honduras. *Journal of Field Archaeology* 19:419–442.

Finlay, Nyree
2000 Outside of Life: Traditions of Infant Burials in Ireland from Cillin to Cist. *World Archaeology* 31(3):407–422.

Folan, William
1969 Dzibilchaltun, Yucatán, Mexico: Structures 384, 385, and 386: A Preliminary Interpretation. *American Antiquity* 34(4):434–61.

Folan, William J., Ellen Kintz, and Lorraine A. Fletcher
1983 *Coba: A Classic Maya Metropolis*. New York: Academic Press.

Fortuny Loret de Mola, Patricia
2009 Transnational Hetzmek: From Oxkutzcab to San Francisco. In *Religion at the Corner of Bliss and Nirvana: Politics, Identity, and Faith in New Migrant Communities*, eds. L. Lorentzen, J. Gonzalez, K. Chun, and H. Duc Do, 207–242. Durham: Duke University Press.

Freidel, David
1981 Continuity and Disjunction: Late Postclassic Settlement Patterns in Northern Yucatan. In *Lowland Maya Settlement Patterns*, ed. Wendy Ashmore, 311–332. Albuquerque: University of New Mexico Press.

Freidel, David A., Barbara MacLeod, and Charles K. Suhler
2003 Early Classic Maya Conquest in Words and Deeds. In *Ancient Mesoamerican Warfare*, eds. M. K. Brown and T. W. Stanton, 189–215. Walnut Creek: AltaMira Press.

Freidel, David, Kathryn Reese-Taylor, and David Mora-Marin
2002 The Origins of Maya Civilization: The Old Shell Game, Commodity, Treasure and Kingship. In *Ancient Maya Political Economies*, eds. Marilyn Masson and David Freidel, 41–86. Walnut Creek: AltaMira Press.

Freidel, David A., and Jeremy Sabloff
1984 *Cozumel: Late Maya Settlement Patterns*. New York: Academic Press.

Freidel, David A., and Linda Schele
1989   Dead Kings and Living Temples: Dedication and Termination Rituals among the Ancient Maya. In *Word and Image in Maya Culture: Explorations in Language, Writing, and Representations*, eds. William Hanks and Don S. Rice, 233-243. Salt Lake City: University of Utah Press.

Freidel, David A., Charles K. Suhler, and Rafael Cobos P.
1992   *The Selz Foundation Yaxuna Project: Final Report of the 1991 Field Season*. Dallas: Department of Anthropology, Southern Methodist University.
1998   Termination Ritual Deposits at Yaxuna: Detecting the Historical in Archaeological Contexts. In *The Sowing and the Dawning: Termination, Dedication, and Transformation in the Archaeological and Ethnographic Record of Mesoamerica*, ed. S. B. Mock, 135-144. Albuquerque: University of New Mexico Press.

Freidel, David A., Charles K. Suhler, and Ruth Krochock
1990   *A Report of the 1989 Field Season and Final Report of Phase One*. Dallas: Department of Anthropology, Southern Methodist University.

Gallegos, Miriam Judith, and Armando Gómez
2006   Actividades y atavíos del hombre maya: La representación masculina en Tabasco, Mexico. In *XIX Simposio de Investigaciones Arqueológicas en Guatemala, 2005*, eds. J. P. Laporte, B. Arroyo, and H. Mejía, 559-570. Guatemala: Museo Nacional de Arqueología y Etnología.

Gardner, Andrew
2007   *An Archaeology of Identity: Soldiers and Society in Late Roman Britain*. Walnut Creek: Left Coast Press.

Garza Tarazona de Gonzalez, Silvia, and Edward B. Kurjack
1980   *Atlas Arqueológico del Estado de Yucatan*. México, D.F.: Instituto Nacional de Antropologia Historía.

Gates, William (trans.)
1978 [1566]   *Yucatan Before and After the Conquest by Friar Diego de Landa*. New York: Dover Publications.

Geller, Pamela
2009   Identity and Difference: Complicating Gender in Archaeology. *Annual Review of Anthropology* 38:65-81.
2011   The Sacrifices We Make of and for Our Children: Making Sense of Pre-Columbian Maya Practices. In *Breathing New Life into the Evidence of Death: Contemporary Approaches to Bioarchaeology*, eds. Aubrey Baadsgaard, Alexis T. Boutin, and Jane E. Buikstra, 79-108. Santa Fe: School for Advanced Research Press.
2012   Parting (with) the Dead: Body Partibility as Evidence of Commoner Ancestor Veneration. *Ancient Mesoamerica* 23:115-130.

Gendrop, Paul
1984   El tablero-talud en la arquitectura mesoamericana. *Cuadernos de arquitectura mesoamericana* 2:5-27.

Gerry, John, and Meredith S. Chesson
2000   Classic Maya Diet and Gender Relationships. In *Gender and Material Culture in Archaeological Perspective*, eds. Moira Donald and Linda Hurcombe, 250–265. New York: St. Martin's Press.

Giddens, Wendy L.
1995   Talud-Tablero Architecture as a Symbol of Mesoamerican Affiliation and Power. Master's thesis, University of California, Los Angeles.

Gillespie, Susan
1991   Ballgames and Boundaries. In *The Mesoamerican Ballgame*, eds. Vernon Scarborough and David Wilcox, 317–346. Tucson: University of Arizona Press.
2000   Rethinking Ancient Maya Social Organization: Replacing "Lineage" with "House." *American Anthropologist* 102(3):467–484.
2001   Personhood, Agency and Mortuary Ritual: A Case Study from the Ancient Maya. *Journal of Anthropological Archaeology* 20(1):73–112.

Goldberg, Marilyn Y.
1999   Spatial and Behavioral Negotiation in Classical Athenian City Houses. In *The Archaeology of Household Activities*, ed. Penelope Allison, 142–161. London: Routledge.

Golden, Charles, and Andrew K. Scherer
2013   Territory, Trust, Growth, and Collapse in Classic Period Maya Kingdoms. *Current Anthropology* 54(4):397–435.

Gonzalez de la Mata, Rocio, and Anthony P. Andrews
1998   Navigation and Trade on the Eastern Coast of the Yucatán Peninsula. In *Maya Civilization*, eds. P. Schmidt, M. de la Garza, and E. Nalda, 450–467. New York: Thames and Hudson.

Gosden, Chris, and Yvonne Marshall
1999   The Cultural Biography of Objects. *World Archaeology* 31(2):169–178.

Gottlieb, Alma
2004   *The Afterlife Is Where We Come From: The Culture of Infancy in West Africa*. Chicago: University of Chicago Press.

Götz, Christopher M.
2008   Coastal and Inland Patterns of Faunal Exploitation in the Prehispanic Northern Maya Lowlands. *Quaternary International* 191:154–169.
2010   Appendix 1: The Faunal Materials from Yaxuna, Yucatan, Mexico. In *Excavations at Yaxuna, Yucatan, Mexico*, eds. Travis Stanton et al., 267–284. Oxford: Archaeopress/British Archaeological Reports.
2011   Una mirada zooarqueológica a los modos alimenticios de los mayas de las tierras bajas del norte. In *Identidades y cultura material en la región maya*, eds. Héctor A. Hernández Alvarez and Marcos Pool Cab, 89–109. Mérida: Universidad Autónoma de Yucatán.

Götz, Christopher M., and Travis W. Stanton
2013   The Use of Animals by Pre-Hispanic Maya of the Northern Lowlands.

In *The Archaeology of Mesoamerican Animals*, eds. Christopher Götz and Kitty F. Emery, 191-232. Atlanta: Lockwood Press.

Gowland, Rebecca

2006 Aging the Past: Examining Age Identity from Funerary Evidence. In *Social Archaeology of Funerary Remains*, eds. Rebecca Gowland and Christopher Knusel, 143-154. Oxford: Oxbow Press.

Graff, Don, and Gabrielle Vail

2001 Censers and Stars: Issues in the Dating of the Madrid Codex. *Latin American Indian Literatures Journal* 17(1):58-95.

Halbwachs, Maurice

1992 *On Collective Memory*. Chicago: University of Chicago Press.

Hall, Martin

2001 Social Archaeology and the Theatres of Memory. *Journal of Social Archaeology* 1:50-61.

Hanks, William F.

1990 *Referential Practice: Language and Lived Space among the Maya*. Chicago: University of Chicago Press.

Harrison-Buck, Eleanor

2012 Architecture as Animate Landscape: Circular Shrines in the Ancient Maya Lowlands. *American Anthropologist* 114(1):64-80.

Hegmon, Michelle

2013 The Archaeology of Human Experience. SAA *Archaeological Record* 13(5):16-19.

Hendon, Julia A.

1992 Hilado y tejido en la epoca prehispanica: Technología y relaciones sociales de la producción textil. In *La indumentaria y el tejido mayas a través del tiempo*, eds. Linda Asturias de Barrios and Dina García, 7-16. Guatemala City: Museo Ixchel del Traje Indígena.

1996 Archaeological Approaches to the Organization of Domestic Labor: Household Practice and Domestic Relations. *Annual Review of Anthropology* 25:45-61.

1997 Women's Work, Women's Space, and Women's Status among the Classic-Period Maya Elite of the Copan Valley, Honduras. In *Women in Prehistory: North America and Mesoamerica*, eds. Cheryl Claassen and Rosemary Joyce, 33-46. Philadelphia: University of Pennsylvania Press.

2010 *Houses in a Landscape: Memory and Everyday Life in Mesoamerica*. Durham: Duke University Press.

Hernández Álvarez, Héctor

2011 Identidades de genero masculino entre los mayas prehispanicos. In *Localidad y globalidad en el mundo maya prehispanico e indigena contemporaneo: Estudios de espacio y genero*, eds. Miriam Judith Gallegos G. and Julia Hendon, 139-158. México, D.F.: Instituto Nacional de Antropologia e Historia.

Hernández Álvarez, Héctor, and Gustavo Novelo Rincón
2007   Una visión diacrónica de la arquitectura doméstica de Yaxuná, Yucatán. In *Los investigadores de la cultura maya* 15, tomo 1, 279-292. Campeche: Universidad Autónoma de Campeche.

Hervik, Peter
2003   *Mayan People Within and Beyond Boundaries: Social Categories and Lived Identities in Yucatan*. New York: Routledge.

Heyden, Doris, and Paul Gendrop
1980   *Pre-Columbian Architecture of Mesoamerica*. New York: Electa/Rizzoli.

Hixson, David R.
2005   Measuring a Maya Metropolis. *Institute of Maya Studies Newsletter* 34(1): 1-4.
2011   Settlement Patterns and Communication Routes of the Western Maya Wetlands: An Archaeological and Remote-Sensing Survey, Chunchucmil, Yucatan, Mexico. PhD diss., Tulane University.

Hodder, Ian, and Scott R. Hutson
2003   *Reading the Past: Current Approaches to Interpretation in Archaeology*. Cambridge: Cambridge University Press.

Hoffman, Warren
2009   *The Passing Game: Queering Jewish American Culture*. Syracuse: Syracuse University Press.

Holloway, Karla F. C.
2011   *Private Bodies, Public Texts: Race, Gender, and a Cultural Bioethics*. Durham: Duke University Press.

Hostettler, Ueli
2001   Milpa, Land and Identity: A Central Quintana Roo Mayan Community in a Historical Perspective. In *Maya Survivalism*, eds. Ueli Hostettler and Matthew Restall, Acta MesoAmericana 12:239-262. Germany: Verlag Anton Sauerwein.

Houston, Stephen
2009   A Splendid Predicament: Young Men in Classic Maya Society. *Cambridge Archaeological Journal* 19(2):149-178.

Houston, Stephen D., and David Stuart
1989   The Way Glyph: Evidence for Co-Essence among the Classic Maya. *Research Reports on Ancient Maya Writing*, no. 30. Washington, DC.

Hutson, Scott R.
2006   Children Not at Chunchucmil: A Relational Approach to Young Subjects. In *The Social Experience of Childhood in Ancient Mesoamerica*, eds. Traci Ardren and Scott R. Hutson, 103-132. Boulder: University Press of Colorado.
2010   *Dwelling, Identity, and the Maya: Relational Archaeology at Chunchucmil*. Walnut Creek: AltaMira Press.
In prep   *Ancient Maya Merchants: Multidisciplinary Research at Chunchucmil*.

Hutson, Scott R., David Hixson, Aline Magnoni, Daniel E. Mazeau, and Bruce H. Dahlin
2008   Site and Community at Chunchucmil and Ancient Maya Urban Centers. *Journal of Field Archaeology* 33(1):19–40.
Hutson, Scott R., and Aline Magnoni
2011   Identidad social en el mosaico urbano de Chunchucmil, Yucatán. In *Localidad y globalidad en el mundo maya prehispánico e indígena contemporáneo, estudios de espacio y género*, eds. Miriam Judith Gallegos and Julia Ann Hendon, 65–77. México, D.F.: Instituto Nacional de Antropologí e Historia.
Hutson, Scott R., Aline Magnoni, and Bruce Dahlin
2000   Intra-Site Settlement Patterns at Chunchucmil, Yucatán, Mexico. Paper presented at the 65th Annual Meeting of the Society for American Archaeology, Philadelphia.
Hutson, Scott R., Aline Magnoni, Daniel Mazeau, and Travis W. Stanton
2006   The Archeology of Urban Houselots at Chunchucmil, Yucatán, Mexico. In *Lifeways in the Northern Maya Lowlands: New Approaches to Archaeology in the Yucatán Peninsula*, eds. J. P. Mathews and B. A. Morrison, 77–92. Tucson: University of Arizona Press.
Hutson, Scott R., Aline Magnoni, and Travis W. Stanton
2004   House Rules? Social Organization and Ritual Practice at Classic Period Chunchucmil, Yucatán, Mexico. *Ancient Mesoamerica* 15:74–92.
Hutson, Scott R., Travis W. Stanton, Aline Magnoni, Richard Terry, and Jason Craner
2007   Beyond the Buildings: Formation Processes of Ancient Maya Houselots and Methods for the Study of Non-Architectural Space. *Journal of Anthropological Archaeology* 26(3):442–473.
Isbell, William
2000   What We Should Be Studying: The "Imagined Community" and the "Natural Community." In *The Archaeology of Communities: A New World Perspective*, eds. Marcello Canuto and Jason Yaeger, 243–266. New York: Routledge.
Janusek, John Wayne
2004   *Identity and Power in the Ancient Andes: Tiwanaku Cities through Time.* New York: Routledge.
Jiménez, Socorro
In prep   Chronology and Site Dynamics. In *Ancient Maya Merchants: Multidisciplinary Research at Chunchucmil*, ed. Scott R. Hutson.
Johnson, Jim (B. Latour)
1988   Mixing Humans with Non-Humans: Sociology of a Door-Closer. *Social Problems* 35:298–310.
Johnson, Matthew
1999   *Archaeological Theory: An Introduction.* Malden: Blackwell.

Johnston, Kevin
2001 Broken Fingers: Classic Maya Scribe Capture and Polity Consolidation. *Antiquity* 75(288):373-381.

Johnstone, David
1993 Test Excavations in Non-Elite Residential Structures, Yaxuna. In *The Selz Foundation Yaxuna Project: Final Report of the 1992 Field Season*, eds. Charles Suhler and David Freidel, 114-140. Dallas: Department of Anthropology, Southern Methodist University.

Jones, Sian
1997 *The Archaeology of Ethnicity: Constructing Identities in the Past and Present*. New York: Routledge.

Joyce, Rosemary
1993 Women's Work: Images of Production and Reproduction in Pre-Hispanic Southern Central America. *Current Anthropology* 34:255-274.
1999 Social Dimensions of Pre-Classic Burials. In *Social Patterns in Pre-Classic Mesoamerica*, eds. David C. Grove and Rosemary Joyce, 15-48. Washington, DC: Dumbarton Oaks.
2000a *Gender and Power in Prehispanic Mesoamerica*. Austin: University of Texas Press.
2000b A Pre-Columbian Gaze: Male Sexuality among the Ancient Maya. In *Archaeologies of Sexuality*, eds. Robert Schmidt and Barbara Voss, 263-283. New York: Routledge.
2000c Girling the Girl and Boying the Boy: The Production of Adulthood in Ancient Mesoamerica. *World Archaeology* 31(3):473-483.
2001 Negotiating Sex and Gender in Classic Maya Society. In *Gender in Pre-Hispanic America*, ed. Cecelia Klein, 109-142. Washington, DC: Dumbarton Oaks.

Kamp, Kathryn (ed.)
2002 *Children in the Prehistoric Puebloan Southwest*. Salt Lake City: University of Utah Press.

Kellogg, Susan
2005 *Weaving the Past: A History of Latin America's Indigenous Women from the Prehispanic Period to the Present*. Oxford: Oxford University Press.

Kepecs, Susan M.
1998 Diachronic Ceramic Evidence and Its Social Implications in the Chinkinchel Region, Northeast Yucatán, Mexico. *Ancient Mesoamerica* 9(1):121-136.
2003 Salt Sources and Production. In *The Postclassic Mesoamerican World*, eds. M. E. Smith and F. Berdan, 126-130. Salt Lake City: University of Utah Press.

Kepecs, Susan, and Marilyn Masson
2003 Political Organization in Yucatán and Belize. In *The Postclassic Meso-*

american World, eds. M. Smith and F. Berdan, 40-44. Salt Lake City: University of Utah Press.

Killion, Thomas W., Jeremy A. Sabloff, Gair Tourtellot, and Nicholas P. Dunning
1989 Intensive Surface Collection of Residential Clusters at Terminal Classic Sayil, Yucatan, Mexico. *Journal of Field Archaeology* 16(3):273-294.

Knowlton, Timothy W.
2010 *Maya Creation Myths: Words and Worlds of the Chilam Balam*. Boulder: University Press of Colorado.

Knox, Paul L., and Peter J. Taylor (eds.)
1995 *World Cities in a World System*. Cambridge: Cambridge University Press.

Kopytoff, Igor
1986 The Cultural Biography of Things: Commoditization as Process. In *The Social Life of Things: Commodities in Cultural Perspective*, ed. Arjun Appadurai, 64-94. Cambridge: Cambridge University Press.

Kowalski, Jeff Karl
2003 Evidence for the Functions and Meanings of Some Northern Maya Palaces. In *Maya Palaces and Elite Residences: An Interdisciplinary Approach*, ed. Jessica Joyce Christie, 204-252. Austin: University of Texas Press.

Kowalski, Jeff Karl, Rhonda Silverstein, and Mya Follensbee
2002 Seats of Power and Cycles of Creation: Continuities and Changes in Iconography and Political Organization at Dzibilchaltun, Uxmal, Chichen Itza, and Mayapan. *Estudios de Cultura Maya* 22:87-111.

Lacan, Jacques
1977 *Écrits: A Selection*. New York: W. W. Norton.

Lally, Mike, and Traci Ardren (eds.)
2008 Little Artefacts: Rethinking the Constitution of the Archaeological Child. *Childhood in the Past* 1(1):62-77.

Lally, Mike, and Alison Moore
2011 (Re)Thinking the Little Ancestor: New Perspectives on the Archaeology of Infancy and Childhood. *International Series* 2271. Oxford: Archaeopress/British Archaeological Reports.

Lancy, David
2008 *The Anthropology of Childhood: Cherubs, Chattel, Changelings*. Cambridge: Cambridge University Press.

Landa, Diego D. (trans. William Gates)
1566/1978 *Yucatan Before and After the Conquest*. New York: Dover.

Latour, Bruno
1993 *We Have Never Been Modern*. New York: Harvester-Wheatsheaf.
1999 *Pandora's Hope: Essays on the Reality of Social Sciences*. Cambridge: Harvard University Press.
2005 *Reassembling the Social: An Introduction to Actor-Network-Theory*. Oxford: Oxford University Press.

Lee, Benjamin, and Edward LiPuma
2002   Cultures of Circulation: The Imaginations of Modernity. *Public Culture* 14(1):191-213.

Leventhal, Richard M.
1983   Household Groups and Classic Maya Religion. In *Prehistoric Settlement Patterns: Essays in Honor of Gordon R. Willey*, eds. E. Vogt and R. Leventhal, 55-76. Cambridge: Peabody Museum of Archaeology and Ethnology, Harvard University.

LiPuma, Edward, and Thomas Koelble
2005   Cultures of Circulation and the Urban Imaginary: Miami as Example and Exemplar. *Public Culture* 17(1):153-180.

Lucero, Lisa J.
2006   *Water and Ritual: The Rise and Fall of Classic Maya Rulers*. Austin: University of Texas Press.
2010   Materialized Cosmology among Ancient Maya Commoners. *Journal of Social Archaeology* 10(1):138-167.

Lucy, S. J.
1994   Children in Early Medieval Cemeteries. *Archaeological Review from Cambridge* 13:21-34.

Lyall, Victoria I.
2012   The Effigy Censers of Mayapan. In *Children of the Plumed Serpent: The Legacy of Quetzalcoatl in Ancient Mexico*, eds. Virginia Fields, John M. D. Pohl, and Victoria I. Lyall, 128-132. Los Angeles: Los Angeles County Museum of Art.

Magnoni, Aline
2007   Population Estimates at the Ancient Maya City of Chunchucmil, Yucatán, Mexico. In CAA *2006: Computer Applications and Quantitative Methods in Archaeology*, ed. J. Clark, 160-167. Oxford: BAR International Series.

Magnoni, Aline, Traci Ardren, and Scott Hutson
2007   Tourism in the Mundo Maya: Inventions and (Mis)Representations of Maya Identities and Heritage. *Archaeologies* 3(3):353-383.

Magnoni, Aline, Traci Ardren, Scott Hutson, and Bruce Dahlin
2014   The Production of Space and Identity at Classic Period Chunchucmil, Yucatán, Mexico. In *Making Ancient Cities: Space and Place in Early Urban Societies*, eds. Andrew Creekmore and Kevin D. Fisher, 145-180. Cambridge: Cambridge University Press.

Magnoni, Aline, Scott Hutson, and Bruce Dahlin
2012   Living in the City: Settlement Patterns and the Urban Experience at Classic Period Chunchucmil, Yucatán, Mexico. *Ancient Mesoamerica* 23(2):313-343.

Magnoni, Aline, Scott Hutson, and Travis Stanton
2008   Landscape Transformations and Changing Perceptions at Chunchucmil, Yucatán. In *Ruins of the Past: The Use and Perception of Abandoned*

Structures in the Maya Lowlands, eds. Aline Magnoni and Travis Stanton, 193-222. Boulder: University of Colorado Press.

Maldonado Cardenas, Ruben

1995   Proyecto arqueológico Dzibilchaltun, la estructura 44. *Revista de la Universidad Autonoma de Yucatan* 192:67-75.

2001   La exploracion y restauracion de la subestructura 44, de Dzibilchaltun. In *Yucatan a traves de los siglos: Memorias del 49th congreso internacional de americanistas*, eds. Ruth Gubler and Patricia Martel, 67-76. Mérida: Universidad Autonoma de Yucatán.

Maldonado Cardenas, Ruben, Angel Gongora, and Alexander Voss

2002   Kalom Uk'Uw, Senor de Dzibilchaltun. In *La organizacion social entre los mayas prehispanicos, coloniales, y modernos. Memoria del tercera mesa redonda de Palenque*, eds. Vera Tiesler, Rafael Cobos, and Merle Greene Robertson, 79-100. México, D.F.: Universidad Autonoma de Yucatán and Instituto Nacional de Antropología e Historia.

Manahan, T. Kam, and Traci Ardren

2008   Cambios y conflictos en la region Cupul: Resultados preliminares de la temporada 2006 en Xuenkal, Yucatán. In *Los investigadores de la cultura maya encuentro* 16, tomo 2, ed. M Rosario Dominguez C., 255-266. Campeche, Mexico: Universidad Autónoma de Campeche.

Manahan, T. Kam, Traci Ardren, and Alejandra Alonso Olvera

2012   Household Organization and the Dynamics of State Expansion: The Late Classic-Terminal Classic Transformation at Xuenkal, Yucatán, Mexico. *Ancient Mesoamerica* 23(2):345-364.

Mansell, Eugenia B., Robert H. Tykot, David Freidel, Bruce Dahlin, and Traci Ardren

2006   Early to Terminal Classic Maya Diet in the Northern Lowlands of the Yucatán, Mexico. In *Histories of Maize: Multidisciplinary Approaches to the Prehistory, Biogeography, Domestication, and Evolution of Maize*, eds. J. E. Staller, R. H. Tykot, and B. F. Benz, 173-185. Academic Press: New York.

Marcus, Joyce

1983   On the Nature of the Mesoamerican City. In *Prehistoric Settlement Patterns: Essays in Honor of Gordon Willey*, eds. E. Z. Vogt and R. M. Leventhal, 195-242. Albuquerque: University of New Mexico Press.

1987   The Inscriptions of Calakmul: Royal Marriage at a Maya City in Campeche, Mexico. *Technical Report* 21. Ann Arbor: Museum of Anthropology, University of Michigan.

Marquina, Ignacio

1964   *Arquitectura Prehispanica*. 2nd ed. México, D.F.: Instituto Nacional de Antropologia e Historia.

Martin, Kathleen Rock

2007   *Discarded Pages: Araceli Cab Cumi, Maya Poet and Politician*. Albuquerque: University of New Mexico Press.

Martin, Simon, and Nikolai Grube
1995   Maya Superstates. *Archaeology* 48(6):41-46.
Masson, Marilyn
2000   *In the Realm of Nachan Kan*. Boulder: University Press of Colorado.
Masson, Marilyn, Timothy Hare, and Carlos Peraza Lope
2006   Postclassic Maya Society Regenerated at Mayapan. In *After Collapse: The Regeneration of Complex Societies*, eds. Glenn Schwartz and John J. Nichols, 188-207. Tucson: University of Arizona Press.
Masson, Marilyn, and Carlos Peraza Lope
2010   Evidence for Maya-Mexican Interaction in the Archaeological Record of Mayapan. In *Astronomers, Scribes and Priests: Intellectual Interchange between the Northern Maya Lowlands and Highland Mexico in the Late Postclassic Period*, eds. Gabrielle Vail and Christine Hernandez, 77-114. Washington, DC: Dumbarton Oaks.
2014   *Kukulkan's Realm: Urban Life at Ancient Mayapan*. Boulder: University Press of Colorado.
Mazeau, Daniel
2002   Non-Local Resource Dependency: Economy and the Lithic Assemblage of Chunchucmil, Yucatan, Mexico. Paper presented at the Society for American Archaeology Annual Meeting, Denver.
Mazeau, Daniel, and Jamie E. Forde
2003   The Lithic Industries of Chunchucmil: Chipped Stone Tools in a Market Economy. Paper presented at the Society for American Archaeology Annual Meeting, Milwaukee.
McAnany, Patricia
1995   *Living with the Ancestors: Kinship and Kingship in Ancient Maya Society*. Austin: University of Texas Press.
2010   *Ancestral Maya Economies in Archaeological Perspective*. Cambridge: Cambridge University Press.
McAnany, Patricia, and Shannon Plank
2001   Perspectives on Actors, Gender Roles, and Architecture at Classic Maya Courts and Households. In *Royal Courts of the Ancient Maya*, eds. Takeshi Inomata and Stephen D. Houston, 1:84-129. Boulder: Westview Press.
McKerr, Lynne, Eileen Murphy, and Colm Donnelly
2009   I Am Not Dead, but Do Sleep Here: The Representation of Children in Early Modern Burial Grounds in the North of Ireland. *Childhood in the Past* 2:109-131.
McKillop, Heather
2002   *Salt: White Gold of the Ancient Maya*. Gainesville: University Press of Florida.
Meskell, Lynn
2001   Archaeologies of Identity. In *Archaeological Theory Today*, ed. Ian Hodder, 187-213. Cambridge: Polity.

2004 *Object Worlds in Ancient Egypt: Material Biographies Past and Present.* Oxford: Berg.

Meskell, Lynn, and Rosemary Joyce

2003 *Embodied Lives: Figuring Ancient Maya and Egyptian Experience.* New York: Routledge.

Milbrath, Susan, and Carlos Peraza Lope

2003 Revisiting Mayapan: Mexico's Last Maya Capital. *Ancient Mesoamerica* 14:1-46.

Miller, Jeffrey

1974 Notes on a Stela Pair Probably from Calakmul, Campeche, Mexico. In *Primera Mesa Redonda de Palenque, Part 1*, ed. Merle Greene Robertson, 149-161. Pebble Beach: Robert Louis Stevenson School.

Mock, Shirley B.

1998 *The Sowing and the Dawning: Termination, Dedication, and Transformation in the Archaeological and Ethnographic Record of Mesoamerica.* Albuquerque: University of New Mexico Press.

Montgomery, Heather

2009 *An Introduction to Childhood: Anthropological Perspectives on Children's Lives.* Malden: Wiley-Blackwell.

Moore, Henrietta

1986 *Space, Text and Gender: An Anthropological Study of the Marakwet of Kenya.* Cambridge: Cambridge University Press.

1994 *A Passion for Difference: Essays in Anthropology and Gender.* Bloomington: Indiana University Press.

Morrison, Kenneth M.

1994 Native American Religions: Creating through Cosmic Give and Take. In *Native America: Portrait of the Peoples*, ed. Duane Champagne, 441-474. Detroit: Visible Ink.

Mountjoy, Joseph B., and Mary K. Sanford

2006 Burial Practices during the Late Formative/Early Classic in the Banderas Valley Area of West Mexico. *Ancient Mesoamerica* 17(2):313-327.

Ochoa R., Jose Manuel

2007 Las esferas ceramicas tases del postclasico en el norte de la peninsula de Yucatán. In *La Producción alfarera en el mexico antiguo*, eds. Beatriz Merino C. and Angel Garcia C., 5:383-406. México, D.F.: Instituto Nacional de Antropologia e Historia.

Okoshi, Tsubasa

1995 Revisión crítica de la organización política de la provincial de Ah Canul en vísperas de la invasión Española. In *Memorias del Segundo Congreso Internacional de Mayistas, Mérida, Yucatán*: 60-69. México, D.F.: Centro Estudios Mayas, Universidad Nacional Autónoma de México.

Olivier, Laurent (trans. Arthur Greenspan)
2011   *The Dark Abyss of Time: Archaeology and Memory*. Walnut Creek: AltaMira.

Orser, Charles E.
2001   *Race and the Archaeology of Identity*. Salt Lake City: University of Utah Press.

Osorio, Jose F.
2004   El conjunto de los falos en Chichen Itza: el reflejo de una vida palaciega. In *XVII Simposio de Investigaciones Arqueologicas en Guatemala, 2003*, eds. J. P. Laporte, B. Arroyo, H. Escobedo, and H. Mejia, 1025-1034. Guatemala: Museo Nacional de Antropologia e Etnologia.

Paris, Elizabeth H.
2008   Metallurgy, Mayapan, and the Postclassic Mesoamerican World System. *Ancient Mesoamerica* 19:43-66.

Pauketat, Timothy R., and Susan M. Alt
2003   Mounds, Memory, and Contested Mississippian History. In *Archaeologies of Memory*, eds. Ruth Van Dyke and Susan Alcock, 151-179. Malden: Blackwell.

Pearson, Mike Parker
1999   *The Archaeology of Death and Burial*. College Station: Texas A&M University Press.

Peraza L., Carlos, and Susan Milbrath
2010   El Escribano de Mayapan, Yucatan. *Arqueologia Mexicana* 18(104):18-20.

Perez de Heredia, Eduardo, Gabriel Euan Canul, Francisco Perez Ruiz, Jose F. Osorio, and Jose Manuel Arias
2004   Un patron de entierros infantiles en vasijas durante la transicion del clasico tardio al terminal en Chichen Itza, Yucatán. Paper presented at the 18th Simposio de Investigaciones Arqueológicas in Guatemala City, Guatemala.

Pohl, Mary, and Larry H. Feldman
1982   The Traditional Role of Women and Animals in Lowland Maya Economy. In *Maya Subsistence: Studies in Memory of Dennis E. Puleston*, ed. Kent V. Flannery, 295-313. New York: Academic Press.

Pollock, Harry E. D.
1962   Introduction to Mayapan, Yucatán, Mexico, *Carnegie Publication 619*, eds. H. Pollock, R. Roys, T. Proskouriakoff, and A. Smith, 1-24. Washington, DC: Carnegie Institution of Washington.

Pool Cab, Marcus Noé
2013   La cuestion etnica en Chichen Itza e Isla Cerritos. Paper presented at the 9th Congreso Internacional de Mayistas, San Francisco de Campeche, Campeche, Mexico.

Preucel, Robert W., and Lynn Meskell
2004 Knowledges. In *A Companion to Social Archaeology*, eds. Lynn Meskell and Robert W. Preucel, 3-22. Malden: Blackwell.

Quezada, Sergio
1993 *Pueblos y caciques Yucatecos, 1550-1580*. México, D.F.: El Colegio de México.
1998 Political Organization of the Yucatan Mayas during the Eleventh to Sixteenth Centuries. In *Maya Civilization*, eds. P. Schmidt, M. de la Garza, and E. Nalda, 468-481. New York: Thames and Hudson.

Renfrew, Colin
1984 *Approaches to Social Archaeology*. Edinburgh: Edinburgh University Press.

Resic, Sanimir
2006 From Gilgamesh to Terminator: The Warrior as Masculine Ideal — Historical and Contemporary Perspectives. In *Warfare and Society: Archaeological and Social Anthropological Perspectives*, eds. T. Otto, H. Thrane, and H. Vandkilde, 423-433. Aarhus: Aarhus University Press.

Restall, Matthew
1995 He Wished It in Vain: Subordination and Resistance among Maya Women in Post-Conquest Yucatan. *Ethnohistory* 42(4):577-595.
1997 *The Maya World: Yucatec Culture and Society, 1550-1850*. Stanford: Stanford University Press.
1998 *Maya Conquistador*. Boston: Beacon Press.
2004 Maya Ethnogenesis. *Journal of Latin American Anthropology* 9(1):64-89.

Restall, Matthew, and John F. Chuchiak IV
2002 A Reevaluation of the Authenticity of Fray Diego de Landa's Relacion de las cosas de Yucatan. *Ethnohistory* 4(3):651-669.

Reyes-Cortes, Beatriz, and Timoteo Rodriguez
2007 Mayab Bejlae: Yucatan Today. *Kroeber Anthropological Society Papers no. 96*. Berkeley: Kroeber Anthropological Society, University of California.

Ringle, William M., and George J. Bey III
2001 Post-Classic and Terminal Classic Courts of the Northern Maya Lowlands. In *Royal Courts of the Ancient Maya*, eds. T. Inomata and S. Houston, 2:266-307. Boulder: Westview Press.

Rivera Dorado, Miguel
1989 *Oxkintok 2*. Madrid: Mision Arqueologica de Espana en Mexico.
2000 Las tierras bajas de la zona maya en el Posclásico. In *Historia Antigua de Mexico*, vol. 3, *El Horizonte Posclásico*, eds. L. Mazanilla and L. Lopez L., 127-159. México, D.F.: Instituto Nacional de Antropologia e Historia.

Robertson, Donald
1970 The Tulum Murals: The International Style of the Late Post-Classic. In *Verhandlungen des XXXVIII Internationalen Amerikanistenkongresses*,

Stuttgart-Munchen, 1968, 2:77-88. Munich: Kommissionsverlag Klaus Renner.

Robles Castellanos, J. Fernando

1976   Ixil, centro agricola de Coba. *Boletín de la Escuela de Ciencias Antropológicas de la Universidad de Yucatán* 4(20):13-43.

1990   *La secuencia ceramica de la region de Coba, Quintana Roo*. México, D.F.: Instituto Nacional de Antropologia e Historia.

Robles Castellanos, J. Fernando, and Anthony P. Andrews

1986   A Review and Synthesis of Recent Postclassic Archaeology in Northern Yucatan. In *Late Lowland Maya Civilization: Classic to Postclassic*, eds. J. Sabloff and E. W. Andrews V, 53-98. Albuquerque: University of New Mexico Press.

Rodning, Christopher

2001   Mortuary Ritual and Gender Ideology in Protohistoric Southwestern North Carolina. In *Archaeological Studies of Gender in the Southeastern United States*, eds. Jane Eastman and Christopher Rodning, 77-100. Gainesville: University Press of Florida.

Rodriguez-Shadow, Maria, and Miriam López Hernández

2011   *Las mujeres mayas en la antigüedad*. México: Centro de Estudios de la Antropologia de la Mujer.

Roman Berrelleza, Juan Alberto, and Ximena Chavez Balderas

2006   The Role of Children in the Ritual Practices of the Great Temple of Tenochtitlan and the Great Temple of Tlatelolco. In *The Social Experience of Childhood in Mesoamerica*, eds. Traci Ardren and Scott Hutson, 233-248. Boulder: University Press of Colorado.

Rowlands, Michael J.

1993   The Role of Memory in the Transmission of Culture. *World Archaeology* 25(2):141-151.

Roys, Ralph

1957   The Political Geography of the Yucatan Maya. *Carnegie Institution Publication 613*. Washington, DC: Carnegie Institution of Washington.

Ruz Lhuillier, Alberto

1989   *Costumbre funerarias de los antiguos mayas*. México, D.F.: Fondo de Cultura Economica.

Sabloff, Jeremy, and E. Wyllys Andrews V (eds.)

1986   *Late Lowland Maya Civilization: Classic to Postclassic*. Santa Fe: School of American Research.

Sanders, William T., and David Webster

1988   The Mesoamerican Urban Tradition. *American Anthropologist* 90:521-546.

Schele, Linda

1984   Some Suggested Readings for the Event and Office of Heir-Designate at Palenque. In *Phoneticism in Mayan Hieroglyphic Writing*, eds. J. S. Justeson and L. Campbell, 287-305. Institute for Mesoamerican Studies Publication 9. Albany: State University of New York.

Schele, Linda, and David Freidel
1990 *A Forest of Kings: The Untold Story of the Ancient Maya.* New York: William Morrow and Company.

Schele, Linda, and Mary Miller
1986 *The Blood of Kings: Dynasty and Ritual in Maya Art.* Dallas: George Braziller and Kimball Art Museum.

Schmidt, Peter
2007 Birds, Ceramics, and Cacao: New Excavations at Chichen Itza. In *Twin Tollans: Chichen Itza, Tula, and the Epiclassic to Early Postclassic Mesoamerican World*, eds. J. K. Kowalski and C. Kristan-Graham, 151-204. Washington, DC: Dumbarton Oaks.

Shafer, Harry J., and Thomas R. Hester
1983 Ancient Maya Chert Workshops in Northern Belize, Central America. *American Antiquity* 48(3):519-543.

Shanks, Michael
1992 *Experiencing the Past: On the Character of Archaeology.* London: Routledge.
2001 *Theatre/Archaeology.* London: Routledge.

Shaw, Justine M.
1998 The Community Settlement Patterns and Community Architecture of Yaxuna from A.D. 600-1400. PhD diss., Southern Methodist University.

Sheets, Payson
2002 *Before the Volcano Erupted: The Ancient Ceren Village in Central America.* Austin: University of Texas Press.
2006 *The Ceren Site: An Ancient Village Buried by Volcanic Ash in Central America.* Belmont: Thompson, Wadsworth.

Sierra Sosa, Thelma N.
1994 *Contribución al estudio de los asentamientos de San Gervasio, Isla de Cozumel.* México, D.F.: Instituto Nacional de Antropología e Historia.

Sigal, Pete
2000 *From Moon Goddesses to Virgins: The Colonization of Yucatecan Maya Sexual Desire.* Austin: University of Texas Press.

Silva Rhoads, Carlos, and Concepción Maria del Carmen Hernandez
1991 Estudios de patrón de asentamiento en Playa del Carmen, Quintana Roo. *Serie Arqueología.* México, D.F.: Instituto Nacional de Antropología e Historia.

Smith, Monica L.
2003 Introduction: The Social Construction of Ancient Cities. In *The Social Construction of Ancient Cities*, ed. Monica L. Smith, 1-36. Washington, DC: Smithsonian Institution Press.

Smith, Robert E.
1971   The Pottery of Mayapan. *Papers of the Peabody Museum of Archaeology and Ethnology* 66. Cambridge: Harvard University.

Smyth, Michael P., and Daniel Rogart
2004   A Teotihuacan Presence at Chac II, Yucatán, Mexico. *Ancient Mesoamerica* 15(1):17-47.

Sofaer, Joanna R.
2006   Gender, Bioarchaeology and Human Ontogeny. In *Social Archaeology of Funerary Remains*, eds. Rebecca Gowland and Christopher Knusel, 155-167. Oxford: Oxbow Press.

Sørensen, Mary Louise Stig
2000   *Gender Archaeology*. Cambridge: Polity Press.

Soustelle, Jacques
1961   *Daily Life of the Aztecs on the Eve of the Spanish Conquest*. Stanford: Stanford University Press.

Stanton, Travis
2005   Taluds, Tripods, and Teotihuacanos: A Critique of Central Mexican Influence in Classic Period Yucatán. *Mayab* 18(2005):17-35.

Stanton, Travis, and Traci Ardren
2005   The Middle Formative of Yucatán in Context: The View from Yaxuna. *Ancient Mesoamerica* 16:213-228.

Stanton, Travis W., M. Kathryn Brown, and Jonathon B. Pagliaro
2008   Garbage of the Gods? Squatters, Refuse Disposal, and Termination Rituals among the Ancient Maya. *Latin American Antiquity* 19(3):227-248.

Stanton, Travis, David Freidel, Charles Suhler, Traci Ardren, James Ambrosino, Justine Shaw, and Sharon Bennett
2010   Excavations at Yaxuna, Yucatán, Mexico. *International Series* 2056. Oxford: Archaeopress/British Archaeological Reports.

Stanton, Travis W., and Tomás Gallareta Negrón
2001   Warfare, Ceramic Economy, and the Itzá: A Reconsideration of the Itzá Polity in Ancient Yucatán. *Ancient Mesoamerica* 12:229-246.

Stanton, Travis W., and Aline Magnoni (eds.)
2008   *Ruins of the Past: The Use and Perception of Abandoned Structures in the Maya Lowlands*. Boulder: University Press of Colorado.

Stavrakopoulou, Francesca
2004   *King Manasseh and Child Sacrifice: Biblical Distortions of Historical Realities*. New York: Walter de Gruyter.

Stewart, T. Dale
1974   Human Skeletal Remains from Dzibilchaltun, Yucatan, Mexico, with a Review of Cranial Deformity Types in the Maya Region. In *Archaeological Investigations on the Yucatan Peninsula*, eds. E. Wyllys Andrews et al., 31:199-225. New Orleans: Middle American Research Institute, Tulane University.

Strathern, Marilyn

1988 *The Gender of the Gift: Problems with Women and Problems with Society in Melanesia.* Berkeley: University of California Press.

2005 *Kinship, Law and the Unexpected: Relatives Are Always a Surprise.* Cambridge: Cambridge University Press.

Strauss, Claudia

2006 The Imaginary. *Anthropological Theory* 6(3):322–344.

Stuart, David

1996 Kings of Stone: A Consideration of Stelae in Ancient Maya Ritual and Representation. RES: *Anthropology and Aesthetics* 29/30:148–171.

1998 The Fire Enters His House: Architecture and Ritual in Classic Maya Texts. In *Function and Meaning in Classic Maya Architecture*, ed. S. Houston, 373–426. Washington, DC: Dumbarton Oaks.

Suhler, Charles

1996 Excavations at the North Acropolis, Yaxuna, Yucatán, Mexico. PhD diss., Southern Methodist University.

Suhler, Charles, Traci Ardren, and Dave Johnstone

1998 The Chronology of Yaxuna: Evidence from Excavation and Ceramics. *Ancient Mesoamerica* 9(1):167–182.

Suhler, Charles, and David Freidel

1993 *The Selz Foundation Yaxuna Project: Final Report of the 1992 Field Season.* Dallas: Department of Anthropology, Southern Methodist University.

1994 Excavations in the Structure 6F-3 Locality. In *The Selz Foundation Yaxuna Project: Final Report of the 1993 Field Season.* Dallas: Department of Anthropology, Southern Methodist University.

1998 Life and Death in a Maya War Zone. *Archaeology* 51(3):28–34.

Suhler, Charles, David Freidel, and Traci Ardren

1998 Northern Maya Architecture, Ritual, and Cosmology. In *Anatomia de una civilizacion. Aproximaciones interdisciplinarias a la cultura maya*, eds. Andres Ciudad Ruiz et al., 253–274. Madrid: Sociedad Española de Estudios Mayas.

Sweely, Tracy

1999 Gender, Space, People, and Power at Ceren, El Salvador. In *Manifesting Power: Gender and the Interpretation of Power in Archaeology*, ed. Tracy Sweely, 155–172. New York: Routledge.

Taube, Karl A.

1992 *The Major Gods of Ancient Yucatan.* Studies in Pre-Columbian Art and Archaeology no. 32. Washington, DC: Dumbarton Oaks.

2010 At Dawn's Edge: Tulum, Santa Rita, and Floral Symbolism in the International Style of Late Postclassic Mesoamerica. In *Astronomers, Scribes, and Priests: Intellectual Interchange between the Northern Maya Lowlands and Highland Mexico in the Late Postclassic Period*, eds. Gabrielle Vail and Christine Hernandez, 145–192. Washington, DC: Dumbarton Oaks.

Taylor, Charles
2002 Modern Social Imaginaries. *Public Culture* 14(1):91-124.
2004 *Modern Social Imaginaries.* Durham: Duke University Press.

Tedlock, Dennis
1985 *Popol Vuh: The Mayan Book of the Dawn of Life.* New York: Simon and Schuster.

Thomas, Frank R.
2002 An Evaluation of Central Place Foraging among Mollusk Gatherers in Western Kiribati, Micronesia: Linking Behavioral Ecology with Ethnoarchaeology. *World Archaeology* 34(1):182-208.

Thomas, Julian
2002 Archaeology's Humanism and the Materiality of the Body. In *Thinking through the Body: Archaeologies of Corporeality*, eds. Y. Hamilakis, M. Pluciennik, and S. Tarlow, 29-46. London: Kluwer Academic/Plenum Publishers.

Thompson, J. Eric S.
1938 Sixteenth and Seventeenth Century Reports on the Chol Mayas. *American Anthropologist* 40:584-604.
1970 *Maya History and Religion.* Norman: University of Oklahoma Press.

Tiesler, Vera, Andrea Cucina, T. Kam Manahan, T. Douglas Price, Traci Ardren, and James H. Burton
2010 A Taphonomic Approach to Late Classic Maya Mortuary Practices at Xuenkal, Yucatan, Mexico. *Journal of Field Archaeology* 35(4):365-379.

Toscano H., Lourdes, and David Ortegón Z.
2003 Yaxuna, un centro de acopio del tribute Itza. In *Los investigadores de la cultura maya* 11, tomo 2, 438-445. Campeche: Universidad Autonóma de Campeche.

Townsend, Richard F.
2000 *The Aztecs.* New York: Thames and Hudson.

Tozzer, Alfred M.
1912 A Spanish Manuscript Letter on the Lacondones in the Archives of the Indies at Seville. Proceedings of the International Congress of Americanists, 497-509. London: Harrison and Sons.

Vail, Gabrielle, and Christine Hernandez (eds.)
2010 *Astronomers, Scribes, and Priests: Intellectual Interchange between the Northern Maya Lowlands and Highland Mexico in the Late Postclassic Period.* Washington, DC: Dumbarton Oaks.

Vail, Gabrielle, and Andrea Stone
2002 Representations of Women in Postclassic and Colonial Literature and Art. In *Ancient Maya Women*, ed. T. Ardren, 203-228. Walnut Creek: AltaMira Press.

Van Dyke, Ruth M., and Susan E. Alcock (eds.)
2003 *Archaeologies of Memory.* Malden: Blackwell.

Varela Torrecilla, Carmen
1998   El clasico medio en el noroccidente de Yucatán. *International Series* 739. Oxford: Archaeopress/British Archaeological Reports.

Varela Torrecilla, Carmen, and Geoffrey Braswell
2003   Teotihuacan and Oxkintok: New Perspectives from Yucatán. In *The Maya and Teotihuacan: Reinterpreting Early Classic Interaction*, ed. G. Braswell, 249-272. Austin: University of Texas Press.

Vargas, Ernesto, Patricia S. Santillán, and Marta Vilalta
1985   Apuntes para el análisis del patrón de asentamiento de Tulum. In *Estudios de Cultura Maya* 16:55-83. México, D.F.: Universidad Nacional Autónoma de México.

Varien, Mark D., and James M. Potter (eds.)
2008   *The Social Construction of Communities: Agency, Structure, and Identity in the Prehispanic Southwest*. Lanham: Roman and Littlefield.

Venables, Robert W.
2010   The Clearings and the Woods: The Haudenosaunee (Iroquois) Landscape—Gendered and Balanced. In *Archaeology and Preservations of Gendered Landscapes*, eds. Sherene Baugher and Suzanne Spencer-Wood, 21-56. London: Springer.

Villa Rojas, Alfonso
1934   The Yaxuna-Coba Causeway. *Contributions to American Archaeology* no. 9, Carnegie Institution of Washington Publication 436. Washington, DC: Carnegie Institution of Washington.

Villamil, Laura P.
2007   Creating, Transforming, Rejecting, and Reinterpreting Ancient Maya Urban Landscapes: Insights from Lagartera and Margarita. In *Negotiating the Past in the Past: Identity, Memory, and Landscape in Archaeological Research*, ed. N. Yoffee, 183-214. Tucson: University of Arizona Press.

Vlcek, David T., Silvia Garza de Gonzalez, and Edward B. Kurjack
1978   Contemporary Farming and Ancient Maya Settlements: Some Disconcerting Evidence. In *Pre-Hispanic Maya Agriculture*, eds. P. D. Harrison and B. L. Turner II, 211-223. Albuquerque: University of New Mexico Press.

Voss, Barbara
2008   *The Archaeology of Ethnogenesis: Race and Sexuality in Colonial San Francisco*. Berkeley: University of California Press.

Wadley, Lynn
2000   The Use of Space in a Gender Study of Two South African Stone Age Sites. In *Gender and Material Culture in Archaeological Perspective*, eds. Moira Donald and Linda Hurcombe, 153-168. New York: St. Martin's Press.

Weber, Max (trans. and ed. D. Martindale and G. Neuwirth)
1958   *The City*. Glencoe: Free Press.

Weiner, Annette
1976　　Women of Value, Men of Renown: New Perspectives in Trobriand Exchange. Austin: University of Texas Press.
1992　　Inalienable Possessions: The Paradox of Keeping-While-Giving. Berkeley: University of California Press.

Weiner, Annette, and Jane Schneider (eds.)
1989　　Cloth and the Human Experience. Washington, DC: Smithsonian Institution Press.

Welsh, W. B. M.
1988　　An Analysis of Classic Lowland Maya Burials. *International Series* 409. Oxford: Archaeopress/British Archaeological Reports.

Wilk, Richard, and William Rathje
1982　　Archaeology of the Household: Building a Prehistory of Domestic Life. *American Behavioral Scientist* 25(6):617–640.

Willey, Gordon
1966　　Problems Concerning Prehistoric Settlement Patterns in the Maya Lowlands. In *Ancient Mesoamerica: Selected Readings*, ed. John A. Graham, 127–134. Palo Alto: Peek Publications.

Wirth, Louis
1938　　Urbanism as a Way of Life. *American Journal of Sociology* 44(1):1–24.

Wolpert, Andrew
2002　　*Remembering Defeat: Civil War and Civic Memory in Ancient Athens*. Baltimore: John Hopkins University Press.

Wright, Rita
1996　　Technology, Gender, and Class: Worlds of Difference in Ur III Mesopotamia. In *Gender and Archaeology*, ed. Rita Wright, 79–110. Philadelphia: University of Pennsylvania Press.

Yaeger, Jason
2003　　Untangling the Ties that Bind: The City, the Countryside, and the Nature of Maya Urbanism at Xunantunich, Belize. In *The Social Construction of Ancient Cities*, ed. Monica L. Smith, 121–155. Washington, DC: Smithsonian Institution Press.

Yoffee, Norman
1995　　Political Economy in Early Mesopotamian States. *Annual Review of Anthropology* 24:281–311.

Zeitlin, Robert N.
1993　　Pacific Coastal Laguna Zope: A Regional Center in the Terminal Formative Hinterlands of Monte Albán. *Ancient Mesoamerica* 4(1):85–101.

Zender, Marc
2010　　The Music of Shells. In *Fiery Pool: The Maya and the Mythic Sea*, eds. Daniel Finamore and Stephen D. Houston, 83–86. New Haven: Peabody Essex Museum, Yale University Press.

INDEX

agency, of children, 110; of individuals, 165; of objects, 16-17, 104, 112, 155, 159, 163, 175
Ake, 78
albarradas (boundary walls), 29, 42-43, 50, 124-125, 128
ancestors, 142, 171; as children, 110-111; and civic/monumental architecture, 75, 77; as deceased, 83, 95-96, 104-106; as intellectual forebears, 67
Anderson, Benedict, 112; on nationalism, 9-11, 153-154; on the social imaginary, 3, 10, 13, 44, 109, 136, 147, 165
artists, alternative masculinities of, 143; contemporary, 173; as makers of objects, 18

ball game, 27, 62, 130-131, 163; as gender specific activity, 144; as marker of masculinity, 128, 133, 150-151
blood, 99, 111
bloodletting, 129, 162
bloodlines, 45, 129
boundary walls (*albarradas*), 29, 42-43, 50, 124-125, 128
burials, 17, 48, 53, 62-65, 83-98, 100-103, 105-106, 109-115, 123, 125, 131-132, 134, 140-141, 149-150, 176; architectural context of, 10, 86, 92, 94, 101, 103, 132; and cremation, 45, 50; eastern shrines with, 10; ritual of, 44, 83, 85, 103, 115, 125, 176; of infants, 20; of juveniles, 19, 83-98, 103, 105-106, 109-115; and urns, 84, 92, 98-102, 105, 111, 115

Canbalam, 36, 37
Caste Wars, 62
cenotes (sinkholes), 57, 101, 112, 135, 176
censer, 58-61, 65, 69, 73-79
ceramics, 22, 26, 31, 33, 36, 40, 46-47, 52-55, 57, 59, 61-63, 69, 73, 76-77, 79, 98, 103, 115, 122, 125, 147-148, 158; as animate, 18; in burials, 12, 92-94, 98, 103, 113, 115, 123, 125; as ethnic marker, 7, 54, 69; ritual use, 57, 59, 61, 79, 111, 113, 115, 123; types of, 7, 15; as vessels, 12, 15, 18, 33, 40, 47, 89-93, 99, 101, 111, 113, 123, 125, 135, 143
Chac II, 33
chert, 37, 41, 88, 123, 132
Chichen Itza, 7, 20, 40, 52, 54, 56, 68, 71, 72, 74, 80, 85, 86, 88, 92, 98, 99, 101, 112, 157, 176
childhood, 3, 8, 19-20, 65, 83-115, 119-121, 133, 142, 146-147, 151, 158-162, 166, 170-172, 176
Chunchucmil, 4, 10, 16, 19, 20-50, 117, 122, 124-128, 142, 145, 150, 159, 164, 166-167, 169-170
circulations, 14-16, 18-19, 21, 28, 40-50, 67, 74, 76-77, 79, 85-86, 92, 96, 103-105, 108-109, 112, 115,

117, 119, 121, 136, 141, 145, 151, 163-164, 166; of material culture, 3, 15, 18-19, 40, 46, 76, 92, 96, 109, 163; performative aspect of, 14, 28, 47, 85-86, 103, 117, 141, 145
Coba, 29, 52, 54, 58, 70, 72, 86, 131
codices, 65, 73, 77
Colha, 41
Colonial period, 42, 70-71, 88, 107, 112, 119, 129-130, 133, 160-162, 171, 175
Conil, 69
corn (maize), 11, 23, 38-39, 61, 65, 107, 121, 123, 125-126, 144-145, 172
Cozumel, 56, 69
craft production, 7, 25, 34, 88, 93, 127, 149, 157, 163-165

deer, 65, 87, 89, 95, 109, 113, 115, 120, 123, 133
Dzibilchaltun, 19-20, 33, 83, 86, 88, 90-93, 98-101, 105, 110-112, 114, 117, 133-136, 142, 150

Early Classic period, 22, 25, 27, 30-33, 36-37, 41, 44, 48-49, 53, 56, 58, 63, 86, 125, 127, 130
Ek Balam, 70, 88
elders, 13, 104, 108, 121, 128, 143, 145, 161, 171
El Meco, 69
Emal, 39
ensoulment, 111, 115, 122
ethnicity, 1-2, 8
ethnobotany, 127
ethnohistoric sources, 28, 42, 53, 56, 69-74, 77, 79, 81, 112, 113, 118, 133, 142, 150, 162

food, 10-12, 36, 125-127, 139, 147; as gendered practice, 7, 119-121, 142, 144, 150-151, 161, 172; offerings of, 65, 92, 99; production of, 25; as

ritual of inclusion, 10-12, 34, 107, 147, 165
forgetting, 51-52, 68, 77, 81, 163, 175-176
funerals and funerary ritual, 12, 15, 27, 63, 77, 84-86, 88, 92, 96, 98, 102-106, 110-111, 115, 123, 143

gender, 1-4, 6-10, 12, 16-19-20, 92, 104, 117-151, 153-157, 159-165, 172, 176

h'men (shaman), 61, 172
heritage, 167, 169, 171, 173
Hero Twins, 107
hieroglyphic writing, 18, 24, 32, 111, 125, 139, 146-147, 158, 169
households, 7, 10, 22, 26, 29, 34, 41-43, 48, 52, 69, 76, 92, 109-113, 122-124, 127, 158-165; activities within, 26, 29, 45, 109, 122-124, 127, 158, 165; ancestral space within, 10, 110; gendered practices and, 7, 117, 119, 122-124, 137-138, 142, 144-147, 161
Hunucma, 169, 170

Ichpaatun, 69
Identity Studies, 20, 138, 155-156, 159, 164, 174-175
individual, 10-18, 49, 104-106, 149, 153-155, 174-176; inattention to in archaeology, 7; relation to the Other, 1-3, 8, 11, 41, 96, 102, 104-106, 110, 113, 137, 141, 162-165; as social actor, 8, 10-18, 66, 136, 153-155, 162-165
infants and infancy, 10, 20, 89-92, 98-102, 105, 111-112, 115
Isla Cerritos, 92, 98
Izamal, 98

jade, 17, 53-54, 90-91, 95, 98, 100-102, 111, 115, 123, 125
Jaina, 94, 98

Joyce, Rosemary, on burials and group membership, 105–106; on costume elements, 93–94; on gender, 146; on material culture, 141; on men's houses, 129

kings and kingship, 35, 45, 53, 106, 159

Landa, Bishop Diego de, 112, 118–120, 124, 128–130, 146–147
Latour, Bruno, 16, 155

maize (corn), 11, 23, 38–39, 61, 65, 107, 121, 123, 125–126, 144–145, 172
Maize Deity, 17, 74, 112, 125
masculinity, 2, 13, 118, 129–130, 143, 147–148, 151
Mayan language, 160–161, 166, 170–172
Mayapan, 29, 55, 58–59, 62, 68–81, 160, 175
memory, 3–4, 19, 51–81, 160, 163–165, 168–170, 174–176
merchants, 34, 37, 39–40, 59, 68
Moore, Henrietta, 2, 78–79, 104, 119, 136–139, 143, 150

nationalism, 9–11, 153

object biography, 17–18
obsidian, 15, 26, 36–37, 46–47, 50, 101, 111, 123, 125, 127, 132–133, 135, 158
offerings, 19, 32, 48, 53–54, 56, 58, 61, 63, 65, 73, 75–76, 79–81, 99, 101, 111, 120, 125; to animate architecture, 17, 115, 122; in burials, 48, 53–54, 92–94, 115, 125; of food, 65, 92, 99; as sacrificial, 94, 101; of shells, 93
Okop, 78
Oxkintok, 24, 33, 36, 37, 44, 45, 168, 169

palaces, 24–27, 88, 129–130, 140
phalli, 129, 148, 162

play, 108–109, 128, 158–159
Playa del Carmen, 56, 161
plazas, 25, 63, 69, 124, 131–136, 143; as a setting for art, 129, 136, 148
Popol Vuh, 107, 164
Postclassic period, 19, 22, 29–30, 40, 42, 51–81, 130, 155, 160, 175
power, 4, 9, 13, 17, 27, 35, 56, 62, 66, 75, 77–80, 86, 96, 101–102, 110–112, 121, 129, 130, 133, 137–140, 150–151, 153, 162; ancestral, 99; dynastic, 45, 75, 77, 93; as exercised, 4; inherent in certain substances, 17, 93–94, 101, 111; and numinous, 20, 96, 102; in social relationships, 4, 9, 13, 19–20, 27, 42, 68, 79, 84, 114, 137, 147–148
Preclassic (Formative) period, 22, 30, 43, 53, 55, 61, 88
Puuc region, 24, 27–28, 36–37, 40, 54, 62, 148, 168

quadrangles and quadrangular architecture, 24–31, 41, 43, 45–46, 49–50, 99
queens and queenship, 17

race, 1–2, 156–157
remembering, 51–52, 75, 77–78, 81, 163, 176
Ringle, William, 27–28, 70–71, 74, 76
road systems. *See sacbeob*

Sacbeob (road systems), 29–30, 43, 46, 52, 86, 99, 121, 124, 130, 143, 169; as part of quadrangle, 25, 27; Sacbe 1 of Yaxuna, 54, 58–59, 62–63, 131
sacrifice, 46, 72–73, 99, 101–102, 111–112; of animals, 65; of captives, 63, 72; of children, 19, 102, 112, 114, 162
salt, 23–24, 33–35, 37–41, 47, 50; as trade item, 19, 21, 24, 33, 39–41, 47, 124

sexuality, 129, 147, 161
shaman (*h'men*), 61, 172
shell, 101–103, 111, 113, 133, 159; and connection to children, 94, 102, 113, 115; as craft production, 88; ornaments of, 87, 89–91, 93–95, 103, 113, 123, 125, 133; as tools, 37, 40, 164
shrines, 28, 48, 50, 98–102, 111, 165; domestic, 10, 12, 30, 43, 48, 123, 125–127; and Postclassic, 19, 53, 56–62, 67, 69, 72–81, 175
Siho, 36
soil chemistry, 22, 32, 125, 127, 145

Talud-tablero architecture, 30, 32–33, 45, 50
Tancah, 73
Taylor, Charles, 19, 109, 112, 165; on background understandings, 15, 28, 35–36, 104; and definition of social imaginary, 3, 136, 139, 146; importance of social practices, 10–13, 28, 36, 141, 154
Teotihuacan, 30, 32–33, 36
Terminal Classic period, 15, 22, 40, 54–55, 58–60, 62–63, 72, 77–78, 80, 83–91, 98, 118–119, 122, 124, 133, 148, 150, 157
T'ho, 33

Tikal, 10, 23, 44
trade, 24, 28, 33–34, 36–50, 53–54, 59, 69, 71, 78–79, 80, 86, 124, 127–128, 142, 175; as exchange of items, 14–15, 28, 33, 37, 48, 53–54, 73, 76, 79, 93, 101; and identity, 28, 47, 50; in salt, 19, 24, 39–41, 47
traders, 35, 40, 43, 47
Tulum, 29, 56, 69, 73
Tzeme, 36

urbanism, 10, 21–55, 66–71, 77–81, 85–86, 88, 96, 101, 124–125, 127, 130, 155, 159, 163–164, 166; definitions of, 22, 29, 35; effect on social relations, 16, 19, 21, 41, 163; landscape of, 29, 43, 66, 68, 79, 159

warfare, 71–72, 74, 77, 85, 124, 146, 148, 151, 162
warriors, 133, 148

Xcaret, 56
Xuenkal, 4, 19, 78, 83, 86, 88–95, 98, 110, 112, 114, 124, 157

Yaxuna, 4, 19, 20, 33, 51–81, 83, 86, 87, 92, 93, 96, 97, 110, 112, 114, 117, 122, 124, 130–133, 142, 150, 175
Yaxunah, 166, 170, 171–174

www.ingramcontent.com/pod-product-compliance
Lightning Source LLC
Jackson TN
JSHW020313120426
100741JS00002B/13